PRO/CON VOLUME 22

INTERNATIONAL LAW

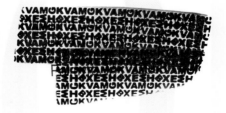

Published 2005 by Grolier,
an imprint of Scholastic Library Publishing
Old Sherman Turnpike
Danbury, Connecticut 06816

Library of Congress Cataloging-in-Publication Data

Pro/con
 p. cm
Includes bibliographical references and index.
 Contents: v. 19. World Politics – v. 20 Religion and Morality – v. 21. U.S.
Judiciary – v. 22. International Law - v. 23. Poverty and Wealth – v. 24. Work and
the Workplace.
 ISBN 0-7172-5950-1 (set : alk. paper) – ISBN 0-7172-5951–X (vol. 19 : alk. paper) –
ISBN 0-7172-5952-8 (vol. 20 : alk. paper) – ISBN 0-7172-5953-6 (vol. 21 : alk. paper)
– ISBN 0-7172-5954-4 (vol. 22 : alk. paper) – ISBN 0-7172-5955-2 (vol. 23 : alk.
paper) – ISBN 0-7172-5956-0 (vol. 24 : alk. paper)
 1. Social problems. I. Scholastic Publishing Ltd Grolier (Firm)

HN17.5 P756 2002
361.1–dc22

                                                              2001053234

Printed and bound in Singapore

SET ISBN 0-7172-5950-1
VOLUME ISBN 0-7172-5954-4

For The Brown Reference Group plc
Project Editors: Aruna Vasudevan, Claire Chandler
Editors: Fiona Plowman, Chris Marshall, Jonathan Dore, Mark Fletcher
Consultant Editor: Kal Raustiala, Acting Professor of Law, University of
California, School of Law, Los Angeles, CA
Designer: Sarah Williams
Picture Research and Permissions: Clare Newman, Susy Forbes
Set Index: Kay Ollerenshaw

Senior Managing Editor: Tim Cooke
Art Director: Dave Goodman
Production Manager: Alastair Gourlay

GENERAL PREFACE

Decisions

Life is full of choices and decisions. Some are more important than others. Some affect only your daily life—the route you take to school, for example, or what you prefer to eat for supper—while others are more abstract and concern questions of right and wrong rather than practicality. That does not mean that your choice of presidential candidate or your views on abortion are necessarily more important than your answers to purely personal questions. But it is likely that those wider questions are more complex and subtle and that you therefore will need to know more information about the subject before you can try to answer them. They are also likely to be questions about which you might have to justify your views to other people. In order to do that, you need to be able to make informed decisions, be able to analyze every fact at your disposal, and evaluate them in an unbiased manner.

What Is *Pro/Con*?

Pro/Con is a collection of debates that presents conflicting views on some of the more complex and general issues facing Americans today. By bringing together extracts from a wide range of sources—mainstream newspapers and magazines, books, famous speeches, legal judgments, religious tracts, government surveys—the set reflects current informed attitudes toward dilemmas that range from the best way to feed the world's growing population to gay rights, from the connection between political freedom and capitalism to the fate of Napster.

The people whose arguments make up the set are for the most part acknowledged experts in their fields, making the vast differences in their points of view even more remarkable. The arguments are presented in the form of debates for and against various propositions, such as "Do extradition treaties violate human rights?" or "Should companies be allowed to relocate abroad?" This question format reflects the way in which ideas often occur in daily life: in the classroom, on TV shows, in business meetings, or even in state or federal politics.

The contents

The subjects of the six volumes of *Pro/Con 4—World Politics, Religion and Morality, U.S. Judiciary, International Law, Poverty and Wealth,* and *Work and the Workplace—* are issues on which it is preferable that people's opinions be based on information rather than personal bias.

Special boxes throughout *Pro/Con* comment on the debates as you are reading them, pointing out facts, explaining terms, or analyzing arguments to help you think about what is being said.

Introductions and summaries also provide background information that might help you reach your own conclusions. There are also tips about how to structure an argument that you can apply on an everyday basis to any debate or conversation, learning how to present your point of view as effectively and persuasively as possible.

VOLUME PREFACE
International Law

International treaties, codes, and laws regulate many different areas, including trade, wars, human rights, commerce, civil and political rights, and children's and women's rights.

A rapid expansion of international law took place after World War II (1939–1945) with the establishment of the United Nations (UN). One of the first things that the UN did was to adopt the Universal Declaration of Human Rights in 1948. It has become one of the cornerstones of international law. Since then the principles of international law have been spread through various international organizations, such as the UN, the International Monetary Fund (IMF), and the World Trade Organization, and their charters, treaties, and conventions.

The global economy could not function without international laws that govern finance, trade, and commerce. In recent years there has been a rapid expansion of international law as a result of greater global economic integration and the growth of international travel, TV, and telecommunications. As more and more people move and communicate internationally, it has become increasingly important to have international laws.

However, the ever-increasing adoption of international laws has created a number of dilemmas. For example, the introduction of the Internet, which is not limited by national boundaries, has increased the need for new laws to protect every individual's privacy. At the same time, international law needs to allow law enforcement agencies access to information in the fight against global organized crime and terrorism. Some countries feel that international laws mean that their sovereignty is limited. A central debate concerns the conflict between nations' legal systems and organizations such the International Criminal Court (ICC). For example, many object to heads of state being tried in an international court of law.

America: A world leader?

The United States' role in international law is particularly important because of its position as the worlds' most powerful country. It also has a long tradition of protecting the rights of its own people. Despite this, the United States is sometimes reluctant to ratify international laws that it believes could be used by other countries against it or that interfere with what it deems acceptable practice within its own boundaries. On the other hand, certain American laws, such as the USA PATRIOT Act, have been criticized for violating some civil rights guaranteed by international law. These issues raise questions of priorities, such as whether a nation's security is more important than the human rights of an individual.

Pro/Con

The purpose of *International Law* is to help the reader reach informed conclusions about important issues in the subject by using primary source material from newspapers, magazines, books, and the Internet to show both sides of each debate.

HOW TO USE THIS BOOK

Each volume of *Pro/Con* is divided into sections, each of which has an introduction that examines its theme. Within each section are a series of debates that present arguments for and against a proposition, such as whether or not the death penalty should be abolished. An introduction to each debate puts it into its wider context, and a summary and key map (see below) highlight the main points of the debate clearly and concisely. Each debate has marginal boxes that focus on particular points, give tips on how to present an argument, or help question the writer's case. The summary page to the debates contains supplementary material to help you do further research.

Boxes and other materials provide additional background information. There are also special spreads on how to improve your debating and writing skills. At the end of each book is a glossary and an index. The glossary provides explanations of key words in the volume. The index covers all 24 books; it will help you find topics throughout this set and previous ones.

background information
Frequent text boxes provide background information on important concepts and key individuals or events.

summary boxes
Summary boxes are useful reminders of both sides of the argument.

further information
Further Reading lists for each debate direct you to related books, articles, and websites so you can do your own research.

other articles in the *Pro/Con* series
This box lists related debates throughout the *Pro/Con* series.

marginal boxes
Margin boxes highlight key points of the argument, give extra information, or help you question the author's meaning.

key map
Key maps provide a graphic representation of the central points of the debate.

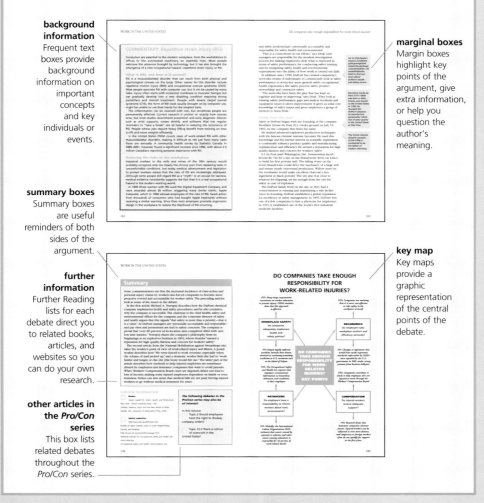

CONTENTS

PART 1
ISSUES IN INTERNATIONAL LAW

Traditionally the basic unit of any legal system is the nation-state. Sovereign countries have the right to self-government, which includes making laws to control the behavior of both citizens and visitors. Nation-states have their own law-enforcement agencies, such as the police or specific intelligence bodies to enforce these codes, judicial systems to apply the law, and their own penal systems for enforcing punishment. However, most nations find certain offenses unacceptable and therefore outlaw them—including murder and crimes against the state—but other acts such as domestic violence, rape within marriage, and sex with children are not always punishable offenses in every legal system.

International law refers to a group of rules, treaties, or conventions that nation-states have agreed to and that are legally binding—also known as the law of nations. For centuries theorists have written about international law. The Dutch humanist and jurist Hugo Grotius (1583–1645) wrote what is considered to be the first comprehensive book on the subject, *De jure belli ac pacis* (*Concerning the Law of War and Peace*), in 1625. Drawing on the Bible and classical texts, Grotius argued that the rules of conduct for nation-states as well as individuals are prescribed by

natural law. He maintained that it is criminal to wage war for anything other than justifiable causes and argued for more humane treatment of individuals during war. The writings of another Dutch theorist, Cornelius van Bynkershoek (1673–1743), were also extremely influential in formulating international law, particularly maritime law. In his 1702 classic *De dominio maris* (*On the Rule of the Seas*) van Bynkershoek first proposed the idea that a nation could claim sovereignty over territorial waters upto a distance of three miles (4.8 km) from shore. Others, such as the English political theorist Thomas Hobbes (1588–1679), opposed the idea of international law as true law since no sovereign organization exists to enforce it.

Despite this interest, before the 20th century international law developed largely in a piecemeal way in response to specific regional or local circumstances: The 1648 Peace of Westphalia, for example, established a precedent in European law that a ruler of one country could not be prosecuted in another for crimes committed during his rule. Over the last one hundred years, however, support has increased for international codes that protect the rights of both individuals and nation-states in every sphere. World War I (1914–1918) and World War II

(1939-1945) had a particular influence on the development of such laws.

In 1914 the tensions within Europe boiled over into World War I. The conflict saw the emergence of pioneering codes such as the Geneva Conventions, which laid down the basic rules to which all nations must adhere during wartime. Over the 20th century international law largely evolved through the attempts of international organizations to regulate relations between nations and to guarantee and protect the rights of individuals. The first of those bodies, the League of Nations, lasted from 1920 to 1939;

show, and that many high-level officials escaped. Despite this, similar tribunals were set up in the 1990s to prosecute crimes committed during conflicts in the former Yugoslavia and Rwanda.

The International Criminal Court (ICC) was further established in 2002 as the world's first permanent body to promote the international rule of law. International tribunals and the ICC have, however, been criticized for having a limited jurisdiction since they do not have any control over people or nations that have not voluntarily signed up to them. Topic 1 asks whether the ICC undermines national sovereignty,

> *"Every government that is committed to the rule of law at home, must be committed also to the rule of law abroad. All States have a clear interest, as well as clear responsibility, to uphold international law and maintain international order."*
> —KOFI ANNAN, UN SECRETARY–GENERAL (2002)

critics believe that it was weakened by the U.S. refusal to join it. They argue that as a result, the league was largely ineffective; it was unable to enforce its own directives or to prevent the outbreak of World War II (1939-1945). Following this war the league was replaced by a similar but stronger body, the United Nations (UN).

International tribunals

The end of the war set an important precedent in international law. Many of the military leaders of Germany and Japan were tried for war crimes and crimes against humanity in specially established tribunals, although critics assert that the trials were largely for

as critics argue. Topics 2 to 4 also examine issues that touch on national versus international responsibility under the law.

Topic 2 considers whether heads of state should be prosecuted for crimes against humanity committed while in office. Topic 3 ask if targeted killing or assassination as a means of government policy is ever right, and Topic 4 questions if it is legitimate for one nation to attack another as a preemptive measure.

The last two topics in this section look at the protection of vulnerable groups: Topic 5 examines women's rights, and Topic 6 looks at international parent–child abduction.

Topic 1

DOES THE INTERNATIONAL CRIMINAL COURT UNDERMINE NATIONAL SOVEREIGNTY?

YES

FROM "ICC—NEW THREAT TO U.S. SOVEREIGNTY"
WWW.NEWSMAX.COM, AUGUST 27, 2003
DAVID DAVENPORT

NO

"THE INTERNATIONAL CRIMINAL COURT WILL STRENGTHEN
AUSTRALIA'S GLOBAL STANDING"
WWW.ONLINEOPINION.COM, JUNE 15, 2002
ANDREW MACLEOD AND GREG BARNS

INTRODUCTION

The International Criminal Court (ICC) is the first permanent body formed to promote the international rule of law and ensure that war crimes, genocide, and crimes against humanity do not go unpunished. Based in The Hague, Netherlands, the ICC was established by the Rome Statute, which was adopted by 120 nations on July 17, 1998. The treaty required ratification by at least 60 countries before it took effect. The 60th ratification came in April 2002, and the statute came into force on July 1, 2002. After that date anyone who committed any of the crimes specified in the statute became liable for prosecution by the ICC. By mid-2004, however, the court was still not fully operational. Among those countries that had failed to sign or to ratify the treaty were the United States, Russia, and China, and most countries in the Middle East and Asia. Supporters of the ICC, however, believe that further ratifications will follow.

The ICC is a court of last resort. That means that it can only prosecute cases that national authorities are unable or unwilling to prosecute themselves. The ICC's jurisdiction applies to crimes committed in the territory of any state that has ratified the treaty, crimes committed by citizens of such states, and cases that are referred to the court by the United Nations Security Council.

The ICC's supporters argue that it will complement existing national and international justice systems. Kofi Annan, UN secretary general, hailed the court's creation by saying, "The missing link in the international justice system is now in place…. Let it be a deterrent to the wicked and a ray of hope to the innocent and helpless." In the view of the court's advocates it merely replaces the ad hoc tribunals previously used to deal with such serious crimes, such as those established to try the leaders of Germany and Japan after World War II (1939–1945) or those set up to prosecute crimes committed during the conflicts in the former Yugoslavia and Rwanda in the 1990s.

> *"The prospects for the ICC as a protector of the ideals of the international community ... become difficult to imagine ... when some states elect to exclude themselves from that vision."*
> —CHERIE BOOTH,
> ENGLISH LAWYER (2002)

Although the creation of the ICC was widely welcomed by human rights groups, the court remains controversial. Numerous nations that have failed to ratify the Rome Statute argue that the ICC threatens national sovereignty— that is, a nation's ability to determine its affairs independently. The most notable critic of the ICC is the United States.

President Bill Clinton's administration was among the original signatories of the Rome Statute, but in May 2002 the government of George W. Bush declared that "the U.S. has no legal obligations arising from its signature" of the treaty, in effect "unsigning" the statute and withdrawing U.S. involvement in the ICC. The Bush administration was concerned that

Americans could be subject to trial without recourse to the protections they are guaranteed by the U.S. Constitution. The government argued that it alone should have the right to try U.S. nationals, and it sought to conclude bilateral immunity agreements to prohibit countries from surrendering any American to the ICC.

Critics of the ICC also fear that it will provide a platform for opponents of the United States to bring politically motivated actions against Americans. Given that the United States has more military personnel involved in overseas operations than any other nation, including, for example, peacekeeping missions on behalf of the UN, some people suggest that its citizens may attract a disproportionate degree of prosecution. The United States initially demanded that personnel from non-ICC countries serving on UN missions be exempt from prosecution but withdrew its proposal to renew the exemption for the third successive year in June 2004.

A further concern is that were the court to appoint a prosecutor who is critical of the United States, the court might look to bring prosecutions in cases that could be dealt with justly under existing national laws. In such circumstances, critics claim, the ICC could become a political tool of opponents of the United States.

Supporters of the ICC counter that as a country whose justice system is open and fair, the United States has nothing to fear from the court. The United States, in turn, argues that either its own judicial system or a series of bilateral agreements with other nations provide the means to deal with any case that would potentially come before the ICC.

The following articles examine these issues in greater detail.

ICC—NEW THREAT TO U.S. SOVEREIGNTY
David Davenport

David Davenport is a research fellow at the Hoover Institution, a think tank at Stanford University dedicated to research in domestic policy and international affairs. This article was published on the NewsMax website in 2003.

In January 2004 an international panel of lawyers and academics called on the ICC to investigate Britain for alleged war crimes in Iraq.

Go to http://www.globalpolicy.org/intljustice/iccl 2003/0606 usbilaterals.htm for an analysis of the bilateral immunity agreements by the Coalition for the International Criminal Court.

YES

☑ … To some, this new court in The Hague is the most significant international institution since the United Nations [UN]. To others, including U.S. policymakers, it represents a major threat to national sovereignty and values.

Consider the tug-of-war between these views of the new world court from this summer's headlines:

• At the request of the United States, the UN Security Council voted 12–0 to exempt U.S. soldiers serving on UN peacekeeping forces from prosecution by the International Criminal Court for one year. UN Secretary-General Kofi Annan protested and France, Syria and Germany abstained in dissent. Supporters of the court claimed that the resolution was inappropriate and illegal.

• The Greek Bar Association filed a complaint with the new court charging British Prime Minister Tony Blair with war crimes in Iraq. President George W. Bush avoided charges because the United States did not sign the treaty, fearing political prosecutions of just this kind.

• The United States seeks bilateral agreements with allies agreeing not to turn American soldiers on their territory over to the International Criminal Court for prosecution. Countries not signing such agreements by July 1 faced the loss of military aid, causing charges that the United States was bullying weaker countries into cooperating with its anti-court crusade.

• When the U.S. president arrived in Senegal, protestors chanted "Bush is a criminal … send Blair to the International Criminal Court."

• Summarizing the U.S. position on the International Criminal Court, a headline in the London-based *Economist* magazine read: "America versus the rest."

A significant threat to American sovereignty

The truth is that the concept of an International Criminal Court could and should represent a strengthening of justice and the rule of law. But the devil is in the details, and the development of this particular court represents a significant threat to American sovereignty.

In 2002 the former Serbian and Yugoslav president, Slobodan Milosevic (1941–), was put on trial for war crimes by the UN International Criminal Tribunal for the Former Yugoslavia. It was the first time an international court had tried a former head of state for such grave crimes.

Sadly, this is no accident. Proponents of the court aggressively expanded its jurisdiction so that it would necessarily undermine national sovereignty and attempt to shift power away from the United States. Now they seem surprised that the United States is resisting this overreach of international power.

Historically, international criminal courts have been established on a case-by-case basis, as needed, and the United States has supported every one. From criminal tribunals in

All previous courts of the ICC's kind, such as the war crimes tribunals after World War II (1939–1945), were set up for a particular purpose and dissolved as soon as they had returned their verdicts.

Nuremberg and Tokyo following World War II, to ad hoc tribunals for Rwanda and the former Yugoslavia in the 1990s, these special courts have prosecuted war crimes, genocide and crimes against humanity.

Overreaching its jurisdiction

The United States not only supported each of these special tribunals, but also the movement to establish a permanent court. But a funny thing happened on the way to Rome in 1998, where diplomats planned to discuss a framework for the ICC. A group of human rights groups such as Amnesty International and Human Rights Watch joined with small- and medium-sized states such as Canada and several of the European Union countries to expand the jurisdiction and powers of the proposed new court.

Do you agree that the ICC should have jurisdiction over citizens of states that have not ratified the treaty? What are the arguments for and against this idea?

Rather than involving the UN Security Council in referring cases, as had been done historically, this group wanted an independent prosecutor who could bring cases more proactively. Whereas international law limits the effect of treaties to those nations that sign them, proponents of the court wanted it to have jurisdiction over citizens of non-party states. And they wanted to add a new, undefined crime of "aggression" to the list of crimes the prosecutor could charge.

The International Law Commission was established by the UN General Assembly in 1947. Go to its website at http://www.un.org/law/ilc/ for more information.

These were overreaches of jurisdiction beyond anything done before and they were out of step with the recommendations of the International Law Commission charged by the United Nations with structuring the court. Therefore, the United States rightly objected to them.

The surprise was not that the United States refused to go along with this expansive agenda for the court, but that proponents of the court rushed it through to approval without the support of major world powers. Even today, fewer than half the nations of the world, representing considerably less than half its population, have ratified the treaty.

As of July 2004, 94 nations had ratified the Rome Statute.

How, then, is U.S. sovereignty affected by a treaty the United States has not ratified? The court purports to have jurisdiction over crimes committed by citizens of states that have ratified the treaty, but also crimes committed on the territory of signatory states. As a result, the United States, which has more troops engaged in peacekeeping and other missions around the world than any other nation, is most vulnerable. Supporters of the court argue it is nonsense for the United States to fear prosecution by the International Criminal Court, since its purpose is to provide justice in areas where local and regional courts are not up to the task.

The new president of the court, Canadian Philippe Kirsch, recently confirmed: "It is not designed [for] democratic leaders." Of course, charges have been filed against Blair for war crimes in Iraq, and no one doubts that similar complaints would be made against U.S. leaders if the United States or Iraq were a party to the court.

Go to http://www. npwj.org/modules. php?name=News& file=print&sid= 1320 to learn more about Kirsch's views.

Belgian courts, which also assert universal jurisdiction over war crimes, genocide and crimes against humanity, have a full docket of democratic leaders, including Gen. Tommy Franks and former President George H.W. Bush.

General Franks was commander of the U.S. armed forces in Iraq until mid-2003. In the wake of the Iraq war 17 Iraqis and 2 Jordanians introduced a lawsuit against him in a Brussels court for war crimes.

The claims of ICC supporters

In fairness, proponents argue, court filings against democratic leaders must nevertheless be reviewed by the prosecutor and may not result in court action. Only time will tell, of course, and no one should doubt that the political pressures that created such expansive jurisdiction for the court, and the anti-American sentiment behind it, will result in great pressure on the prosecutor to pursue such cases. And, as we have learned with special prosecutors in this country, even the filing of charges and subsequent investigation are themselves highly charged and politically powerful.

Davenport is referring to the special prosecutor Kenneth Starr, who investigated allegations against President Bill Clinton in 1998.

Court supporters also claim that the principle of "complementarity," included in the Rome treaty, prevents the International Criminal Court from pursuing cases that local jurisdictions can and do pursue. On closer legal analysis, however, complementarity has holes you could drive a truck through.

If the United States, for example, did not prosecute one of its soldiers for a war crime, the court could easily find the United States "unable or unwilling" to pursue the matter and go forward anyway. Listen to internationalists talk about their views of our military tribunals or the death penalty, and it is easy to see how U.S. courts could be ignored.

An attempt to shift the balance of power

In the end, the International Criminal Court is not just about justice, as it could have been with careful drafting of the Rome statute. It is equally about international politics and altering the balance of power. Small- and medium-power states actively seek to develop international institutions that will proactively balance the economic, military and diplomatic power of the United States. The International Criminal Court is only their latest creation, and the United States is right to oppose its aggressive jurisdictional reach.

Do you agree that states actively seek to balance the power of the United States? What evidence can you find to support your view?

THE INTERNATIONAL CRIMINAL COURT WILL STRENGTHEN AUSTRALIA'S GLOBAL STANDING
Andrew MacLeod and Greg Barns

Andrew MacLeod is a former military negotiator for the International Red Cross. Greg Barns is a writer, lawyer, and a former senior political adviser.

The 1977 protocols to the Geneva Conventions require that war detainees be treated humanely in all circumstances.

In 1994 ethnic fighting in the African nation of Rwanda led to the deaths of around 800,000 Tutsis and moderate Hutus at the hands of Hutu militias.

Why might all these people have been against international courts?

NO

Twenty-five years ago this week Australia, together with the International Red Cross, took the lead in the development of the law on War Crimes. Yet today our nation has members of its government who wish to turn our back on past achievements and run a populist line of 'national sovereignty'. This will ensure that we lose our status as a country committed to the continued development of laws against War Crimes.

On the 11 June 1977, more than 100 states adopted two Protocols to the Geneva Conventions. Nations like Australia had pushed successfully for the Law of War to now cover internal conflicts, wars of National Liberation and to give further protection to innocent civilians caught in the cross fire of conflict.

It is breaches of these Protocols and other laws that have Milosevic and the perpetrators of the Rwandan Genocide facing justice in two ad hoc International Courts.

Australia had no difficulty signing up in 1977 as we recognised the need to bring the world's evil to justice was greater than evil's need to appeal to 'National Sovereignty'. But today we risk being seen to let the world's evil off the hook.

A threat to national sovereignty?

We are being asked to ratify the Rome Statute that would create the first permanent International Criminal Court to try the world's evil—and government backbenchers led by former minister Bronwyn Bishop are refusing.

They claim that the International Criminal Court, with the power to try Australian soldiers, is a threat to our 'National Sovereignty' and not in our 'national interest'. They say that Australia's courts would no longer be the final arbiters of Australia's guilt.

Bishop is not alone in her view. Milosevic, Pinochet, the WWII Japanese leaders, the Nazis and Pol Pot have all been on record at various times saying that international courts

like this should not be supported. So have the Americans—
not surprising given their record in places like Vietnam.

Funnily enough though, those taking the opposing
view, that the court should go ahead, include the
Australian Defence Force, the United Kingdom, Australia's
negotiating team at the ICC Conference, most of the
Commonwealth, modern day Japan, modern day Germany
and ... modern day Yugoslavia.

Admiral Chris Barrie, Chief of the Australian Defence
Force, said that the creation of the ICC would be no threat
to Australian forces, rather the Court's existence would
make Australian soldiers' jobs easier and safer in peacekeeping operations.

Former British Foreign Secretary Robin Cook said that
Britain has ratified the ICC treaty as "it is in Britain's national
interest to do so. A more stable, democratic world is safer to
live, travel and trade in."

Tim McCormack and Helen Durham, who headed
Australia's negotiating team, recently wrote "the suggestion
that if Australia ratifies the Rome Statute the High Court of
Australia will no longer be the highest court of authority in
this country is ludicrous".

Each of the above quotes negate arguments put by Bishop
and highlight how odd it seems that Australia may side with
Milosevic instead of the Australian Defence Force, with the
Japanese WWII leaders instead of the Commonwealth or Pol
Pot instead of our own negotiating team.

Analysing the argument

But rather than just make simple comparisons, let's
analyse Bishop's argument. Does the treaty threaten or
undermine our National Sovereignty, and more importantly,
if it does, should it?

The answer to the first question is 'yes to a degree'. If a
permanent international court is established, and it has the
power to try our soldiers if we do not try them, then our
sovereignty is lessened. Bishop is partly right.

But, wait a second, let's look at that a bit more closely.

The ICC will only try Australians that in the future may
be accused of Genocide or horrendous crimes if, and only
if, Australia refuses to try them in Australia. If an accused
Australian soldier, and one co-author of this article is
an Australian Army Officer, is prosecuted in our system,
then no sovereignty is lost.

No one can take our soldiers away if we have a go at
them first.

In 2002 and 2003 the United States got the United Nations to declare its personnel immune from prosecution by the ICC. In June 2004, however, it dropped a similar request when it became apparent that the UN would refuse it. The change in UN attitude was put down to revelations of mistreatment of prisoners by U.S. personnel in Iraq. Do you think such revelations changed the way other nations see the United States?

Does comparing opponents of the ICC to people who were responsible for genocide such as Milosevic and Pol Pot strengthen the authors' argument or not?

Do you think the United States would ever refuse to prosecute an American accused of such a crime? If so, in what circumstances might this happen?

This leads on to the second question. If an Australian soldier commits or is suspected of committing a horrendous offence and a future government refuses to prosecute them, should an international court step in?

We said that it should with the Germans. We said that it should with the Japanese. We said that it should with the Rwandans. We said that it should with the Serbs, Croats and Bosnians.

This memorial commemorates the victims of Rwanda's 1994 genocide. A UN international criminal tribunal has been investigating war crimes since 1997.

So to Bronwyn Bishop we say "Yes" you are right. A little sovereignty would be lost with the creation of the International Criminal Court, but only if future governments fail to act against atrocities....

But sovereignty in that case not only "should" be lost but "must" be lost. If we don't have the guts to prosecute our own people if they commit crime on a horrendous scale, then someone else must.

Summary

Although David Davenport, the author of the first article, supports the principle of an international criminal court, he believes that the jurisdiction of the ICC is too extensive and represents a threat to national sovereignty. He favors international criminal tribunals that are set up as and when they are needed, such as the war crimes tribunals held in Germany and Japan in the 1940s following World War II and the tribunals for Rwanda and the former Yugoslavia in the 1990s. Davenport believes that the ICC, in seeking to file charges against citizens of states that have not signed up to it, is overreaching its jurisdiction. He points out that the United States has more troops engaged in peacekeeping missions than any other nation and would therefore be particularly vulnerable to cases brought by the court. He disputes the idea that the ICC will not file charges against democratic leaders, arguing that British Prime Minister Tony Blair has already been accused of war crimes in Iraq. Davenport concludes that the ICC is an attempt by smaller states to balance the economic, political, and military power of the United States.

The Australian authors of the second article, Andrew MacLeod and Greg Barns, acknowledge that the ICC will restrict national sovereignty by making states answerable to an international court. In their view, however, that does not present a challenge to any free country because the soldiers of any nation who commit atrocities will be tried by an international court only if the legal system of their native country fails to deal with them first. If a country does fail to prosecute its own citizens who are accused of atrocities, they argue, then it is only fair and right that it should lose its sovereignty in that case.

FURTHER INFORMATION:

Books:

Deller, Nicole, *et al.* (eds.), *Rule of Power or Rule of Law?* New York: Apex Press, 2003.

Schabas, William A., *An Introduction to the International Criminal Court* (2nd edition). New York: Cambridge University Press, 2004.

Sewall, Sarah B., and Carl Kaysen (eds.), *The United States and the International Criminal Court.* Lanham, MD: Rowman & Littlefield, 2000.

Useful websites:

www.icc-cpi.int

International Criminal Court website.

http://www.weltpolitik.net/sachgebiete/zukunft/article/538.html

Article about the ICC and different countries' positions on the national sovereignty debate.

The following debates in the Pro/Con series may also be of interest:

In this volume:

Topic 2 Should heads of state be prosecuted for crimes against humanity?

Topic 14 Does the United States have too much influence on international law?

Topic 16 Is the U.S. War on Terrorism a violation of international law?

DOES THE INTERNATIONAL CRIMINAL COURT UNDERMINE NATIONAL SOVEREIGNTY?

YES: Ad hoc tribunals, such as those set up at the end of World War II or those dealing with Rwanda or former Yugoslavia, are the best way to deal with such serious crimes

YES: By trying citizens of particular nations, the ICC will be doing something that should be done by national courts

REPLACEMENT COURT
Will the ICC take the place of national courts?

NECESSITY
Is there no need for a permanent international criminal court?

NO: The ICC is a court of last resort: It will try only those cases that national courts cannot or will not prosecute

NO: The existence of such a court is an essential indicator that crimes against humanity and war crimes cannot be committed with impunity

DOES THE INTERNATIONAL CRIMINAL COURT UNDERMINE NATIONAL SOVEREIGNTY?

KEY POINTS

YES: National sovereignty is the fundamental principle of international politics. Every nation is entitled to organize its own affairs as it sees fit.

YES: Any attempt by the ICC to try such citizens would overreach the fundamental principles of international law

SOVEREIGNTY
Is national sovereignty an indivisible principle?

NONPARTY STATES
Should it be impossible for the ICC to try citizens of non-ICC states?

NO: If nations choose not to prosecute those accused of crimes against humanity, they do not deserve to preserve their national sovereignty in the case

NO: The ICC has been ratified by the United Nations; it should not be possible for nations to escape its jurisdiction simply by not signing up to it

Topic 2
SHOULD HEADS OF STATE BE PROSECUTED FOR CRIMES AGAINST HUMANITY?

YES
FROM "NEW BID TO ARREST MUGABE"
COMMONWEALTH SUMMIT, BRISBANE, 2002
PETER TATCHELL

NO
"WAR CRIMES TRIALS AND ERRORS"
WWW.LEWROCKWELL.COM, DECEMBER 19, 2003
BUTLER SHAFFER

INTRODUCTION

It is a long-standing principle of international law that a head of state—an elected or unelected governor of a nation—cannot be put on trial in another nation's courts. Depending on specific national laws, a head of state may, however, be prosecuted in his or her home country; heads of state are also subject to prosecution by various international tribunals set up on specific occasions. That precedent was set in 2002 when the International Criminal Tribunal for the Former Yugoslavia began the trial of the former president of Serbia and Yugoslavia, Slobodan Milosevic, for war crimes committed in Croatia, Kosovo, and Bosnia–Herzegovina during the 1990s.

The principle of immunity for heads of state exists to prevent one country from being able to sit in judgment on the actions of another government in its own country. Its historical roots lie in the 1648 Treaty of Westphalia, which concluded the Thirty Years' War (1618-1648) in Europe. The treaty established the principle that heads of sovereign states were free to impose their own rule without interference from any other state. The precedent that one government could not object to the way a foreign ruler treated his or her own people governed international relations for three centuries.

After World War II (1939-1945), which involved civilians to a greater degree than any previous conflict, the rights of individuals began to assume greater importance in relation to the political rights of the state or its rulers. In the war's aftermath international tribunals were set up in Nuremberg and Tokyo, respectively, to try the leaders of Germany and Japan for crimes against peace, war crimes, and crimes against humanity. Since then thousands of individuals have been held accountable for crimes against humanity. According to Article 6 of the charter that established the International Military Tribunal at Nuremberg, such crimes include "murder, extermination, enslavement, deportation, and other inhumane acts committed against any civilian population, before or during the war; or persecution on political, racial, or religious grounds in execution of or in connection with any crime within the jurisdiction of the tribunal, whether or not in violation of the domestic law of the country where perpetrated."

> "Under international law heads of state and government officials are not immune from criminal prosecution."
>
> —AMNESTY INTERNATIONAL

Article 7 of the charter further specified, "The official position of defendants, whether as Heads of State or responsible officials in Government Departments, shall not be considered as freeing them from responsibility or mitigating punishment." Although Adolf Hitler's successor as head of the German state, Admiral Karl Dönitz, was present at Nuremberg, he was tried for his criminal conduct as a military commander, not as a head of state. In Tokyo the United States, as the occupying power, decided not to prosecute the Emperor Hirohito. It preferred to leave him to serve as the unifying figurehead of the new constitutional monarchy.

An important precedent in the treatment of heads of state came in 1998. British authorities detained General Augusto Pinochet, president of Chile from 1974 to 1990, while British courts considered a request from Spain to extradite him to stand trial for the murder of Spanish citizens while he was in office. A panel of judges in the House of Lords eventually decided that immunity from prosecution only applied to what are considered the official duties of a head of state. They ruled that the crimes of which Pinochet was accused, which included genocide and torture, did not fall into that category. In the event, Pinochet was declared too sick to stand trial and returned to Chile. Some experts now argue, however, that a head or former head of state cannot invoke immunity in cases of torture, genocide, war crimes, or crimes against humanity. But others counter that heads of state have to be free to act without fear of future prosecution. Some also contend that it would be impossible for a dignitary to receive a fair trial.

The ongoing trial of Slobodan Milosevic is another test case. He and his supporters argue that the tribunal trying him is illegal. They claim that he was a legitimate head of state who was victimized by other aggressor nations. Prosecutor Justice Louise Arbour, however, has countered that "No credible, lasting peace can be built upon impunity.... The refusal to bring war criminals to account would be an affront to those who obey the law, and a betrayal of those who rely on it for their life and security."

The following articles look at two very different aspects of this question.

NEW BID TO ARREST MUGABE
Peter Tatchell

Peter Tatchell is a gay and human rights campaigner and author. He was born in Melbourne in 1952 and has lived in the United Kingdom since 1971. This article is from his website.

Robert Mugabe (1924–) became prime minister of Zimbabwe in 1980 and president in 1987. He has been criticized for his dictatorial actions, disregard for human rights, and suppression of opposition.

In fact, Tatchell was refused a visa by the Australian government (he has been a British citizen since 1989) until it was too late for him to attend. In the end Mugabe did not attend the summit either.

YES

☑ President Mugabe has beefed up his security ahead of the Commonwealth summit in Brisbane in 2002, with his bodyguards undergoing special Russian-backed training. He fears a repeat of my attempts to arrest him in London in 1999 and in Brussels in 2001. His fear is justified. I am going to Brisbane to seek to have him arrested. International and Australian law are on my side. Mugabe has broken the law against torture; I am endeavouring to enforce it.

Mugabe must be put on trial

At the Commonwealth summit in Brisbane I will attempt to have President Mugabe arrested by the Australian authorities on charges of torture and crimes against humanity—under the international human rights laws that have been used to arrest the ex-Yugoslav President, Slobodan Milosevic. My two previous attempts in London and Brussels failed, but I will keep trying until Mugabe is in jail, which is where he belongs. My motive is to end his tyrannical, homophobic regime and ensure democracy and human rights for all Zimbabweans—black and white, gay and straight.

Mugabe knows what to expect from me. There are no surprises. My objective is to have him arrested under the UN Convention Against Torture 1984. I have nothing to hide. All my plans are in the open. Mugabe is the one who has to hide behind dozens of bodyguards because he fears being arrested and put on trial for human rights abuses. I am not afraid of Mugabe or his henchmen. If he has me beaten up again, that will not save his regime. The international outcry would help hasten his downfall. I will be acting alone, non-violently, and in cooperation with the Australian legal authorities. Why is Mugabe so afraid of me? My only weapons are words and the legal authority of international human rights law.

The legal case against Mugabe

Australia, Britain and most other Commonwealth countries have signed the UN Convention Against Torture 1984. Under

Political activist Peter Tatchell holds a placard satirizing Robert Mugabe as a tyrannical drag queen at the London Gay Pride march in July 2003.

this Convention the signatory states pledge to arrest any person who commits an act of torture anywhere in the world. Australia has incorporated this UN Convention into its own domestic law, the Crimes (Torture) Act 1988. This is the legal basis for my bid to have Mugabe arrested by the Australian authorities. If they refuse, I will try to get a court order for the arrest of Mugabe. My actions will seek to enforce the international law against torture, which Australia has ratified and promised to uphold.

See http://www. irct.org/usr/irct/ home.nsf/unid/ BKEN-5HMKUW for the history and main provisions of the UN Convention against Torture.

Choto–Chavunduka case

Amnesty International, with corroboration from the Zimbabwe High Court, have evidence that in 1999 Mugabe condoned the torture of two black journalists, Ray Choto and Mark Chavunduka of *The Standard* newspaper in Harare:

See http://web. amnesty.org/library/ Index/ENGAFR46002 1999?open&of=ENG -2F3 for Amnesty International's press release on the Choto– Chavunduka case.

Military interrogators beat both men all over their bodies with fists, wooden planks and rubber sticks, particularly on the soles of their feet, and gave them electric shocks all over the body, including the genitals. The men were also subjected to "the submarine"— having their heads wrapped in plastic bags and submerged in a water tank until they suffocated.
—Amnesty International release, 21 January 1999

During his torture, Choto was told that Mugabe had ordered them to be tortured. Mugabe has since publicly refused to condemn their torture, and has tacitly endorsed it, suggesting that the two men got what they deserved.

I will be taking with me to Australia signed affidavits from Ray Choto and Mark Chavunduka, attesting to their torture by the Zimbabwe authorities. These affidavits will be presented to the Attorney-General, with a request that he authorise Mugabe's arrest and trial.

Given this overwhelming evidence, the Australian government has a moral and legal duty to arrest and prosecute President Mugabe on charges of torture.

The myth of head-of-state immunity

The claim that Mugabe has Head of State immunity, and therefore cannot be prosecuted, is a legal fiction. Under the UN Convention Against Torture there are no exemptions. No one is immune.

The Australian government, however, claims that Heads of State have absolute immunity from prosecution for torture under Section 5 (1) of the Crimes (Torture) Act 1988 and Section 3A of the Crimes (Internationally Protected Persons) Act 1976.

This interpretation does not stand legal scrutiny. It is customary law that international human rights statutes take precedence over domestic legislation. In other words, individual states—particularly those that have signed and ratified binding human rights conventions—cannot use national law to invalidate international legislation, especially where crimes against humanity are involved.

Over 50 years ago, following the Nazi atrocities, the Nuremberg Tribunal verdicts established the international human rights principle that nobody is above the law. This principle still applies. It has been recently reiterated in the case of Slobodan Milosevic. He was indicted for war crimes while he was still Head of State. It was recognised in his case that Heads of State do not have immunity from prosecution

The journalists were arrested because they had published a story about a coup plot that had been discovered in the army. Zimbabwe's High Court ordered their release, which did not take place until several days afterward. Chavunduka died after a long illness in November 2002, and Choto now works in the United States.

"Customary law" is rules of conduct widely agreed to be universally applicable. That is why international law outlawing slavery, for instance, could not simply be overruled by a country deciding to legalize slavery.

Slobodan Milosevic was president of Yugoslavia (Serbia and Montenegro) at the time of his arrest in Belgrade by Serb police in April 2001. See Volume 15, Human Rights, The Slobodan Milosevic case, page 206.

26

for crimes against humanity, such as torture. The indictment and arrest of Milosevic has created the precedent under which Mugabe can also be arrested and put on trial....

Mugabe's record of human rights abuses

Mugabe is the key person behind the current terror campaign in Zimbabwe. He is giving the green light to the torture and murder of black farm workers, white farmers and supporters of the opposition Movement for Democratic Change.

Mugabe has a long history of human rights abuses. As well as attacks on the lesbian and gay community, he is implicated in the massacre of up to 20,000 people in Matabeleland during the 1980s, restrictions on strikes and demonstrations, the intimidation of the press and judiciary, infringements of trade union rights, and police brutality against peaceful protesters.

In the single month of July 2001, the Amani Trust in Harare, which monitors human rights abuses, recorded 11 politically motivated murders, 61 disappearances, 104 cases of unlawful detention, and 288 incidents of torture. Nearly all the victims were black opponents of the Mugabe regime, mostly supporters of the democratic opposition, the MDC.

Lesbians and gay men have been frequent targets of Mugabe's wrath. He has denounced gay people as "sexual perverts," "beasts" and "worse than dogs and pigs." Rejecting calls for homosexual human rights, Mugabe says: "we don't believe they have any rights at all." Since his comments, lesbians and gays in Zimbabwe have been beaten, arrested, framed on trumped-up charges, and threatened with death.

Mugabe's homophobic hate campaign began in 1995, when the human rights group Gays And Lesbians of Zimbabwe (GALZ) was banned from exhibiting at the Zimbabwe International Book Fair. The following year at the Book Fair, GALZ members were attacked and threatened by government stooges, forcing them to flee.

In recent months, GALZ's offices in Harare have been vandalised by pro-Mugabe vigilantes. They have ordered GALZ members to leave the country, threatening reprisals if they stay.

President Mugabe has got away with assaults on human rights for too long. The time has come for Australia and the Commonwealth to show him that he cannot terrorise his people with impunity.

If Slobodan Milosevic is to stand trial in The Hague, why shouldn't Mugabe?

Matabeleland is home to the minority Ndebele people, who were associated with the ZAPU party. Mugabe's ZANU (now ZANU-PF) party was associated with the majority Shona. Fighting between the groups continued for years after independence in 1980. This rivalry goes back to the Ndebele conquest of Shona lands in the mid-19th century.

The MDC (Movement for Democratic Change) was formed in 1999 from a coalition of labor, business, church, and women's groups. It is the main opposition to Mugabe's ruling ZANU-PF party.

GALZ was founded in 1989 to provide social support for gays and lesbians in Zimbabwe. See http://www.icon.co.za/stobbs/galz.htm for more information about the organization.

WAR CRIMES TRIALS AND ERRORS
Butler Shaffer

Butler Shaffer is
a professor at
Southwestern
University School of
Law, Los Angeles.
His writings take an
antigovernment
stance from a
libertarian
perspective, shared
by other authors
on the website—
www.lewrockwell.
com—from which
this article comes.

NO

Years ago, a news story reported thefts of inmates'
personal property at a state penitentiary. The prisoners
held an impromptu meeting in the cafeteria, at which one of
the convicts declared: "men, we have a thief among us!" I
recalled this story as I watched the television agents of
disinformation and sophistry chortle over the capture of
Saddam Hussein, and then announce that Hussein would be
prosecuted for "war crimes" or "crimes against humanity!"

Satire has never been more fully expressed than in the
institution of "war crimes trials." Such extravaganzas seek to
bestow legitimacy upon the act of punishing the losing side
in wartime for having done the very acts engaged in by the
victors. Such charades remind me of the posturings in the
Godfather movies, with organized crime leaders embracing
and sanctimoniously pledging their mutual honor, while their
operatives are out on the street killing one another.

Revenge dressed up as justice

After cutting through self-serving legal definitions and
distinctions that obscure the fact that all wars are crimes
against humanity, the essence of a war crime comes down to
this: the winners get to beat up and/or kill the losers. For all
the gilt-edged window-dressing and black-robed magistrates
with which "war crimes trials" are conducted, their
underlying logic is no different than when our ancient
ancestors placed the severed heads of vanquished leaders
on pikes and rode through the streets to cheering throngs.

We delude ourselves that we are too "civilized" to engage
in the barbarities of "victors' justice." Like members of a
lynch mob who, after the fact, are embarrassed to admit to
themselves that they were capable of having their fears
mobilized into angry and murderous expressions, we must
rationalize our support for wars. The fear and hatred of a foe
that was skillfully nurtured by statist propaganda is not easily
dissipated once reason and intelligence returns to our minds.
We need to convince ourselves that there was some noble
purpose, some abiding principle that drove our fury. If there
is to be a "war on terror" with which to frighten men and
women into submitting to state authority, there must be

> In fact, from the
> end of the Roman
> Empire until the
> 20th century it was
> highly unusual for
> defeated rulers to
> be executed.

> Do you agree with
> the author's
> implication that
> war can never have
> a noble purpose?

horrible terrorist acts to be punished. What better mechanism for the completion of this cycle of self-deception than a "war crimes" trial?

You can see how such trials are crucial to the state's efforts to rationalize its viciousness to an otherwise decent public. Lopping off the heads of the conquered will no longer be acceptable to men and women of enhanced sensibilities. In a legalistic age, the appearance of due process must be adhered to, even if the guilt of the accused is a foregone conclusion. The proposition was never better stated than by Lewis Carroll's Queen of Hearts who intoned: "sentence first, verdict afterwards."

The author is referring to the trial scene in Lewis Carroll's novel Alice in Wonderland *(1865).*

Before joining with the Bush administration and its media flunkies for another round of boob-hustling, bear in mind the wholly one-sided nature of "war crimes" prosecutions. Had there ever been a sincere effort to punish those who intentionally inflicted needless death and suffering upon civilian populations, Winston Churchill and Harry Truman would have ended their careers on the hangman's scaffold (as would Roosevelt, had he survived the war). It has been estimated that British and American terror bombings of German cities—directed not at military installations, but civilian targets—killed over half a million people. The fire bombings of Dresden—a city with no more military significance than Beverly Hills—led to the deaths of anywhere from 30,000 to 100,000 or more persons. The attack on Hamburg killed some 40,000; Wurzburg added another 6,000 dead; while the massive raid on Cologne (Köln) added more victims.

The author makes no distinction between those who initiated World War II by invading other countries and those who fought in response. Do you agree that there is no moral distinction between them?

Terrorizing civilians

The British openly defended such attacks as a way of terrorizing the German people into demanding a surrender. The head of the RAF Bomber Command, Arthur "Bomber" Harris, confessed to even more brutal purposes in declaring that bombing raids on German cities occurred simply because the allies had run out of other targets to bomb! Harris' statement that "bombing anything in Germany is better than bombing nothing" summarizes the purpose of such raids. (I am amused by Anglophiles who hold up the British as an example of a "civilizing" influence in the world!)

After the bombing of Hamburg in July 1943 Albert Speer, Hitler's armaments minister, believed that half a dozen more such raids in quick succession would have broken German morale and forced a surrender. If this had happened, and the war had ended two years before it eventually did, would it have justified the policy?

Nor can we overlook what may be the most grievous war crime and act of state terrorism: the American nuclear bombings of Hiroshima and Nagasaki. Some 105,000 were estimated to have been killed outright by these bombs— including American prisoners of war being held in a nearby

In summer 1945 the Japanese cabinet was split: Some wanted to begin peace talks with the Americans, but many military leaders wanted to fight on. The atomic attacks strengthened the peace party's hand, but it is impossible to know whether surrender would have come anyway.

The 2001 book The Trial of Henry Kissinger by Christopher Hitchens actually does make the case for regarding the former secretary of state as a war criminal.

Donald Rumsfeld was President Reagan's special envoy when he met Saddam Hussein, then an ally of the United States, in 1983. They discussed ways of getting Iraqi oil to market after routes controlled by Iran and Syria had been blocked.

prison camp—with many more than that number who subsequently died from radiation burns and secondary diseases. That many Americans continue to assuage themselves with the lie that these bombings brought about an end of the war—the Japanese had been trying to surrender before the attacks—reflects the same need of people to distance themselves from the wrongs of their government as is found in the oft-cited statements of Germans who "didn't know" of the vile practices being engaged in by their Nazi leaders.

If the prosecution of government leaders for the fomenting of war was a truly principled undertaking, the United States could have added more war-crimes defendants to the docks as a result of the Vietnam War. Presidents Johnson and Nixon, and such administration officials as Robert McNamara and Henry Kissinger, would have had much to answer for when it comes to the intentional infliction of death and suffering upon humanity.

Saddam Hussein—friend or foe?

And now we come to the Bush administration's efforts to sanitize its wrongs by prosecuting Saddam Hussein. Was Hussein a butcherous tyrant? Of course he was. His record for viciousness was a matter of record even during the administrations of Ronald Reagan and George H.W. Bush, when the United States cozied up to this thug and authorized the sale of deadly weapons—including chemical and biological agents—to his regime. The *Washington Post* reported that Iraq was using chemical weapons on an "almost daily" basis when Donald Rumsfeld was meeting with Hussein in December 1983. During the prolonged debate over whether Hussein had weapons of mass destruction, I kept expecting George Bush to announce: "we have the evidence; we have the original invoices!" Photos of Rumsfeld shaking hands with Hussein, in 1983, reflect the Janus-faced nature of enemies and allies in our world.

If Hussein is to be prosecuted for employing chemical or biological weapons against his foes, will Bush I and Rumsfeld be indicted as co-defendants? Mr. Reagan is apparently in no condition to stand trial, but ought not these other men who aided and abetted Hussein's efforts by helping the United States supply him with his weapons? If not, will they be permitted to testify as character witnesses on behalf of Hussein?

And what about the current President Bush? Will he be made to answer for his crimes of making unprovoked attacks upon Afghanistan and Iraq? Will his administration's cascades of lies and forged documents be introduced into evidence to support the charge that Mr. Bush, like "Bomber" Harris before him, was intent on bombing any plausible target? And should Mr. Bush plead his "war on terror" as a defense, will he be compelled to confront the fact that the United States has been, for decades now, a leading practitioner of state terror against other nations? Even the Bush administration's prolonged, heavy bombing of Baghdad was an admission of this fact: aptly named "Shock and Awe," this deadly campaign was designed to do to Iraqis what the allied bombing of Germany had sought, namely, to terrorize people, and for what purpose? If, as the neocons and Bush-leaguers had maintained, the Iraq people lived under the tyranny of Saddam Hussein—which, indeed, they had—and eagerly awaited our rescue efforts, then to what end should the Iraqis experience "shock and awe" [from] their alleged "liberators?"

States are to blame

Rather than continuing our participation in these periodic self-righteous, farcical "trials" for "war-crimes" or "crimes against humanity," let us acknowledge that all political systems war against humanity, for they seek to compel people to be what they do not choose to be and to act as they do not choose to act. Every state is a "terrorist state," for each, in varying degrees, threatens people with the infliction of violence or death for failure to abide by its demands.

It is time that we gave up our illusions about "good" guys and "bad" guys in our world, and recognize that political thinking and the systems it spawns will always be destructive of human well-being. The earlier photo of Donald Rumsfeld shaking hands with Saddam Hussein is but one exhibit tending to show the symbiotic relationship that unites all statists in a conspiracy against the human race. Such evidence ought to be carefully considered by a jury of humanity itself in a trial of more encompassing dimensions, namely, mankind versus the state.

> The invasion of Afghanistan in 2001 was launched because the Afghan government was believed to be sheltering the Al Qaeda organization responsible for the 9/11 terror attacks. Does that count as enough provocation to launch an attack?

> The "neocons," or neoconservatives, believe that the United States should use its power to spread democracy and the free market around the world. They formed a powerful influence on George W. Bush's administration.

> Can humans only be free in a system with no government or a new form of government? Who would be the winners and losers from such a change?

Summary

In the first of the two articles writer and gay and human rights activist Peter Tatchell puts forward the case for arresting Robert Mugabe, president of Zimbabwe, for the crime of torture. He describes the case of two journalists who were tortured, allegedly on Mugabe's orders. Tatchell explains how he has tried to perform a citizen's arrest on Mugabe twice before, both times unsuccessfully. Mugabe, among other abuses of human rights, has persecuted the gay community in Zimbabwe. Tatchell argues that the claim that heads of state have immunity is illegitimate. Under international law, he argues, they should be prosecuted for crimes against humanity. He compares the case of Mugabe with that of the former Serbian and Yugoslav President Slobodan Milosevic, who was tried for war crimes before an international tribunal. If Milosevic can stand trial, Tatchell asks, why can't Mugabe?

In the second article Butler Shaffer looks at the December 2003 capture of Saddam Hussein and the announcement that he would face prosecution for war crimes and crimes against humanity. Shaffer argues that all such trials are show trials. If heads of state were really culpable for their actions, he says, leaders such as Winston Churchill and Harry S. Truman would have stood trial for acts such as the dropping of the atomic bomb on Hiroshima during World War II. He also argues that George W. Bush's administration would be attempting to sanitize its own wrongs by putting Hussein on trial. Shaffer goes further by suggesting that states and their leaders attack and terrorize not only other nations but also their own people. He argues that all forms of government are coercive and that all leaders can therefore be considered as criminals to a greater or lesser degree.

FURTHER INFORMATION:

Books:

Gutman, Roy, and David Rieff (eds.), *Crimes of War: What the Public Should Know*. New York: W.W. Norton & Co., 1999.

Maga, Tim, *Judgment at Tokyo: The Japanese War Crimes Trials*. Lexington, KY: University Press of Kentucky, 2001.

Marrus, Michael R., *The Nuremberg War Crimes Trial 1945–46: A Documentary History*. Boston, MA: Bedford Books, 1997.

Useful websites:

http://www.ess.uwe.ac.uk/genocide/war_criminals.htm
Genocide Documentation Centre page on Nuremberg.
http://www.un.org/icty
International Criminal Tribunal for the Former Yugoslavia.

The following debates in the Pro/Con series may also be of interest:

In this volume:

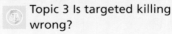

Topic 3 Is targeted killing wrong?

Topic 10 Do extradition treaties violate human rights?

Topic 16 Is the U.S. War on Terrorism a violation of international law?

SHOULD HEADS OF STATE BE PROSECUTED FOR CRIMES AGAINST HUMANITY?

YES: *The Milosevic trial has shown how careful the tribunal has been to make sure that he receives a fair trial*

YES: *If leaders know they will be held accountable for their actions, they may be more circumspect in their respect for human rights*

FAIRNESS
Would heads and former heads of state receive fair trials?

ACCOUNTABILITY
Might the fear of prosecution make political leaders more respectful of their citizens' rights?

NO: *Nations involved in the trial of such people may have hidden agendas, perhaps to deflect attention away from their own actions*

SHOULD HEADS OF STATE BE PROSECUTED FOR CRIMES AGAINST HUMANITY?
KEY POINTS

NO: *The kind of leaders who are prepared to commit crimes against humanity are not likely to care whether they are breaking international laws*

YES: *The crimes for which heads of state can be prosecuted, such as crimes against humanity, can never be justified as part of political obligations*

YES: *The ICC was specifically created to deal with war crimes and crimes against humanity, so heads of state should fall within its jurisdiction*

JUSTIFICATION
Is it wrong for heads of state to justify improper actions by stating that the end justifies the means?

JUDGMENT
Is the International Criminal Court (ICC) the best body to try heads of state?

NO: *Leaders of nations sometimes have to take unpopular measures for the good of the majority. They cannot be expected to do so if they might be open to politically motivated prosecutions.*

NO: *Ad hoc international tribunals have been successfully used to prosecute crimes against humanity in the past; they are less open to political influence than a permanent court*

AUGUSTO PINOCHET: PATRIOT OR WAR CRIMINAL?

*"Not a leaf moves without
my knowing of it."*
—GENERAL AUGUSTO PINOCHET (1975)

In 1973 General Augusto Pinochet staged a military coup that ended in the death of the democratically elected President Salvador Allende. Pinochet remained in power until 1990. Such were the human rights abuses committed during Pinochet's rule, and particularly during the coup itself, that increasing numbers of people have called for his trial for war crimes. During a visit to Britain he was detained and placed under arrest while it was decided whether he should be extradited to Spain, where a warrant had been issued for him to stand trial. His detainment was controversial, bringing to public attention the issue of whether it is right to make heads of state stand trial for crimes committed during their time in power. This article examines Pinochet's case further.

From Valparaiso to president

Augusto Pinochet Ugarte was born in Valparaiso on November 25, 1915. His mother encouraged him to pursue a military career, and he rose quickly through the officer ranks, becoming a general under the left-wing Popular Unity government led by Salvador Allende in the early 1970s. Allende trusted Pinochet and in August 1973 made him army commander-in-chief. On September 11, 1973, Pinochet led the coup against Allende by the military junta, which represented every branch of Chile's armed forces. He was backed by the U.S. government, which feared a socialist government in Chile—even a democratically elected one.

Caravan of death

In October 1973 an army unit toured many villages throughout Chile by helicopter. Officially their job was to "review the War Council proceedings for political prisoners in the regions and bring procedures there in line with Santiago standards." Many of Allende's supporters had turned themselves in voluntarily, but in the course of these visits—the so-called "caravan of death"—around 3,000 Allende supporters were killed, thousands more were tortured, and many thousands more again were forced to flee abroad into exile. Many believe that the unit was acting under Pinochet's direct orders, but his supporters, including his lawyer Ricardo Rivadeneira, deny the charge. After the coup Pinochet suspended the constitution, closed the Chilean parliament, and banned all political and labor union activity. He also imposed curfews and restricted media freedom. He defended his actions by calling himself a patriot who wished to save his country from the chaos that the left-wing government, 150 percent inflation, and inefficient nationalized industries had allegedly brought. In 1974 Pinochet appointed himself president. In 1990 he reluctantly stepped down, having lost a referendum designed to prolong his hold on power, but he ensured that he was appointed a senator for life and commander-in-chief of the army—a post he held until 1998. Critics say he used that position to ensure that no members of the security forces were prosecuted for human rights abuses, and also to block any "radical" political initiatives. Increasingly, human rights groups called for Pinochet's arrest and trial for crimes against humanity.

Investigations in Chile

The Chilean National Commission on Truth and Reconciliation, established by President Patricio Aylwin in April 1990, together with the Chilean government's report to the Committee against Torture, concluded that the intelligence service, DINA (Directorate of National Intelligence), under Pinochet's direct command, played a central role in the policy of systematic and widespread human rights violations in Chile. Similarly, they concluded that DINA developed a variety of criminal tactics, including killings and "disappearances" of Chileans and other nationals in other countries, including a car-bombing carried out in Washington, D.C., in 1976. They found that these violations required intelligence coordination and planning at the highest levels of the state. According to these reports, during the period 1973 to 1977 the DINA reported directly to General Pinochet.

Arrest in Britain

General Pinochet was arrested on October 16, 1998, while visiting the United Kingdom. He was detained on a Spanish arrest warrant, which stated that he had been responsible for the murder of Spanish citizens in Chile when he was president. Other criminal proceedings against Pinochet were initiated in national courts in Belgium, France, Italy, Luxembourg, Sweden, and Switzerland. The international community debated the legitimacy of holding a former head of state responsible for crimes committed during his rule. Some believed that he should be held accountable and extradited to Spain for trial. Others argued that it would set a dangerous precedent for other leaders, including ones of democratic nations, to be held accountable for their actions. Three British High Court judges ruled that Pinochet had immunity for any crime committed as head of state. This judgment was reversed by a panel of five Law Lords. After a fresh hearing in March 1999 a panel of seven Law Lords ruled that Pinochet could be extradited to Spain to face charges, but not for offenses that had allegedly occurred before 1988. Pinochet was finally released and allowed to return to Chile by British Home Secretary Jack Straw in March 2000 on the medical grounds of senility. Since Pinochet had given lucid interviews shortly before and showed no sign of senility on his return to Chile, he is widely believed to have been coached in how to mimic the symptoms of the condition for his medical examination in Britain. In May 2004 a court in Santiago stripped Pinochet of his immunity from prosecution under Chilean law, but the ruling will likely be appealed to the Chilean Supreme Court.

Topic 3

IS TARGETED KILLING WRONG?

YES

"ASSASSINATION AND DISPLAY IN IRAQ: THE KILLINGS OF UDAY AND
QUSAI HUSSEIN IN INTERNATIONAL LAW"
JURIST, JULY 29, 2003
MARJORIE COHN

NO

FROM "REVIVING THE ASSASSINATION OPTION"
THE AMERICAN ENTERPRISE, DECEMBER 2001
DAVID SILVERSTEIN

INTRODUCTION

In the space of little more than a month in 2004 Israeli forces killed both the radical Palestinian leader Sheikh Ahmed Yassin and his successor Abdel Aziz al-Rantissi. The men were leaders of Hamas, a militant group opposed to what it sees as Israeli occupation of Palestinian land. Hamas has been directly implicated in planning terrorist attacks against Israeli civilians. Israel has long seen what it calls "targeted killing" as a legitimate response to dealing with terror groups such as Hamas and Islamic Jihad. Since the start of the second Palestinian uprising, or intifada, in 2000, it has killed dozens of Palestinian leaders.

Opponents of the Israeli action argue that targeted killing is unlawful execution since its targets have not been tried and found guilty by any judicial process. In response to the killing of Sheikh Yassin the United Nations (UN) Security Council drafted a resolution condemning the killing as "the most recent extrajudicial execution committed by Israel." However, the United States vetoed the resolution. It claimed that since the text did not specifically condemn Hamas for its terrorist activities, it was biased. The U.S. veto was widely condemned by other countries.

For centuries nations have used the assassination of political opponents, dissidents, or leaders of potential enemies as an official policy. Their justification is that such actions are for the national good. Ancient thinkers such as Aristotle, Plutarch, and Cicero, for example, justified the practice of tyrannicide—the killing of a tyrant in order to benefit his subjects. The medieval Christian writer Thomas Aquinas also argued that anyone who killed a tyrant should be "praised and rewarded." In such a view the end justifies the means. For example, if someone had assassinated the German Nazi leader Adolf Hitler (1889-1945)— he narrowly survived a bomb attack in July 1944—perhaps World War II

(1939–1945) would have been shortened and many thousands of lives saved. For some people nations should therefore be able use assassination in order to protect their own citizens.

Many other people, however, remain uncomfortable with the practice of targeted killing. A 1998 UN report, for example, stated that "extrajudicial executions can never be justified under any circumstances, not even in time of war." Opponents of targeted killing argue that it might not reflect justice but prejudice: Since it is not part of a legitimate judicial process, it is open to abuse. People can be targeted simply because they disagree with the ruling government. The chances of abuse are increased because many assassination operations are undertaken in secret.

> "*Tyrannicide … is not only lawful, but also laudable.*"
> —JOHN MILTON, ENGLISH WRITER, *THE TENURE OF KINGS AND MAGISTRATES* (1649)

In March 2003 the U.S.-led invasion of Iraq began with a highly visible "decapitation strike." The initial U.S. air strikes on Iraq specifically targeted not only military targets but also the country's leaders, including President, Saddam Hussein (1937–). Although Hussein was eventually captured alive in December 2003, two of his sons, also leading members of the Iraqi regime, had been killed five months earlier in a targeted military campaign. Critics argue that such actions violated not only international law—including the 1937 Convention for the Prevention and Repression of Terrorism, and the 1974 Resolution on Aggression— but also the U.S. Army's guidelines on warfare, which state that the assassination of an enemy, particularly a head of state, is illegal. The U.S. government countered that the Husseins were military as well as political leaders and as such were legitimate targets.

Commentators claim that the United States has used targeted killings in the past. In 1975 a Senate select committee investigation found evidence of U.S. plans to assassinate leaders in the Belgian Congo (now the Democratic Republic of Congo), Cuba, Chile, and South Vietnam, among other countries. The committee concluded that targeted killings were "incompatible with American principles, international order, and morality."

President Gerald Ford (1974–1977) subsequently enacted executive order 11905, which prohibited political assassinations. During the 1980s, however, Pentagon lawyers argued that the executive order did not apply to the killing of people in command positions during times of war. Later other presidents—including Bill Clinton in 1998 and George W. Bush in 2001—were criticized for approving covert targeted killings on a case-by-case basis; they argued that the executive order was not a statute.

Advocates insist that targeted killing can be a legitimate political tool, although critics maintain not only that it is ineffective, but that it can also exacerbate existing resentment, hostility, or opposition toward any government that practices it.

The following two articles examine this question further.

ASSASSINATION AND DISPLAY IN IRAQ...
Marjorie Cohn

Marjorie Cohn, a professor of law at Thomas Jefferson School of Law in San Diego, is executive vice president of the National Lawyers Guild.

YES

Last week [on July 22, 2003] the US military assassinated Uday and Qusai Hussein in a villa in Mosul, Iraq. Hundreds of troops armed with automatic weapons, rockets, rocket-propelled grenades, and tow missiles, and dozens of vehicles and aircraft, attacked four people armed with AK-47 automatic rifles. Mustapha, the 14-year old son of Qusai, was also killed in the operation, along with another individual who was apparently a bodyguard.

The subsequent firestorm of media coverage momentarily diverted public attention from the Bush administration's failing Iraq war—its vain attempts to find any weapons of mass destruction or link between Saddam Hussein and Al Qaeda, the White House's admission that the President used false information in his State of the Union address, and the continuing deaths of American soldiers in an occupation with no end in sight.

The false information in question was a claim that Saddam Hussein tried to buy uranium ore from the West African country of Niger. Such material can be used in the manufacture of nuclear weapons. Bush's information was later shown to be based on forged documents.

Gloating, or important evidence?

The assassinations prompted chest-thumping and back-slapping all around. Even Senator Ted Kennedy joined British Prime Minister Tony Blair, *The New York Times* and the *Washington Post*, in congratulating Bush on the good news. Then, after reportedly reflecting on the pros and cons, Secretary of Defense Donald Rumsfeld gave the go-ahead to display the grisly photographs of the Hussein brothers' reconstructed bullet-riddled faces. The Pentagon didn't want to appear to be "gloating," but Rumsfeld thought the photos would convince skeptical Iraqis that Uday and Qusai were indeed dead, which would reduce the attacks on U.S. troops and encourage informants to come forward without fear of retaliation by the old regime.

The media in many countries do not have the same reservations as U.S. media about showing the dead and other victims of violence and warfare. Do you think Americans would think differently about military action if they were allowed to see its consequences? Could failing to show such scenes be considered a form of media censorship?

Both the targeted assassinations and the photographic display violated well-established principles of international law. Targeted, or political, assassinations are extrajudicial executions. They are unlawful and deliberate killings carried out by order of, or with the acquiescence of, a government, outside any judicial framework. Extrajudicial executions are unlawful, even in armed conflict. In a 1998 report, the United Nations Special Rapporteur on extrajudicial, summary or arbitrary executions noted that "extrajudicial executions can never be justified under any circumstances, not even in time of war."

The International Covenant on Civil and Political Rights, a treaty ratified by the United States, prohibits the arbitrary denial of the right to life, a right so fundamental, there can be no derogation from it even in "time of public emergency which threatens the life of the nation." The UN General Assembly and Human Rights Commission, as well as Amnesty International, have all condemned extrajudicial executions.

After the Senate Select Committee on Intelligence disclosed in 1975 that the CIA had been involved in several murders or attempted murders of foreign leaders, President Gerald Ford issued an executive order banning assassinations. Although every succeeding president has renewed that order, the Clinton administration targeted Osama Bin Laden in Afghanistan, but narrowly missed him.

Unjustifiable change of position

In July 2001, the U.S. Ambassador to Israel denounced Israel's policy of targeted killings, or "preemptive operations." He said "the United States government is very clearly on the record as against targeted assassinations. They are extrajudicial killings, and we do not support that."

Yet after September 11, former White House press secretary Ari Fleischer invited the killing of Saddam Hussein: "The cost of one bullet, if the Iraqi people take it on themselves, is substantially less" than the cost of war. Shortly thereafter, George W. Bush issued a secret directive, which authorized the CIA to target suspected terrorists for assassination when it would be impractical to capture them and when large-scale civilian casualties could be avoided. In November 2002, Bush reportedly authorized the CIA to assassinate a suspected Al Qaeda leader in Yemen. He and five traveling companions were killed in the hit, which Deputy Defense Secretary Paul Wolfowitz described as a "very successful tactical operation."

U.S. opposition

Nearly sixty years ago, the U.S. government opposed the extrajudicial executions of Nazi officials who had committed genocide against millions of people. U.S. Supreme Court Justice Robert H. Jackson, who served as chief prosecutor at the Nuremberg War Crimes Tribunal, told President Harry Truman: "We could execute or otherwise punish [the Nazi leaders] without a hearing. But undiscriminating executions

The International Covenant on Civil and Political Rights was adopted by the UN General Assembly in 1966; it came into effect in 1976. Go to http://www.hrweb.org/legal/cpr.html for the text of the covenant.

Go to http://www.ford.utexas.edu/library/speeches/760110e.htm to read President Ford's executive order 11905 of February 18, 1976.

This statement was made after an attack on July 31, 2001, in which an Israeli helicopter fired three missiles into an office building in Nablus, killing Jamal Mansour and Jamal Salim, members of Hamas, and six other people, including two children.

Qaed al-Harethi, a suspected Al Qaeda operative, was killed along with five others traveling in a car through the desert in Yemen. The car was blown up by a Hellfire missile fired by a pilotless Predator aircraft operated by the CIA.

COMMENTARY: Killing Escobar

Ever since the Colombian drug baron Pablo Escobar (1949–1993) was shot dead in 1993, there has been great debate about how much involvement the United States had in what was essentially the targeted killing of one of the most-wanted criminals in the world.

Escobar rose from a background of extreme poverty and petty crime through the ranks of the drug cartel in the Colombian city of Medellín to become its eventual leader. Escobar's operations were highly lucrative: At the height of his power he was organizing about five trips a week of small aircraft into remote places in the United States. He netted millions of dollars in profit per trip since each plane carried around around 880 to 1,100 lbs. (400–500 kg) of cocaine. Escobar, however, craved political power. In 1986 he ran for and won a seat in the Colombian congress, much to the anger of many legitimate politicians. Escobar subsequently launched a violent campaign against his opponents, He was responsible for the murder of policemen, government ministers, and in 1989, the popular Liberal Party presidential candidate, Luis Galán.

Escobar, Search Bloc, and the Americans

The U.S. government was extremely interested in curtailing Escobar's activities in order to cut down drug smuggling into America. As a result, America provided military advisers to the Colombians in order to help capture Escobar. They trained the Colombian Search Bloc, a group of special police units under the command of Colonel Hugo Martinez. A number of commentators, however, argue that U.S. involvement went beyond advice. They insist that the U.S. counterterrorist unit Delta Force and an army intelligence unit known as Centra Spike actively assisted Martinez's men.

U.S. complicity?

In 1991 the Colombian government struck a deal with Escobar to send him to jail. The deal obstructed America's intended extradition of Escobar to stand trial. It quickly became clear that Escobar was playing both the Colombian and American governments for fools since he continued to run his drug operation from his luxury prison. In 1992 he escaped. Soon afterward a group of people called "Los Pepes" began assassinating Escobar's associates. Rumors closely linked Los Pepes with Search Bloc, although Martinez denied this. Even after the U.S. joint chiefs of staff ordered all U.S. military units out of Colombia, some experts believe that Delta Force had dealings with Search Bloc and may even have given tip-offs to Los Pepes.

On December 2, 1993, Escobar was shot dead on the roof of his hideout by Colombian forces. Some experts say that America was not only complicit in the killing but that a Delta Force sniper may have fired the fatal shot.

or punishments without definite findings of guilt, fairly arrived at, would ... not set easily on the American conscience or be remembered by children with pride."

Sow the wind, reap the whirlwind

Americans should not feel pride in the public display of the gruesome photos of the assassinated Hussein brothers. The First Geneva Convention requires combatants to ensure that the dead are not despoiled. Reconstruction of their faces violates this treaty, which also provides that the dead be honorably interred; Islamic law requires immediate burial. When Iraqis displayed images of captured U.S. troops, Bush demanded that the POWs be treated humanely, and he warned that anyone who mistreated them would be tried for war crimes. But Bush didn't complain when American media outlets featured Iraqi prisoners down on their knees, blindfolded and handcuffed. What's good for the goose is good for the gander.

Uday and Qusai Hussein should have been arrested and tried in Iraqi courts or an international tribunal for their alleged crimes. George W. Bush cannot serve as judge, jury and executioner. This assassination creates a dangerous precedent, which could be used to justify the targeted killings of U.S. leaders. The display of the photographs may backfire and turn the brothers into martyrs who stood against the foreign invaders. It could also result in even more violence against U.S. troops.

The author is referring to the treatment of Iraqi prisoners in the immediate aftermath of the invasion in 2003. This was before the later revelations of prisoner abuse at Abu Ghraib prison and elsewhere.

Do you think that there was any justification in showing photographs of Uday and Qusai Hussein after they had been killed? Has this undermined the United States' position as a leading champion of human rights?

REVIVING THE ASSASSINATION OPTION
David Silverstein

David Silverstein is a member of the Foundation for the Defense of Democracies, based in Washington, D.C. This article was written soon after the September 11 terrorist attacks in 2001.

NO

… "Assassin" is actually an Arabic word, linked to the fanatical Muslim killers who targeted Christian crusaders nine hundred years ago. In modern usage, assassination has usually come to mean the killing of a government official, generally using secret or treacherous means. It is a tool of war that America has used successfully in the past.

Most recently, there was the Phoenix Program run jointly by the CIA and South Vietnamese agencies. This was an operation for uncovering and then neutralizing members of the Viet Cong who were secretly directing subversion and terror campaigns in South Vietnam—communists who aimed to undercut the stability of South Vietnam's evolving proto-democracy. Working with a strong intelligence network, commando teams captured many of these Viet Cong members. They tried to extract knowledge of enemy plans, and to "turn" or imprison the agents.…

In the Vietnam War (1964–1975) the United States and its South Vietnamese allies fought communist North Vietnam and its guerrilla supporters, the Viet Cong.

See http://www. military.com/ Content/ MoreContent1/ ?file=vn_phoenix and http://www.iusb. edu/~journal/ 1998/Paper2.html for varying perspectives on the Phoenix Program.

Successful in Vietnam

The Phoenix Program turned out to be highly effective in eliminating terror and subversion in South Vietnam.… The ranks of Viet Cong terrorists were thinned so drastically that the war became less of a counter-guerilla battle and more a struggle against invading regular North Vietnamese troops.

Like so much else in the Vietnam era, however, the Phoenix Program inspired domestic political opposition in the U.S. Disregarding the program's clear operational successes, the Senate Intelligence Committee, under the direction of its dovish chairman, Senator Frank Church, held hearings beginning in January 1975 which attempted to discredit and embarrass the CIA and the other U.S. intelligence services on many levels.

The very idea of the U.S. conducting undercover operations was challenged.… And the Church Committee report stated without qualification that "assassination is unacceptable in our society." The CIA was raked over the coals for its role in the Phoenix Program. A great stink was generated over indirect American involvement in the killings of Congolese strongman Patrice Lumumba, Dominican Republic dictator

Is assassination always unacceptable? Is it ever justifiable to take one life in order to save many lives? Who should make that decision?

Rafael Trujillo, and Vietnamese official Ngo Dinh Diem. The Committee revealed that the U.S. had considered exotic plans to kill Fidel Castro with an exploding sea shell, a poison cigar, or a wet suit impregnated with toxic fungus.... Given the political climate at the time, it was clear that assassination was going to be eliminated as a tool of American state power.

Outlawed by presidential order

But Congress never specifically outlawed the practice. Instead, it relied on a ban on assassination contained in President Gerald Ford's 1976 Presidential Executive Order 11905, later expanded in President Ronald Reagan's 1981 Presidential Executive Order 12333. The later version of this directive reads: "No person employed by or acting on behalf of the United States Government shall engage in, or conspire to engage in, assassination."

See http://www.cia.gov/cialinformation/eo12333.html for the text of President Reagan's executive order 12333.

Every successive President has followed these bans, and with the Church Committee muckraking in mind, our intelligence and military operatives have been kept on a very short leash. Just the same, our executives are not completely hamstrung in this area. A great advantage of the executive orders is that they can be repealed by the President at any time without Congressional action. Moreover, Congress never required that any bans on "assassination" formally define the term. This fact has given subsequent Presidents considerable latitude when contemplating actions that might result in the death of enemy officials.

There have been at least four or five cases in the last 25 years where it can reasonably be argued that the American military, or an ally working with our assistance, was implicitly targeting a leading foreign enemy for elimination. One example was the 1985 car bombing in a Beirut suburb that targeted Sheikh Mohammed Hussein Fadlallah, the leader of the Hezbollah group which had murdered 241 Marines in that city in 1983. Another example is the 1986 air strike against Muammar Qadaffi's personal compound in Libya, which was launched by President Reagan in the face of evidence of Libyan terrorism. Two further cases were the missile attacks on Saddam Hussein's command bunkers in Iraq in 1991 and 1993. A final instance was the 1993 killing of Colombian drug baron Pablo Escobar by local soldiers operating with American intelligence, training, and assistance. In each of these instances, our Commanders in Chief have scrupulously followed the letter of the law contained in the executive orders against assassination. Yet they effectively managed to skirt the ban. (Only one of these efforts was

Note that Silverstein only says that his case can be "reasonably argued." Is that a high enough standard of proof? How else could proof be established?

Saddam Hussein built many heavily armored bunkers deep underground in Iraq, mainly beneath Baghdad. Missile attacks succeeded in damaging some of them, but Saddam was not in them at the time.

Do you think that public support should be taken into account when deciding an ethical question such as the use of assassination?

See http://www. trialbriefs.com/ HR19.htm for the text of the Terrorist Elimination Act. The bill was not passed. A similar bill, H.R. 356, was introduced in the 108th Congress in January 2003 by representative Terry Everett of Alabama.

Note how Silverstein uses the phrase "has had to be" to imply that the Israelis had no choice but to use assassination. Do you believe that this is true? Should arrest and trial also be considered as options?

Would Silverstein's argument be more convincing if he provided further evidence that the killings have headed off "untold" attacks?

successful, however—that against Escobar.) Importantly, potential critics said little about these strikes, even though they verged on violating the assassination ban, because they were strongly supported by popular opinion.

Today, as Americans call for strong reprisals against the terrorists responsible for the September 11 attacks, even liberal politicians are suddenly showing a new willingness to consider the merits of assassination as a means of responding to sworn enemies. Members of both parties in the House and Senate, including the new chairman of the Senate Intelligence Committee, Senator Bob Graham (D-FL), openly predict a possible lifting of the U.S. ban on the use of assassination. Indeed, a previously moribund bill to repeal the prohibition —H.R. 19, the Terrorist Elimination Act of 2001—recently gained 14 co-sponsors, all enrolled after September 11. Recognizing the emasculated self-defense capabilities created by the ban, President Bush signed an order the same month as the attacks, which explicitly directs the CIA to engage in covert—and deadly—operations against Osama Bin Laden as well as the Al Qaeda organization.

Israel—an example to follow

Amidst this newfound realism, it might be useful to examine Israel's experience with assassination, where the policy has had to be implemented more than perhaps any other place. Surrounded by hostile dictatorships and plagued by a fifth column of Israeli and Palestinian Arabs, Israel has repeatedly been beset by terrorism at home and abroad. One response to this existential threat has been the development of an aggressive policy of state-sponsored assassination of terrorists—referred to as "targeted killings" or "active self-defense."…

Since the start of the first Palestinian uprising or intifada in December 1987, and continuing through the latest uprising that began in September 2000, Israel's targeted killings of terrorists have been restricted to the Middle East, and mostly within its own borders. Employing techniques ranging from sniping to helicopter gunship strikes on moving cars to tiny bombs hidden in cell phones, Israeli operatives have planned pin-point strikes that kill criminals, usually without harming innocent people around them. According to Palestinian sources, Israel has killed more than 60 Palestinians over the past year in this way, heading off untold numbers of attacks. Compared to America's penchant for going after terrorists with cruise missile strikes it can be argued that a pinpoint assassination is

actually much more humane, controlled, and gentle
on non-combatants.…

Israel's "targeted killing" policy has yielded mixed results.
Suicide bombings, drive-by shootings, and random sniping
attacks against Israelis have not been eliminated. In mid
October, Palestinian radicals actually killed an Israeli cabinet
minister in what they said was revenge for a targeted killing.
Meanwhile, foreign governments continue to complain
bitterly over Israeli pre-emptive killings of even the most
violent terrorists.

Israeli counter-terrorism authorities do report,
however, that targeted killings have succeeded in deterring
and short-circuiting attacks, including potential suicide
bombings, and that they have reduced the numbers of
terrorist leaders and skilled bomb-makers. Among other
things, this has resulted in poorer execution of attacks,
and many more premature detonations that kill bombers
before they can fully assemble their explosives or maneuver
them into position.

Do you think that targeted killing should be treated differently than murder?

Assassinations would make us safer

Whether U.S. forces borrow a page from the Israeli playbook
and start knocking off terrorists in quiet pre-emptive hits
remains to be seen. In any case, killing Osama Bin Laden is
likely to be a very different operation from rooting out
bombers in Gaza.…

A policy permitting U.S. assassination efforts will force
terrorist leaders to go deeper underground. It will deter
casual sympathizers from becoming involved in these
movements. It will discourage national leaders like Saddam
Hussein, Muammar Qaddafi, and Mullah Mohammed Omar of
the Taliban from sponsoring terrorism in the future, knowing
that it could cost them their own lives.

An American policy of selective assassination offers far
more certain results than trying to rely on fuzzy international
police efforts. It is also far less costly, in both dollars and
soldiers' lives, than trying to capture terrorists and bring them
to justice, or rout them in conventional battles. Targeted
killings also avoid creating near-martyrs sitting in American
jails, who could inspire future attackers. And assassination
is a morally superior alternative to carpet bombing.…

The use of assassination may be one of the most effective
ways to stop today's plague of Islamic fundamentalist
terror. Applied with precision, it can give us the advantage
we need in a deadly serious war, without leading us away
from our humane traditions.

Muammar Qaddafi, leader of Libya, established improved relations with the United States in 2003; Mullah Omar escaped the 2001 war in Afghanistan and went into hiding.

Can an assassination policy be squared with U.S. traditions and values?

Summary

In the first article law professor Marjorie Cohn considers the killing of Uday and Qusai Hussein and the publication of photographs of their bodies in the media in December 2001. Both actions, she argues, violated principles of international law. She claims that targeted assassinations are "extrajudicial executions." Such executions, because they do not follow due process of the law, are clearly unlawful even during times of war. The display of the bodies also contravened the Geneva Conventions on the treatment of the dead. Cohn states that under various international agreements adhered to by the United States, such killing is wrong. She claims that Uday and Qusai Hussein should have been tried by Iraqi or international courts, and that their execution does not reflect well on the United States. She also claims it may result in further violence by resentful Iraqis.

David Silverstein, on the other hand, argues that targeted killing should be adopted officially as a U.S. policy in the so-called War on Terrorism. He argues that it is a tool of war that the United States has used effectively in the past. He examines the Phoenix Program, adopted by CIA agents and South Vietnamese agencies, which targeted specific individuals who were infiltrating South Vietnamese villages on behalf of communist North Vietnam. Although presidents Ford and Reagan later explicitly rejected assassination as a political tool, Silverstein argues, it has been useful for the United States in the past. He says that the example of Israel shows how useful it can be in fighting terrorism. He claims that targeted killings have prevented "untold" terrorist attacks on innocent Israelis, and that there are the lesser of two evils.

FURTHER INFORMATION:

Books:

Bowden, Mark, *Killing Pablo: The Hunt for the World's Greatest Outlaw.* New York: Atlantic Monthly Press, 2001.

Grossman, David, *et al.*, *Death as a Way of Life.* New York: Farrar, Straus and Giroux, 2003.

Lentz, Harris M., *Assassinations and Executions: An Encyclopedia of Political Violence, 1900 Through 2000,* (Revised edition). Jefferson, NC: McFarland, 2002.

Useful websites:

http://www.commondreams.org/views03/0725-05.htm
Article on the killing of Uday and Qusai Hussein.

http://www.law.mcgill.ca/quid/archive/2003/03032513.html
An analysis of the implications of assassination in U.S. law.

The following debates in the Pro/Con series may also be of interest:

In this volume:

   Topic 2 Should heads of state be prosecuted for crimes against humanity?

   Augusto Pinochet: Patriot or war criminal?, pages 34–35

   Topic 16 Is the U.S. War on Terrorism a violation of international law?

IS TARGETED KILLING WRONG?

YES: Unlawful killing is immoral. Tyrants should be arrested and tried according to law.

YES: Targeted killing is not subject to any judicial process and is therefore no more acceptable than any other form of murder

TYRANNICIDE
Is the killing of tyrants wrong?

LEGALITY
Is targeted killing legally the same as murder?

NO: Throughout history writers, politicians, and philosophers have justified tyrannicide on the grounds that it is a small crime that can prevent great evil

NO: Targeted killing is a legitimate preventive action that is justified by its results

IS TARGETED KILLING WRONG?
KEY POINTS

YES: The War on Terrorism can be won by diplomacy, financial investigation, international law, and legitimate military action. It is not necessary to use illegal killing.

YES: Various states have used assassination or targeted killing to remove political opponents. As the case of Israel shows, it just leads to further conflict, resentment, and death.

TERRORISM
Is it wrong to use targeted killing as a weapon in the War on Terrorism?

VIOLENCE
Does targeted killing lead to further violence?

NO: Terrorists such as Al Qaeda are a new type of enemy. In a war against an enemy that thinks nothing of using assassination, it is vital to be able to use the same tactics in return.

NO: The evidence of the Israeli operation actually suggests that targeted killing has prevented untold numbers of terrorist attacks

Topic 4
IS IT LEGAL FOR ONE NATION TO ATTACK ANOTHER PREEMPTIVELY?

YES

FROM "INTERNATIONAL LAW AND THE PREEMPTIVE USE OF FORCE AGAINST IRAQ"
CONGRESSIONAL RESEARCH SERVICE, MARCH 22, 2003
DAVID M. ACKERMAN

NO

"MAKE WAR, NOT LOVE"
THE PROGRESSIVE, SEPTEMBER 2003
EDUARDO GALEANO

INTRODUCTION

A "preemptive attack" is a military attack launched in order to prevent an enemy launching an imminent attack of its own. In military terms it is often a highly useful tactic. It not only neutralizes a threat before it is realized; it often also allows the attacker to achieve the advantage of surprise.

In terms of international law, however, the status of preemptive action is highly ambiguous. By tradition, international law sanctions the use of force by a state only in self-defense against an actual rather than a potential threat. The use of force when no imminent threat exists is known as a preventive attack and is illegal in international law. A preemptive attack therefore occupies a poorly defined legal area that lies between self-defense and a preventive attack. In many cases its status depends on the precise interpretation of words such as "imminent." It is also true that few nations have been dissuaded from

military action by the threat of having their actions deemed illegal.

In 1967, for example, Israel launched an attack on its Arab neighbors and won a rapid victory in the Six Day War. Israel's attack came after the open massing of enemy troops around its borders. Much of the international community accepted that the attack was justified as self-defense. In 1981, however, the United Nations (UN) Security Council condemned Israel when it attacked a new nuclear reactor in Iraq, which the Israelis also saw as a threat. This time the Security Council did not recognize that there was an imminent threat: Israel's action was therefore illegal, even though it was intended to prevent a future threat becoming manifest.

The legitimacy of using preemptive force in self-defense was first promulgated by U.S. Secretary of State Daniel Webster after British troops attacked the U.S. vessel *Caroline* in

1837 because it was carrying supplies for rebels fighting British rule in Canada. Webster argued that the attack was illegal. He asserted that a nation may only invoke the right of self-defense when a threat is instant, overwhelming, and leaves no choice of other responses. Webster's criteria remained widely accepted for over a century and a half.

The legality of self-defense was underlined again in Article 51 of the 1945 UN Charter, but the article did not specifically mention preemptive action. It reads: "Nothing in the present charter shall impair the inherent right of individual or collective self-defense if an armed attack occurs against a Member of the UN." Commentators have read the clause as both including and excluding preemptive action.

"We must adapt the concept of imminent threat to the capabilities and objectives of today's adversaries."

—NATIONAL SECURITY STRATEGY, SEPTEMBER 2002

After the terror attacks on the United States on September 11, 2001, many people argued that it was necessary to redefine the criteria for what constitutes a preemptive strike. They argue that in the past military action was far more visible: Nations could usually tell when an enemy was preparing an attack. The 9/11 attacks, they claim, prove that there is no longer any guarantee of warning of an attack. They maintain that countries should be allowed to strike in self-defense well before a hostile enemy attacks them.

The Bush administration introduced such a doctrine in September 2002 as part of its National Security Strategy (NSS). The government claimed that the effectiveness of its War on Terrorism relied on its ability to strike first at terrorist groups and states that harbor them, and also at so-called rogue states that might present a later threat.

Many critics argue that the different targets should involve different criteria. When the United States attacked Afghanistan in 2001, for example, citing Afghan support for the Al Qaeda terrorist group, the action was widely supported around the world. When the United States invaded Iraq in 2003, however, claiming that it was a rogue state that presented a threat to U.S. interests, much of the international community condemned the action as preventive rather than preemptive. They argue that Iraq, although hostile to the United States, did not represent an imminent threat.

Critics also claim that any broadening of the definition of self-defense by the United States will have dangerous implications for international law and global security. They argue that the precedent might be used to justify military action in other troublespots around the world—for a Chinese attack on Taiwan, for example, or an Indian one on Pakistan. Critics also argue that at least in regard to action against other states, it is still generally possible to anticipate impending attacks so that there is no need to redefine the nature of preemptive action.

The following articles consider different views on the debate.

INTERNATIONAL LAW AND THE PREEMPTIVE USE OF FORCE...
David M. Ackerman

David Ackerman wrote this piece in March 2003 for the Congressional Research Service (CRS). The CRS was set up in 1914 to provide unbiased analysis and information to members of Congress on subjects such as American law, foreign policy, and social issues.

YES

✓ Until recent decades customary international law deemed the right to use force and even to go to war to be an essential attribute of every state....

Within that framework customary international law also consistently recognized self-defense as a legitimate basis for the use of force:

> *An act of self-defense is that form of self-protection which is directed against an aggressor or contemplated aggressor. No act can be so described which is not occasioned by attack or fear of attack. When acts of self-preservation on the part of a State are strictly acts of self-defense, they are permitted by the law of nations, and are justified on principle, even though they may conflict with the ... rights of other states.*

Dutch scholar Hugo Grotius (1583–1645) formulated many provisions of international law in his 1625 work De jure belli ac pacis (On the Laws of War and Peace).

Moreover, the recognized right of a state to use force for purposes of self-defense traditionally included the preemptive use of force, i.e., the use of force in anticipation of an attack. Hugo Grotius, the father of international law, stated in the seventeenth century that "[i]t be lawful to kill him who is preparing to kill."

Emmerich de Vattel (1714–1767) was a Swiss jurist who wrote a classic work in 1758, Le Droit des gens (The Law of Nations).

De Vattel a century later similarly asserted:

> *The safest plan is to prevent evil, where that is possible. A Nation has the right to resist the injury another seeks to inflict upon it, and to use force ... against the aggressor. It may even anticipate the other's design, being careful, however, not to act upon vague and doubtful suspicions, lest it should run the risk of becoming itself the aggressor.*

The classic formulation of the right of preemptive attack was given by Secretary of State Daniel Webster in connection with the famous *Caroline* incident. In 1837 British troops under the cover of night attacked and sank an American ship, the *Caroline*, in U.S. waters because the ship was being used to provide supplies to insurrectionists against British rule in Canada headquartered on an island on the Canadian side of the Niagara River. The U.S. immediately protested this "extraordinary outrage" and demanded an apology and reparations. The dispute dragged on for several years before the British conceded that they ought to have immediately offered "some explanation and apology."

The British were protecting their legitimate government in Canada. Should they have had to apologize for doing what they thought was necessary? What else might they have done?

But in the course of the diplomatic exchanges Secretary of State Daniel Webster articulated the two conditions essential to the legitimacy of the preemptive use of force under customary international law. In one note he asserted that an intrusion into the territory of another state can be justified as an act of self-defense only in those "cases in which the necessity of that self-defense is instant, overwhelming, and leaving no choice of means and no moment for deliberation."

In another note he asserted that the force used in such circumstances has to be proportional to the threat …

The International Court of Justice declared the threat or use of nuclear weapons illegal in 1996. Go to http://www.prop1. org/2000/ialana.htm for details of its decision.

In its advisory opinion on the Legality of the Threat or Use of Nuclear Weapons, the International Court of Justice stated that "[t]he submission of the exercise of the right of self-defence to the conditions of necessity and proportionality is a rule of customary international law."

Effect of the United Nations Charter

… With the founding of the United Nations, the legitimacy of the use of force by individual states under international law has been substantially narrowed. The Charter of the UN states in its Preamble that the UN is established "to save succeeding generations from the scourge of war"; and its substantive provisions obligate the Member States of the UN to "settle their international disputes by peaceful means" (Article 2(3)) and to "refrain in their international relations from the threat or use of force against the territorial integrity or political independence of any State, or in any manner inconsistent with the Purposes of the United Nations" (Article 2(4)). In place of the traditional right of states to use force, the Charter creates a system of collective security in which the Security Council is authorized to "determine the existence of any threat to the peace, breach of the peace, or act of aggression" and to "decide what measures shall be taken … to maintain international peace and security" (Article 39). Although nominally outlawing most uses of force in international relations by individual States, the UN Charter does recognize a right of nations to use force for the purpose of self-defense. Article 51 of the Charter provides:

Nothing in the present Charter shall impair the inherent right of individual or collective self-defence if an armed attack occurs against a Member of the United Nations, until the Security Council has taken measures necessary to maintain international peace and security.

The exact scope of this right of self-defense, however, has been the subject of ongoing debate. Read literally, Article 51's articulation of the right seems to preclude the preemptive use of force by individual states or groupings of states and to reserve such uses of force exclusively to the Security Council. Measures in self-defense, in this understanding, are legitimate only *after* an armed attack has already occurred. Others contend that Article 51 should not be construed so narrowly and that "it would be a travesty of the purposes of the Charter to compel a defending state to allow its assailant to deliver the first, and perhaps fatal, blow...."

> Many experts believe that the right to self-defense includes the right to preemptive action, as defined by Daniel Webster's criteria.

To read Article 51 literally, it is said, "is to protect the aggressor's right to the first strike." Consequently, to avoid this result, some assert that Article 51 recognizes the "inherent right of individual or collective self-defence" as it developed in customary international law prior to adoption of the Charter and preserves it intact. The reference to that right not being impaired "if an armed attack occurs against a Member of the United Nations," it is said, merely emphasizes one important situation where that right may be exercised but does not exclude or exhaust other possibilities.

Cold War realities

> Does it really matter how the international community evaluates particular actions? How does condemning a military action after it has happened help? Does it make any difference to the aggressor?

In further support of this view, it is argued that the literal construction of Article 51 simply ignores the reality that the Cold War and other political considerations have often paralyzed the Security Council and that, in practice, states have continued to use force preemptively at times in the UN era and the international community has continued to evaluate the legitimacy of those uses by the traditional constraints of necessity and proportionality. The following examples illustrate several aspects of these contentions:

• In 1962 President Kennedy, in response to photographic evidence that the Soviet Union was installing medium range missiles in Cuba capable of hitting the United States, imposed a naval "quarantine" on Cuba in order "to interdict ... the delivery of offensive weapons and associated material." Although President Kennedy said that the purpose of the quarantine was "to defend the security of the United States," the U.S. did not rely on the legal concept of self-defense either as articulated in Article 51 or otherwise as a justification for its actions....

• In 1967 Israel launched a preemptive attack on Egypt and other Arab states after President Nasser had moved his army across the Sinai toward Israel, forced the UN to withdraw its peacekeeping force from the Sinai border, and closed the port of Aqaba to Israeli shipping, and after Syria, Iraq, Jordan, and Saudi Arabia all began moving troops to the Israeli borders. In six days it routed Egypt and its Arab allies and had occupied the Sinai Peninsula, the West Bank, and the Gaza Strip. Israel claimed its attack was defensive in nature and necessary to forestall an Arab invasion. Both the Security Council and the General Assembly rejected proposals to condemn Israel for its "aggressive" actions.

• On June 7, 1981, Israel bombed and destroyed a nuclear reactor under construction in Iraq.... Israel claimed that "in removing this terrible nuclear threat to its existence, Israel was only exercising its legitimate right of self-defense within the meaning of this term in international law and as preserved also under the United Nations Charter."

Nonetheless, the Security Council unanimously "condemn[ed] the military attack by Israel in clear violation of the Charter of the United Nations and the norms of international conduct"....

Current situation

Thus, in both theory and practice the preemptive use of force appears to have a home in current international law; but its boundaries are not wholly determinate. Its clearest legal foundation is in Chapter VII of the UN Charter. Under Article 39 the Security Council has the authority to determine the existence not only of breaches of the peace or acts of aggression that have already occurred but also of threats to the peace; and under Article 42 it has the authority to "take such action by air, sea, or land forces as may be necessary to maintain or restore international peace and security." These authorities clearly seem to encompass the possibility of the preemptive use of force. As a consequence, the preemptive use of force by the United States against Iraq or any other sovereign nation pursuant to an appropriate authorization by the Security Council would seem to be consonant with international law. Less clear is whether international law currently allows the preemptive use of force by a nation or group of nations without Security Council authorization....

Gamal Abdel Nasser (1918–1970) came to power in Egypt as a nationalist determined to remove foreign influence from the country. He was also president of the United Arab Republic, the political union of Egypt and Syria between 1958 and 1961.

Is there a difference between a nuclear reactor and a nuclear weapons program? Or do you agree with the Israeli implication that one can inevitably lead to the other?

Although critics condemned the U.S. decision to invade Iraq in 2003 without the backing of the UN Security Council, some lawyers argued that the invasion was justified due to Iraq's failure to comply with earlier UN resolutions.

MAKE WAR, NOT LOVE
Eduardo Galeano

Uruguayan-born Eduardo Galeano (1940–) is one of Latin America's leading social critics and writers. He wrote this piece for The Progressive, a magazine founded in 1909 to promote "peace and social justice."

NO

Of all forms of professional murder, war pays the best. And of all forms of war, preemptive war provides the best alibis. Like "zero tolerance," it punishes the defenseless not for what they have done or are doing but for what they might have done or could do.

Patenting preemptive war

President Bush cannot patent preemptive war, though. It was invented well before him. Other practitioners can be found in not-so-distant history: Al Capone sent many people from Chicago to the afterworld because he knew that it is better to prevent than to cure, Stalin imposed his purges on the basis of suspicion, Hitler invaded Poland proclaiming that Poland could invade Germany, and the Japanese attacked Pearl Harbor because they could have been attacked from there.

"War is being imposed upon us," Hitler used to say, as he pushed ahead with his vast criminal project. A majority of Germans believed him and went right along, just as a huge chunk of Americans believed that Saddam Hussein was a co-author of September 11 and an imminent threat. The language of warring powers hasn't changed.

They all repeat the same phrase: Evil is forcing us to defend ourselves. In reality, Iraq was no threat to world peace, but in the speeches of Bush, Blair, and Aznar it was. The real weapons of mass destruction are the words that brought them into existence.

In June 2004 the national commission investigating the September 11, 2001, attacks declared that there was no connection between Iraq and the attacks. Do you think that fact changes the legitimacy of the 2003 war on Iraq?

A laboratory of future wars?

Donald Rumsfeld defined Iraq as "a laboratory of future wars." Bush, while he crosses the globe preaching sexual abstinence, is busy minting new threats of war. Make war, not love.

Like nine Presidents before him, Bush sees red when it comes to Cuba. Referring to Cuba, he said not long ago, "The best way to make America more secure is to find the enemy before the enemy comes to you and that's what we will do."

The President, a specialist in involuntary plagiarism, was repeating one of Stalin's phrases: "We must eliminate our enemies before they eliminate us."

As leader of the Soviet Union, Joseph Stalin (1879–1953) was responsible for the deaths of up to 20 million political opponents and other Soviet citizens. Is such a comparison useful to Galeano's argument?

Al Capone (1899–1947) authorized the murder of many enemies, including the victims of the 1929 St. Valentine's Day Massacre.

The concept was Al Capone's: "Kill before they kill you."

The proof of Cuba's dangerousness is in plain view in cinemas around the world. In his most recent film, *Die Another Day*, James Bond, pursued as ever by bombs and bikinis, infiltrated Havana and discovered there a secret high-tech cell for the recycling of terrorists.

Do movies like James Bond reflect reality, or do they shape what people believe to be real?

55

Saddam Hussein, former president of Iraq, was handed over to the Iraqi interim government in July 2004 to stand trial for war crimes.

But there is other, equally irrefutable proof against additional countries, and the list of candidates is long.

Which will be the next victim of mass murder cloaked as humanitarian action? North Korea, Syria, Iran?

There is one factor, one temptation, that tilts the scales toward Iran: The country is sitting atop the world's second largest natural gas reserves, which gives the situation a certain urgency.

Like Iraq's oil, this gas will never be mentioned by the invaders if Iran turns out to be the chosen target.

North Korea and Iran were both named by George W. Bush as members of an "axis of evil" alongside Iraq. Do you think that U.S. military action is dictated by the availability of natural resources? And if so, is that a legitimate aim of U.S. foreign policy?

A license to kill: Preemptive law

It turns out the president of the planet, like James Bond, has a license to kill. And with higher-level authorization: He incarnates Good by divine command. And Good cannot be judged.

The International Criminal Court (ICC) should busy itself with the war crimes of Milosevic and Saddam Hussein, but the instruments of God are untouchable.

Like all criminals, these armored archangels need impunity to work without troublesome intrusions spoiling their lives.

To guarantee impunity for preemptive war, nothing works better than a preemptive law. Bush signed it on August 2 last year, after it was approved by the House and Senate.

It's called the Service Members Protection Act.

It is the official response to the threatening creation of the International Criminal Court.

The law prevents the arrest, trial, or imprisonment of American military and allied personnel, "especially when they are stationed or deployed around the world to protect the vital national interests of the United States."

It authorizes the President "to use all means necessary and appropriate to bring about the[ir] release."

It sets no limit on the use of these means.

Given the experience of history and present reality, this would allow for the invasion of Holland. If the judges of the International Criminal Court behave badly, it would be legally possible for the United States to send troops to The Hague to liberate other soldiers who had fallen into their hands.

The International Criminal Court (ICC) was created in 2002 to deal with crimes against humanity, genocide, and war crimes. The United States refused to join the court on the grounds that its military and peacekeeping personnel might be subject to malicious prosecutions. Do you think the government is right to risk international disapproval in order to protect U.S. personnel overseas? See Topic 1 Does the International Criminal Court undermine national sovereignty?

Words speak louder than actions

A couplet from Calvin Trillin:

"We think that God has never made
A country we should not invade."

Summary

In the first article attorney David M. Ackerman argues that customary law makes it legal for one nation to attack another preemptively as long as traditional requirements of necessity and proportionality are met. He cites the Arab–Israeli War of 1967 as an example of a preemptive attack being appropriate but admits that it can sometimes be difficult to determine what situations meet the test of necessity. Ackerman says that most analysts recognize that in some cases some kind of anticipatory self-defense may be a matter of national survival. He acknowledges that if Article 51 of the UN Charter is read literally, it seems to forbid the preemptive use of force but quotes an opinion that it would be a "travesty … to compel a defending state to allow its assailant to deliver the first, and perhaps fatal, blow." Ackerman concludes that the preemptive use of force appears to have a home in international law, although its boundaries are not absolutely clear.

In the second article the Latin American writer Eduardo Galeano argues against preemptive strikes being legal and justified. He says that preemptive war "punishes the defenseless not for what they have done or are doing but for what they might have done or could do." Galeano notes echoes between George W. Bush's policy and the belief of Russian dictator Joseph Stalin that "We must eliminate our enemies before they eliminate us." The writer argues that Iraq was not a real threat to peace, and that "the real weapons of mass destruction are the words that brought them into existence." Galeano is critical of the Service Members Protection Act, which he describes as a preemptive law preventing the arrest, trial, or imprisonment of American military personnel deployed around the world to protect U.S. interests. The law authorizes the president to use all means necessary to secure their release and sets no limits on the use of these means.

FURTHER INFORMATION:

Books:

Hamilton, John, *Behind the Terror (War on Terrorism)*. Edina, MN: Abdo and Daughters, 2002.

Useful websites:

http://www.amconmag.com/10_21/iraq.html
Article on preemptive war by Paul W. Schroeder, published on *The American Conservative* site.
http://www.cdi.org/news/law/preemptive-war.cfm
Article by Stephen C. Welsh looking at international law and preemptive strikes.
http://www.prospect.org/print/V13/17/galston-w.html
2002 *American Prospect* article by William Galston. Looks at the U.S. position regarding an attack on Iraq.

The following debates in the Pro/Con series may also be of interest:

In this volume:
Part 1: Issues in international law, pages 8–9

In *U.S. Foreign Policy*:
Topic 15 Should the United States use military force against nations that harbor terrorists?

IS IT LEGAL FOR ONE NATION TO ATTACK ANOTHER PREEMPTIVELY?

YES: Preemptive action is legal when it is in self-defense against an instant and overwhelming threat

INTERNATIONAL LAW

Is preemptive action legal according to customary international law?

NO: It is often difficult to determine clearly, according to law, whether military action always constitutes self-defense

YES: The destructiveness of even a single weapon in the hands of terrorists or rogue states makes it even more vital to be able to strike first in self-defense

IS IT LEGAL FOR ONE NATION TO ATTACK ANOTHER PREEMPTIVELY?

KEY POINTS

YES: Preemptive attacks are a legitimate response to the new dangers democratic countries face from terrorists and rogue states

NEW DOCTRINE

Is the doctrine of preemption in the National Security Strategy legal?

NO: The new doctrine of preemption expands the rules of self-defense and could lead to an escalation of violence

YES: Article 51 acknowledges the right of nations to defend themselves, which in customary law includes justified preemptive strikes

WEAPONS OF MASS DESTRUCTION

Do new weapons necessitate a change in the definition of preemptive action?

NO: The invasion of Iraq in 2003 was based on erroneous intelligence about weapons of mass destruction; the episode underlined how important it is to stick to traditional criteria about preemptive action

ARTICLE 51

Does the United Nations sanction preemptive action?

NO: Article 51 makes no specific mention of preemptive action; therefore, a literal interpretation suggests that it does not sanction the preemptive use of force

Topic 5
ARE WOMEN ADEQUATELY PROTECTED BY INTERNATIONAL LAW?

YES
"INTERNATIONAL JUSTICE FOR WOMEN: THE ICC MARKS A NEW ERA"
HUMAN RIGHTS WATCH BACKGROUNDER, JULY 1, 2002
HUMAN RIGHTS WATCH

NO
FROM "15 STEPS TO PROTECT WOMEN'S HUMAN RIGHTS"
WWW.AMNESTY.ORG
AMNESTY INTERNATIONAL

INTRODUCTION

In 2004 the human rights group Amnesty International declared that violence against women is the "hidden human rights scandal of our time." It claimed that at least one in every three women has been beaten, coerced into sex, or abused during her lifetime.

Some observers believe that violence is just one of the ways in which women are treated unfairly. They assert that women make up the majority of the world's poor, and that they are discriminated against at work, in the home, in times of armed conflict, and at every level of society. Other commentators, however, point to various international laws passed since 1948 to safeguard women's rights. Such laws, to which most nations adhere, have made illegal offenses ranging from sex crimes to human trafficking.

Some commentators suggest that women's rights have in fact been legally protected for as long as international humanitarian law has existed since

women are implicitly protected by laws that protect "people," "citizens," or "humans," and also by those that explicitly include females. The 1864 Geneva Convention for the Amelioration of the Condition of the Wounded in Armies in the Field, for example, protected women if they were wounded, while annexes to the Hague Conventions of 1899 and 1907 on the Laws and Customs of War on Land safeguarded women if they became prisoners of war. In 1929 the international community recognized women's contribution to World War I (1914–1918) in its adoption of the Geneva Convention on the Treatment of Prisoners of War, which stated that "Women shall be treated with all the regard due to their sex."

World War II (1939–1945) involved women in greater numbers, although they were seldom present in active combat. The effect of the war on civilians led to a growing campaign for human rights, especially those of vulnerable groups, to be enshrined in law. The Universal Declaration of Human Rights (UDHR), adopted by the United Nations (UN) in 1948, established the rights to which people were entitled regardless of their gender, race, age, or other factors. Some critics contend, however, that such measures have failed to protect women properly. They argue that even the language of the UDHR—it uses words such as "brotherhood" and "himself"—displays its inherent sexism.

> *"The human rights of women and of the girl-child are an unalienable, integral, and indivisible part of universal human rights."*
> —THE VIENNA DECLARATION AND PROGRAM OF ACTION (1993)

Opponents argue that the language of the declaration is not at issue: What is important is the role of international law and international agencies in protecting women. One of the most important of the agencies is the Commission on the Status of Women (CSW), founded by the UN in 1946. The CSW monitors the situation of women around the world, preparing reports, making recommendations, and campaigning for immediate action to end abuses. The commission has 45 members from Africa, Asia, eastern and western Europe, Latin America, the Caribbean, and other regions. It has played a major role in alerting UN agencies to specific concerns. The CSW has analyzed the participation of women in politics and decision-making, and it has recommended changes relating to women's employment and education. Its work has also led to the adoption of key UN declarations, such as the 1993 Declaration on the Elimination of Violence against Women.

Similarly, world conferences have played an important role in highlighting women's rights. The 1993 UN World Conference on Human Rights in Vienna, Austria, focused on problems such as sexual violence in war. Despite attempts to make rape a war crime in the wake of World War II, it was not until 1998 that the Rome Statute of the International Criminal Court (ICC) declared that sexual crimes were war crimes. This enabled the prosecution of perpetrators in the International Criminal Tribunals for Former Yugoslavia and Rwanda. Thousands of women were sexually abused and raped during conflicts in these countries in the 1990s.

Other experts agree that international law protects women in theory but argue that in real life women are not as protected as they should be. For them the problem is not one of law but one of enforcement. For example, the *International Review of the Red Cross* has argued that "The international community will not succeed in remedying this situation merely by adopting new rules. Most of all, it must see that the rules already in force are respected. The responsibility to apply the provisions giving special protection to women, and for that matter all the rules of international humanitarian law, is a collective one."

The following articles examine this issue in greater detail.

INTERNATIONAL JUSTICE FOR WOMEN: THE ICC MARKS A NEW ERA
Human Rights Watch

Human Rights Watch is an independent, nongovernmental organization comprising lawyers, journalists, and academics dedicated to protecting international human rights. It is the largest human rights organization based in the United States.

The International Criminal Court (ICC) was established by the Rome Statute on July 17, 1998, when 120 states adopted it. The ICC was established to ensure that the most serious international crimes are punished. The statute came into force in July 2002. Go to www.icc-cpi.int for more about the ICC.

YES

I. Introduction

Women's rights activists throughout the world—of every political stripe, faith, sexual orientation, nationality, and ethnicity—mobilized at each step of the International Criminal Court (ICC) process. They have worked to create an independent court to afford women greater protection from violations of human rights and humanitarian law.

Women's rights activists participated in every major United Nations preparatory meeting on the ICC. They worked to ensure that the range of abuses that happen to women was accurately reflected in the list of crimes over which the ICC would have jurisdiction. They worked to ensure that the rules and procedures governing how the court functions would be responsive to gender-specific crimes.

Activists held in-country workshops to educate other women and policy makers about the benefits of ICC adoption and ratification. They lobbied their home country officials to sign and then ratify the Rome Statute, which outlined the establishment and structure of the ICC.

That the ICC has come into force today and is potentially a powerful instrument for protecting women's rights is a testament to this indefatigable activism and determination.

Thanks to women around the world, violence and persecution of women will be treated as the serious criminal and humanitarian law violations that they are. The ICC offers a dramatic and long-awaited improvement in how international crimes against women are treated and greatly increases the possibility for redress. Moreover, it provides witness protection and other measures desperately needed to afford women the greatest level of protection.

II. How the ICC protects women's rights

• Codification of Crimes. The Rome Statute of the ICC (the Statute) criminalizes sexual and gender violence as war crimes and crimes against humanity. Accordingly, war crimes and crimes against humanity include rape, sexual slavery (including trafficking of women), enforced prostitution,

COMMENTARY: Violence against women

The Platform for Action, adopted by the Fourth World Conference on Women held in Beijing in 1995, identified violence against women as one of 12 critical areas of concern requiring the special attention of the international community and civil society.

Violence against women takes many different forms, including domestic violence by a family member, rape, trafficking in women and girls, forced prostitution, and violence in armed conflict. Included in the last are acts such as murder, systematic rape (see Volume 15, *Human Rights*, pages 126–127), sexual slavery, and forced pregnancy. Violence against women also includes dowry-related violence, female infanticide, and female genital mutilation. In the words of UN Secretary-General Kofi Annan: "Violence against women is perhaps the most shameful human rights violation. It knows no boundaries of geography, culture or wealth. As long as it continues, we cannot claim to be making real progress towards equality, development, and peace."

Protecting women and girls in law

During the second half of the 20th century the international community introduced a number of codes and laws to eliminate violence against women either specifically as a gender or generally as human beings:

- The Universal Declaration of Human Rights in 1948 states that human rights apply to all people "without distinction of any kind." The UDHR asserts that no one shall be subjected to torture, "cruel, inhuman, or degrading treatment of any kind."
- The Convention on the Elimination of All Forms of Discrimination against Women (CEDAW), adopted by many states in 1979, endorsed General Recommendation 19 in 1992. It defines violence against women as discrimination and requires governments to prevent and punish these acts.
- The 1993 Declaration on the Elimination of Violence against Women, adopted by the UN General Assembly, states that violence against women is a violation of human rights and a form of discrimination against women.
- An Optional Protocol to the Convention on the Elimination of All Forms of Discrimination against Women, adopted by the UN General Assembly on October 6, 1999, gives women the right to seek redress for violations of their human rights, including gender-based violence.
- The Rome Statute of the International Criminal Court, adopted in July 1998, specifically addresses gender-based crimes, including rape and forced sterilization and pregnancy.
- In 2000 the UN's Protocol to Prevent, Suppress, and Punish Trafficking in Persons, Especially Women and Children requires states to protect victims of human trafficking, particularly women and children.

The article focuses heavily on sexual violence. Do you think we should understand gender-based crimes more broadly? If so, what other crimes should be included?

forced pregnancy, enforced sterilization, other forms of grave sexual violence, and persecution on account of gender.

• Procedural Protections for Victims and Witnesses. Women victims and witnesses before the ICC can expect procedures designed to address their needs. The ICC Statute and Rules of Procedure and Evidence (Rules) offer important protections for victims and witnesses, particularly those who suffered sexual or gender violence. The court is required to protect the safety, physical and psychological well-being, dignity, and privacy of victims and witnesses, with special regard to factors such as their gender and whether the crime involved sexual or gender violence. The Statute and Rules also establish a Victims and Witnesses Unit to provide protection, security, counseling, and other assistance. The court can institute measures to protect victims and witnesses during trials and pre-trial proceedings. The court is also required to be vigilant in controlling the questioning of witnesses to avoid harassment or intimidation, especially in sexual violence cases.

Protection and expertise

Why do you think the ICC considers it so important that evidence regarding a victim's or witness's general sexual conduct should be inadmissible?

• Rules of Evidence to Protect Victims of Sexual Violence. The Rules are designed to shield victims of sexual violence from damaging or intrusive attacks on their sexuality or credibility. The court cannot admit evidence of a victim or witness's prior or subsequent sexual conduct or require corroboration of testimony concerning sexual violence. The Rules outline principles to guide the court in handling sexual violence cases, making clear that a victim's consent cannot be inferred where the perpetrator took advantage of a coercive environment (such as a detention center), and requiring special procedures for presenting evidence of consent to acts of sexual violence.

The statute requires a "fair representation" of males and females in the selection of permanent judges. Does the sex of a judge really matter since he or she is meant to be impartial? Does the same logic suggest that black judges would be better at trying cases involving black suspects and victims?

• Staff Expertise on Gender and Sexual Violence. The Statute requires that the ICC prosecutor appoint advisers with legal expertise on sexual and gender violence and that the Victims and Witnesses Unit, to be housed within the ICC registry, include staff with experience in trauma related to sex crimes. The Statute also requires states, in electing judges, to take into account the need for "fair representation" of female and male judges, and requires that the prosecutor and registrar do the same when hiring staff.

• Victim Participation in the Proceedings. The ICC Statute and Rules facilitate victims' direct participation in the court's proceedings. Victims can express their views, in accordance with the Statute and the Rules, giving them a chance to tell their stories even if they are not called as witnesses. This will allow individual women's voices, sometimes overlooked in international prosecutions, to emerge.

III. Why the United States should support the ICC

For millennia, perpetrators of what today would be called war crimes and crimes against humanity directed at women have enjoyed impunity. Now, there is finally a court that can make a real difference for women around the world. International humanitarian and criminal law no longer ignore the experiences of women who are raped, subjected to sexual mutilation and sexual slavery, trafficked, forced to bear the children of their rapists, and persecuted by other horrendous acts of sexual violence. The ICC is a significant milestone in the struggle to end impunity for crimes of sexual and gender violence. To oppose and undermine the ICC is to squander an important opportunity to safeguard women's human rights around the world.

Why would the voices of individual women be overlooked in international prosecutions? Should the authors have explained more about this?

The United States has refused to ratify the ICC because it argues that it will undermine national sovereignty. See Topic 1 Does the International Criminal Court undermine national sovereignty?

15 STEPS TO PROTECT WOMEN'S HUMAN RIGHTS
Amnesty International

Go to http://www.un.org/ womenwatch/daw/ beijing/platform/ plat1.htm for more information about the Platform for Action.

The Convention for the Elimination of All Forms of Discrimination against Women (CEDAW) has been described as an international bill of rights for women. It allows states to ratify the treaty with reservations to particular articles provided they are not incompatible with the aims of the convention. Reservations can be made on the grounds of national law, tradition, religion, or culture.

NO

Human rights for women … are protected in international law. Yet women suffer the full range of human rights violations known to the modern world. Women and girl-children also face human rights violations solely or primarily because of their sex. The international community can play a decisive role in protecting human rights through vigilant and concerted action.…

1. Rights are universal and indivisible

The Platform for Action adopted by the Fourth United Nations (UN) World Conference on Women reflects the commitment made by governments in the Vienna Declaration and Programme of Action of the 1993 UN World Conference on Human Rights that "[t]he human rights of women and of the girl-child are an inalienable, integral and indivisible part of universal human rights".

2. Ratification of international instruments

Governments should ratify international legal instruments which provide for the protection of the human rights of women and girl-children, such as: the International Covenant on Civil and Political Rights (ICCPR).… Governments should also ratify regional standards which protect the human rights of women and girl-children. Governments who have already ratified these instruments should examine any limiting reservations, with a view to withdrawing them. This is particularly important in the case of the Convention on the Elimination of All Forms of Discrimination against Women, where the commitment of many governments is seriously undermined by the extent of their reservations.…

3. Eradicate discrimination

Governments should recognize that discrimination against women, including lesbians and girl-children, is a key contributory factor to human rights abuse such as torture, including rape and other forms of custodial violence. Governments should initiate a plan of action against such discrimination. Governments should ensure that women are treated equally in law; a woman's evidence should have the same weight as a man's in all judicial proceedings and women should not receive harsher penalties than a man would for the same offence....

4. Women's human rights during armed conflict

... The UN should ensure that personnel deployed in UN ... operations observe the highest standards of ... human rights law and receive information on local cultural traditions. They should respect the rights and dignity of women at all times, both on and off duty. Human rights components of UN field operations should include experts in the area of violence against women, including rape and sexual abuse, to ensure that prisons and places of detention where women are held are clearly identified and properly investigated and that victims of rape and other custodial violence have suitable and confidential facilities to meet investigators....

Do you think that international law should always respect local cultural traditions? What about countries that practice punishments such as death by stoning, for example? Should they have the right to follow their own customs and laws?

5. Stop rape, sexual abuse and other torture

Take effective steps to prevent rape, sexual abuse and other torture and ill-treatment in custody. Conduct prompt, thorough and impartial investigations into all reports of torture or ill-treatment. Any law enforcement agent responsible for such acts, or for encouraging or condoning them, should be brought to justice. Any form of detention or imprisonment and all measures affecting the human rights of detainees or prisoners should be subject to the effective control of a judicial authority. All detainees should have [prompt and regular] access to family members and legal counsel....

There should be no contact between male guards and female detainees and prisoners without the presence of a female guard. Female detainees and prisoners should be held separately from male detainees and prisoners. All detainees and prisoners should be given the opportunity to have a medical examination promptly after admission to the place of custody and regularly thereafter....

Men can also be victims of rape. Do you think Amnesty International should acknowledge this possibility?

Victims of rape and sexual abuse and other torture or ill-treatment in custody should be entitled to fair and adequate compensation and appropriate medical care.

6. Prevent "disappearances"

Conduct prompt, thorough and impartial investigations into all reports of "disappearances", extrajudicial executions and deaths in custody and bring to justice those responsible.

The "disappeared" are people who have been killed by a government or army and whose bodies have not been found.

Ensure that the commission of a "disappearance" or extrajudicial execution, or causing the death of a prisoner in custody is a criminal offence…. Inform families immediately of any arrest and keep them informed of the whereabouts of the detainee or prisoner at all times…. Provide … redress to relatives of victims of "disappearance", extrajudicial execution and death in custody, including financial compensation….

7. Stop persecution because of family connections

Any woman detained, imprisoned or held hostage solely because of her family connections should be immediately and unconditionally released. The practice of killing, abducting, or torturing women in order to bring pressure on their relatives should not be tolerated….

8. Safeguard the health rights of women

Provide all women under any form of detention or imprisonment with adequate medical treatment, denial of which can constitute ill-treatment. Provide all necessary pre-natal and post-natal care and treatment for women in custody and their infants. The imprisonment of a mother and child together must never be used to inflict torture or ill-treatment on either by causing physical or mental suffering….

Many American states require the shackling of women prisoners during childbirth. Go to http://www.amnestyusa.org/women/custody/abuseincustody.html for an Amnesty International report about this.

9. Release all prisoners of conscience

… No woman should be detained or imprisoned for peacefully attempting to exercise basic rights and freedoms enjoyed by men. Governments should review all legislation and practices, which result in the detention of women because of their homosexual identity …

10. Ensure prompt and fair trials

Stop unfair trials which violate the fundamental rights of political prisoners in all parts of the world. Ensure that all political prisoners charged with a criminal offence receive a prompt and fair trial by a competent, independent and impartial tribunal….

AI's 10th point applies to political prisoners of either sex. Would the argument have been stronger if it was limited only to women-specific recommendations?

11. Prevent violations against women refugees

No one should be forcibly returned to a country where she or he can reasonably be expected to be imprisoned as a prisoner of conscience, tortured, including by being raped, "disappeared" or executed. Governments should remove all barriers … to women seeking political asylum on the basis of persecution based on sexual identity. Every woman refugee or asylum-seeker should be given the opportunity of an individual hearing.... Governments should take measures to protect women's physical safety and integrity by preventing torture, including rape, and ill-treatment of refugee women and asylum-seekers in the country of asylum.... Governments should thoroughly and impartially investigate human rights violations committed against refugees and asylum-seekers in the country of asylum, and bring to justice those responsible.

In procedures for the determination of refugee status governments should provide interviewers trained to be sensitive to issues of gender and culture....

12. Abolish the death penalty

... Legislation which allows a woman to be put to death for an offence for which a man would receive a lesser sentence should be abolished. In countries which retain the death penalty, the law should provide that executions will not be carried out against pregnant women and new mothers ...

In Nigeria in 2002 Amina Lawal was convicted of adultery and sentenced to death by stoning under Islamic Sharia law. Lawal's case became the focus of human rights groups around the world, and her conviction was overturned on appeal in 2004. See Volume 20, Religion and Morality, Topic 8 Should adultery be a criminal offense?

13. Support the work of agencies

Governments should publicly state their commitment to ensuring that the intergovernmental bodies which monitor violations of human rights suffered by women ... have adequate resources to carry out their task effectively....

14. Promote women's rights as human rights

Governments should ensure all law enforcement personnel and other government agents receive adequate training on national and international standards which protect the human rights of all women.... Law enforcement personnel and other governments agents should be instructed that rape of women in their custody is an act of torture and will not be tolerated. A special emphasis should be given to education designed to make women aware of their rights and to make society at large conscious of its duty to respect the human rights and fundamental freedoms of women and girl-children....

This is a key issue in this debate. No matter what laws are made protecting women, there is still a responsibility for all members of society to make sure that in reality those rights are protected.

Governments and intergovernmental organizations should make available human rights education materials which promote women's rights as human rights....

15. Armed political groups should safeguard women's human rights

Armed political groups should take steps to prevent abuses by their members such as hostage-taking, torture, and ill-treatment, including rape, and ... killings, and to hold those responsible for such abuses to account.

Summary

The article by civil rights organization Human Rights Watch (HRW) looks specifically at how the International Criminal Court (ICC) has affected the position and treatment of women in society. The ICC is an independent court set up in part "to afford women greater protection from violations of human rights and humanitarian law." HRW argues that women's groups have worked hard to make sure that the ICC lives up to its pledge. The ICC preserves women's rights through the Rome Statute, which identifies sexual crimes committed during armed conflicts as war crimes and therefore punishable as criminal offenses under international law. The statute also protects witnesses and victims of sexual crimes, provides guidelines on how to treat evidence to make sure that witnesses and victims are not unnecessarily exposed to unfair or brutal questioning, and provides experienced staff to deal sensitively with them. HRW concludes that "there is finally a court that can make a real difference for women around the world."

Amnesty International (AI) recognizes that governments are addressing the issue of women's rights but claims that women still suffer from abuses. AI argues that the world community can play a decisive role in protecting women and suggests 15 specific ways in which it could be done. Ratifying international treaties, safeguarding women's rights during times of conflict, and protecting the human rights of refugees are positive ways in which governments could better serve women. AI concludes, however, that one of the fundamental problems is the attitudes of both men and of women themselves. It argues, therefore, that emphasis should be put on education to make women and men more aware of women's rights and freedom.

FURTHER INFORMATION:

Books:

Gaughen, Shasta (ed.), *Women's Rights.* San Diego, CA: Greenhaven Press, 2002.

Useful websites:

http://hrw.org/wr2k1/women/

HRW 2001 World Report on Women's Human Rights.

http://www.law.harvard.edu/programs/hrp/Publications/radhika.html

Article on women's rights as human rights.

http://www.un.org/womenwatch/daw/cedaw/

Site for the Convention on the Elimination of All Forms of Discrimination against Women.

www.wld.org

Site of Women, Law, and International Development, a women's human rights nongovernmental organization.

The following debates in the Pro/Con series may also be of interest:

In this volume:

 Part 1: Issues in international law

In *Individual and Society*:

 Topic 3 Are women still the second sex?

In *Human Rights*:

Topic 9 Are human rights women's rights?

ARE WOMEN ADEQUATELY PROTECTED BY INTERNATIONAL LAW?

YES: All laws that apply to male rights, such as the Universal Declaration of Human Rights (UDHR), also protect the rights of women

YES: During the 20th century many laws forbade all types of discriminatory or violent behavior toward women

HUMAN RIGHTS
Do women have equal rights?

VIOLENCE
Does international law protect women against violence?

NO: Declarations and laws can only go some way to granting rights to women. In reality, cultural attitudes mean that women in many societies are still treated as an inferior sex.

NO: According to Amnesty International, at least one in every three women has been beaten, coerced into sex, or abused. This suggests that laws do not act as a deterrent.

ARE WOMEN ADEQUATELY PROTECTED BY INTERNATIONAL LAW?
KEY POINTS

YES: The Rome Statute of the ICC defines specific sexual and war crimes against women, and the court will try perpetrators

YES: Many international agencies implement specific programs aimed at protecting women's rights

LEGAL REDRESS
Will the International Criminal Court (ICC) ensure that violators of women's rights are punished?

WOMEN'S GROUPS
Does the work of international agencies protect women's rights?

NO: Since the ICC lacks international support, particularly from the United States, it will not be effective in punishing any violators, not only those of women's rights

NO: Many international agencies are dominated by men; more importantly, the governments with which they have to deal are often dominated by men. This undermines their effective protection of women's rights.

71

Topic 6

IS THE HAGUE CONVENTION EFFECTIVE IN SETTLING INTERNATIONAL PARENT–CHILD ABDUCTION DISPUTES?

YES
FROM "STATEMENT OF MAURA HARTY, ASSISTANT SECRETARY, BUREAU OF CONSULAR AFFAIRS, UNITED STATES DEPARTMENT OF STATE ON INTERNATIONAL CHILD ABDUCTION BEFORE THE SUBCOMMITTEE ON HUMAN RIGHTS AND WELLNESS COMMITTEE ON HOUSE GOVERNMENT REFORM," JULY 9, 2003
MAURA HARTY

NO
"GERMANS DON'T BUDGE EVEN AFTER PLEA BY CLINTON"
CHICAGO TRIBUNE, JULY 9, 2000
RAY MOSELEY

INTRODUCTION

The breakdown of a marriage often results in a question of custody, or which parent gets to look after any children from the marriage. Often both parents feel they have a claim. Within the United States or other countries such disputes can be settled by custody suits in which a judge decides with which parent the child or children live and the access rights of the other parent. However, in cases of cross-cultural relationships, or those between people from different countries, the situation can be more complicated. One or other parent may abduct a child and take him or her to a different country, or alternatively he or she may detain the child in a different country during a visit. This may sometimes be caused by a custody verdict with which the abductor does not agree.

Historically, parents who abducted their children often fled abroad since it was easy to hide from local authorities, especially if the abductor had extended family or friends in the region. More importantly, most governments lacked a legal framework that could force the return of the abducted child to its other parent. In some cases this meant that the parent with legal custody knew where the child was living but had no legal way to have him or her returned.

Politicians, civil rights advocates, and parental rights organizations pushed for the establishment of an international legal system to help parents reclaim their children from other nations. In 1980 the Hague Convention on the Civil Aspects of International Child Abduction—known more simply as the Hague Convention—was created for the purpose. It aimed to discourage parental child abduction and to ensure that abducted children are returned to their country of normal residence. The terms of the convention are that parents can apply for the return of a child if he or she is under the age of 16 and resided in a convention country immediately prior to the abduction, and if the applicant had a "right of custody" at the time of the abduction. Around 70 countries have adopted the convention since it came into existence more than 20 years ago, and that has enabled thousands of parents and children to be reunited.

> *"The issue of child abduction is a prime example of the limitations of international cooperation in the judicial area."*
> —CATHERINE MEYER, EXPERT ON THE HAGUE CONVENTION (1998)

Critics of the Hague Convention argue that it is ineffectual, inefficient, and open to interpretation by member nations. Despite legal and diplomatic progress, far too many cases remain unresolved. Some observers claim that although the aims of the convention are well-defined, it lacks clear procedural requirements. This often results in member states applying the treaty too slowly, interpreting procedures in quite different ways, and ignoring them if they conflict with issues of national sovereignty. In addition, critics point out, the convention only applies to countries that have ratified the treaty. In nonconvention nations private—usually expensive—lawsuits often remain the only option for parents seeking the return of abducted children.

Another criticism of international parent–child recovery is that countries do not react quickly enough to reported abductions, which gives abductors more of a chance of retaining custody. Under the Hague Convention courts can refuse treaty applications if a child has resided in the country for more than a year, if returning the child is judged detrimental to his or her well-being, or the child is old enough to choose where he or she wants to live. Courts in some countries have ruled that children as young as three are able to make such decisions.

Although some observers have suggested applying sanctions against nations that do not comply with the treaty, Hague Convention expert Catherine Meyer disagrees. Since 1994 she has been trying to reclaim her two sons from Germany, where her estranged former husband retained them after a visit. Meyer, who heads the group Parents and Abducted Children Together (PACT), advocates using legal methods to address the problem. She also organizes conferences to examine the convention's weaknesses and suggest ways to correct them.

While the Hague Convention has been criticized, many people argue that it still serves a purpose. Others believe it should be replaced with something more effective and enforceable in every country around the world.

The following articles examine whether the Hague Convention has been effective or not in more depth.

STATEMENT ... ON INTERNATIONAL CHILD ABDUCTION
Maura Harty

YES

Mr. Chairman, Members of the Subcommittee:
I am pleased to be here today to report on the work done by the Department of State in the area of international child abduction. I believe that you can understand a lot about a society by the way it treats its most vulnerable members and I think that the time, energy, and attention devoted to this problem at the Department of State and within the U.S. Government reflects well upon the United States as a society. We at the Department of State are rapidly approaching the tenth anniversary of the creation of the Office of Children's Issues [CA/OCS/CI]—where we handle matters of international adoptions, abductions, and the return of children to their habitual residence under the Hague Convention....

The United States and the Hague Convention

Since the U.S. became party to the Hague Convention on the Civil Aspects of International Child Abduction in 1988, the Department of State has worked to improve the Convention's implementation in this country. During the first year we created a new child custody division to coordinate our work in this area. In 1994 we consolidated our efforts on behalf of children abroad in our Office of Children's Issues, now an office of 28 people who devote all their time to helping in the international adoption process and assisting in the return of children wrongfully taken and/or retained abroad. Over the years, we have expanded our cooperative arrangement with the National Center for Missing and Exploited Children (NCMEC), formalized in an agreement between the Department of State, the Department of Justice, and NCMEC and signed on September 1, 1995, to provide additional assistance for parents and children in all international child abduction cases. They are our partners and our friends; NCMEC is an extraordinary organization.

When a parent takes or keeps a child from his or her home, and prevents the child from having a relationship with the other parent, the trauma to the child is immediate and compounded each day the child is not returned home. International child abductions are often complicated by the fact that many abducted children are from multi-cultural and multinational families. The children themselves are often citizens of both the United States and the country to which they were abducted. Our position, which I have made clear in my meetings with foreign government officials, is that a child abducted from the U.S. in violation of custody rights recognized under U.S. law should be returned. The taking parent should not be allowed to benefit from the abduction. Ultimately, however, the fate of these children is decided by the courts or other authorities in the countries to which they have been abducted, or in which they have been wrongfully retained. U.S. court orders, as we all know, are often not enforceable abroad. Even when everyone involved is a U.S. citizen, these cases are often difficult to resolve once the child has been removed from the United States.

Do you think that a court of law is the best place to resolve a child abduction issue? What other ways might there be?

How the Hague Convention works

Recognizing that abductions are individual tragedies that the courts of most countries legitimately wish to resolve in good faith for the benefit of the affected children, the United States has long taken a lead in creating a mechanism for the return of children abducted internationally. The United States was instrumental in the negotiation of the Hague Convention. The Convention provides a civil legal mechanism in the country where the child is located for parents to seek the return of, and access to, their child. It applies only to cases where children habitually resident in a Hague Convention country have been abducted to, or wrongfully retained in, another country party to the Convention. The Bureau of Consular Affairs' Office of Children's Issues acts as the Central Authority for the Convention in the United States.

Go to http://www.travel.state.gov/hague_childabduction.html for the text of the Hague Convention.

   Under the Convention, a Hague proceeding does not decide custody; instead, it decides in which country a custody determination should be made. A Hague proceeding should, with very few and limited exceptions, result in an order from the court where the abducted child is located for return to the country of habitual residence so that the parents may pursue the resolution of custody there. While the Convention is far from 100% successful, it does provide a legal channel for left-behind parents in a foreign court, and results in children's return to the United States. We also believe that the existence of the Convention's return mechanism has deterred an untold number of abductions.

Is there really any way to measure things that do not happen or might not happen? How can the author know that the convention will deter "untold" abductions?

Go to http://www.travel.state.gov/ hague_list.html to find out which countries participate in the Hague Convention.

Approximately 60% of the cases in which we provide assistance are now covered by the Convention. When the U.S. joined the Convention in 1988, only nine other countries were party. Today the Convention is in effect between the U.S. and 52 other countries. We encourage countries which embrace the Convention's basic principles to become members as the best possible means of protecting children from the harmful effects of abduction. As we look to improve the Convention's effectiveness, we must remember the many parents who wish that they had even this less-than-perfect mechanism to seek return of their children.

An imperfect system

While The Hague Convention has facilitated the return of many children to the United States, and while it is a vast improvement over the lack of any international mechanism whatsoever, it is an imperfect instrument. The Hague Convention does not guarantee a satisfactory result for every left-behind parent. Compliance with the Convention varies among foreign jurisdictions. Even when the left-behind parent has filed an application in a timely fashion, hired legal counsel, and literally done everything "right", that parent, and the United States, may be bitterly disappointed with the result. There have been some decisions by foreign courts in Hague cases with which we do not agree. However, these decisions are made by independent judiciaries in independent sovereign states. The Hague Convention cannot make a biased judicial system fair, or a nationalistic judge more objective, nor can it remove gender bias from a society or its judicial system.

In some nonconvention countries children are regarded as the property of men rather than women. Do you think that women are still unfairly discriminated against? For further information go to Volume 1, Individual and Society, Topic 3 Are women still the second sex? and Volume 15, Human Rights, Topic 9 Are human rights women's rights?

While the Hague Convention does not guarantee the return of all abducted or wrongfully retained children, the Convention provides us [with] an invaluable tool that is absent in our efforts to resolve abduction cases from countries such as Saudi Arabia that are not Hague signatories and whose judicial system, cultural traditions, and family law are often radically different from our own. The Department, when dealing with such countries, works with other federal and state agencies and the foreign governments concerned to explore ways to recover the children. This may include withholding or revoking the U.S. visas of abducting parents, people who support them, and their family members; revoking U.S. passports at the request of federal law enforcement authorities if a federal warrant is issued for the arrest of a U.S. citizen; and pressing foreign governments for assistance in returning children and either deporting or extraditing their abductors. We also seek to visit abducted children to verify their well-being and facilitate communication between the parents. In some countries with legal systems and practices that vary drastically from those of the U.S., we are exploring the viability of bilateral consular arrangements that could improve mediation and access assistance provided to parents, even as we continue to seek mechanisms for a child's return. We are working to expand and revise our Standard Operating Procedures to provide more comprehensive service to left-behind parents. We will soon establish a Prevention Unit within CA/OCS/CI to focus more attention on this important function.

Returning children to the United States

Let me be completely clear on the main question here: we see no difference between the rights of left-behind parents in cases involving Hague and non-Hague countries and our aim is always the same, the return of the child to the United States. We must, however, work in the manner most likely to be effective in pursuing that aim and we should not neglect those measures that, while they fall short of meeting our ultimate goal of return, nonetheless enable the left-behind parent to have a place in their child's life. Children, as they grow older, are far more likely to exert useful pressure towards reunion with the left-behind parent if that parent is known to and important to them.

Importance of diplomacy

Let me close my discussion … with an observation that is perhaps obvious, but whose implications are not necessarily self-evident: every situation in this area is unique and there is no tailor-made solution that should be applied across the board. The legal tools we have at our disposal are vitally important and we will not hesitate to use them when we, and the left-behind parents, believe them to be relevant and likely to promote a positive outcome. Often, however, the most effective way to handle these cases is through the consistent use of our most vital resource: the persuasive power of our diplomatic efforts abroad. Our Ambassadors and their staff will push foreign governments to recognize the rights of left-behind parents, facilitate visitation, help advance Hague compliance where that remedy is available, and constantly remind foreign interlocutors that the U.S. government cares about, supports, and works for the rights of left-behind parents whose children have been wrongfully removed from the U.S. and retained abroad.

> It can strengthen your argument if you clearly highlight the central issue of the debate. Harty states that the ultimate aim of the U.S. government is to return a child regardless of whether it is from a Hague or non-Hague country.

> Is it really the job of U.S. officials to help solve family disputes? Should they be concentrating on the interests of the nation as a whole?

GERMANS DON'T BUDGE EVEN AFTER PLEA BY CLINTON
Ray Moseley

Ray Moseley is a U.S.-born journalist who spent the last decade of his 40-year career in the United Kingdom, where he was chief European correspondent for the Chicago Tribune. *He is now retired. This piece was published in the* Chicago Tribune *in July 2000.*

NO

BERLIN—When President Clinton recently met here with German Chancellor Gerhard Schroeder and urged him to help return abducted American children to their parents, Schroeder commented that the cases were "tragic." Clinton called them "heart-rending."

Words of sympathy notwithstanding, there has been little evidence since then to suggest Germany will return to the U.S. the children of 59 American parents whose cases are outstanding.

An election issue?

Shortly after Clinton's visit, Schroeder said he would not interfere in affairs of the German Justice Ministry, and Justice Minister Herta Daeubler-Gmelin suggested that members of Congress who have raised a storm of protest about the issue of parental abductions were politically motivated.

"This stirring up of opinion in the election season is not in order," she said.

A European diplomat with experience in abduction cases commented: "She is a problem."

State Secretary Hans-Juergen Geiger, the second-ranking official in the Justice Ministry, said Germany is eager to speed procedures for handling child-abduction cases. But he said it was unlikely the existing cases would be resolved by returning the children to the U.S.

Is it important to have an independent judiciary, or should politicians be able to influence judicial decisions? Go to Volume 21, U.S. Judiciary to look at this issue further.

"We can't change the decisions of our judges," he said. "The courts are independent, and we cannot interfere."

Calls for sanctions

Still, the child-abduction issue threatens to embitter relations between the two close allies. Some members of Congress have spoken of imposing economic sanctions against Germany if abducted American children are not sent home.

Economic sanctions against Germany might hurt the U.S. economy. Is it worth it to help only 59 American children? When do the rights of the individual take precedence?

"We go after countries that steal our products or violate patent or copyright laws, but not when they are supporting the theft of American children," said Sen. Mike DeWine (R-Ohio). "What does that say about us as a country?"

First Lady Hillary Rodham Clinton also has backed the American parents' cause. She said the cases are not just about individual children and victimized parents, but "a question of human rights."

Go to http://www.insight mag.com/main.cfm? include=details& storyid=209162 for an article about Hillary Clinton and the international child abduction issue.

Statistics on child abduction

Germany's Justice Ministry says that about two-thirds of abducted American children are returned to the U.S. The State Department said that in the past three years German courts ordered the return of 18 children in Hague convention cases and refused to return 26. In 22 other cases, it said, children were returned voluntarily by the parents who abducted them.

In cases where children are not returned, German courts usually base their decisions on two articles of the 1980 Hague convention on child abduction.

These articles allow judges to refuse to return a child if the child has lived in Germany more than a year and is "settled in its new environment," if the child would be exposed to "physical or psychological harm" by returning to the U.S., or if the child is mature enough to decide that he or she does not want to go back.

Criticism of German courts

Catherine Meyer, wife of the British ambassador to Washington and a leading figure in the battle over abducted children, said German courts, by delaying decisions, create a situation in which a child becomes settled in Germany and give time to abducting parents to indoctrinate the child against the other parent.

She also said German courts have accepted that children as young as 3 and 5 are mature enough to decide where they want to live.

Do you think that children of this age are old enough to make such decisions?

"The German courts create a situation which entirely favors the abducting parent," said Meyer, whose two sons were abducted by her former German husband in 1994.

"It's a vicious circle, and we find ourselves in a Catch-22 situation," Meyer said.

Geiger said delays were partly the fault of the State Department, which takes up to 22 months to forward applications for return of children to the U.S.

Mary Marshall, head of the Office of Children's Issues in the State Department, agreed that applications are sometimes delayed, either because American parents are not able to establish that their children are in Germany or are slow in producing the necessary paperwork.

"Catch-22" means a no-win situation in which whatever option you choose, you will lose. The phrase comes from the title of Joseph Heller's (1923–1999) novel published in 1961.

Even if the clock is stopped in law, the children concerned are already settling into their new lives. Should cases therefore be heard as quickly as possible?

But she said the U.S. government believes that time spent in getting cases to court "should not accrue to the benefit of the abductor."

"According to the Hague convention, the clock should stop until the cases have been filed with the court," Marshall said.

Geiger said a 1999 German law should help speed the handling of cases. Currently more than 600 German courts are responsible for child abduction cases, but the law will reduce that to just 24 specialized courts.

If this is the case, should the international community put more investment into training judges adequately in international law?

Lack of German knowledge

Whatever the number, American parents complain that German judges aren't familiar with the international rules. Kerstin Niethammer-Juergens, a German lawyer who has represented American and German parents in abduction cases, said, "We don't have enough Hague convention-educated lawyers or judges in Germany. A judge in a small court may know nothing about the convention."

American parents also say they often have no access to abducted children because German courts, unlike those in the U.S., have no power to enforce visitation rights. Geiger denied that, but two German judges, Geert Mackenroth and Angelika Peters, said the American parents were correct.

"Enforcement is a problem," said Mackenroth, spokesman for the German Federal Association of Judges and a judge in Itzehoe, near Hamburg. "We don't have the possibility to enforce court orders. That applies to German parents as well as foreigners involved in abduction cases. The only difference in the international cases is that the court can impose a fine on a parent who doesn't obey an order."

But he conceded that rarely happens, and said enforcement powers "should be regulated in the Hague convention.... We need a new law."

Some observers argue that such indoctrination is child abuse. But is it just the natural result of the bond between a parent and a child?

Problem of lengthy judicial proceedings

Mackenroth and Peters agreed that the length of judicial proceedings is a problem, and they recognized that this gives time to abducting parents to indoctrinate children. But they defended the German procedures.

Mackenroth said it can take three to six months to bring a case to court or, in extreme instances, up to two years.

Both German judges said courts have to determine if a child has been abused by an American parent before returning him or her to the U.S. In none of the cases of American parents interviewed for this article have the abducting parents claimed children were abused by their American spouses.

The child's interests

At least one American parent said he debated with himself whether it would be better for his children, who have lived in Germany several years, to give up his fight to regain custody.

But Ursula Kodjoe, a Karlsruhe University psychologist who has worked with American parents, said they should never give up because it is essential to a child's welfare to have normal access to both parents.

She said children who have been alienated from one parent grow up with a basic mistrust of other people and often a loss of self-worth.

"The result is destructive, with young people not believing in life," she said. "Some become seriously ill. A lot are not able to work. Some are suicidal, and they are nine times as likely as others to have accidents."

A child who has been told lies by the abducting parent, she said, will almost always try to find the "lost" parent when he or she reaches adulthood, she said.

Geiger said German officials were considering setting up a German–American mediation commission to deal with abduction cases, as already has happened with the French.

But French officials and French parents whose children have been abducted are less than satisfied with the work of their mediation commission, which has the power only to try to bring parents to agreement. Since their first meeting in January, no French child has been returned to France.

Jean-Francois Bohnert, a French liaison magistrate working with the German ministry, said that there are about 40 outstanding French cases but that the commission did help one French father gain a week's visitation.

European Union officials, Bohnert said, also are concerned over problems with the Hague convention. The EU plans to set up a European Court of Appeal for civil cases in Luxembourg, and its decisions will be binding. But even that, he conceded, would not help American parents.

Do you believe that a child's welfare depends on access to both parents? What about the many single parents who successfully raise healthy children? Go to Volume 11, Family and Society, Topic 4 Is the two-parent family best?

Go to http://www.pact-online.org/pdf/nigel_france.pdf for a country report on child abduction in France by the Center for International Family Law Studies.

Summary

Maura Harty, assistant secretary of the U.S. Bureau of Consular Affairs, argues that the Hague Convention, which the United States was instrumental in creating, has helped deter international parental child abduction and enabled many parents to regain custody of their children. She claims that its existence also makes it easier for parents to seek the return of, and access to, their children. Harty contrasts the improved procedures for resolving abduction cases with those countries that have signed the convention with the difficulties facing such efforts in countries that have not signed, and that have different judicial systems, cultural traditions, and family laws than the United States. She admits that the convention is an "imperfect instrument" but says that it is better than having no international instrument in place.

Journalist Ray Moseley focuses on the abduction of U.S. children to Germany. Despite being a signatory to the Hague Convention, Germany has been criticized for not implementing the treaty properly. German politicians argue that they cannot influence the judiciary. Moseley also argues that the convention itself allows exemptions that German judges can interpret differently than U.S. judges might. He repeats allegations made by U.S. parents that many German judges are not expert in child-abduction law, and that Germany's own laws give courts only limited powers to enforce any decisions. He also argues that the length of time that abduction cases take to get to court—which can be up to two years or more—favors abductors, who have time to indoctrinate their children, who in turn are, in any case, inevitably becoming more settled in their new country.

FURTHER INFORMATION:

Books:

Hutchinson, Anne-Marie, and Henry Setright, *International Parental Child Abduction*. Bristol, England: Family Law, 1998.

Useful websites:

http://findthekids.org/testimonies.html
Testimonies dealing with missing and abducted children on the Committee for Missing Children site.
http://www.icmec.org/missingkids/servlet/ResourceServlet?
LanguageCountry=en_X1&PageId=1278
Report by the International Centre for Missing and Exploited Children on "Good Practice in Handling Hague Abduction Convention Return Applications."
http://www.insightmag.com/main.cfm?include=detail&
storyid=213401
Article about nations that ignore the Hague Convention.

The following debates in the Pro/Con series may also be of interest:

In this volume:

 Part 1: Issues in international law, pages 8–9

In *Family and Society*:

 Topic 4 Is the two-parent family best?

 Topic 7 Should fathers have more parental rights?

IS THE HAGUE CONVENTION EFFECTIVE IN SETTLING INTERNATIONAL PARENT–CHILD ABDUCTION DISPUTES?

YES: The Hague Convention provides signatories with guidelines and procedures on how to take action in abduction cases

YES: The convention is an important practical tool for recovering abducted children from signatory countries

CODE OF CONDUCT
Does the Hague Convention provide an enforceable code of conduct?

IDEAL VS. REALITY
Is the Hague Convention as strong in theory than in practice?

IS THE HAGUE CONVENTION EFFECTIVE IN SETTLING INTERNATIONAL PARENT–CHILD ABDUCTION DISPUTES?

KEY POINTS

NO: In practice the Hague Convention is open to a wide range of interpretations, which signatories apply according to their own laws and culture

NO: In practice the convention is undermined by time delays and weaknesses in national legal systems

YES: It is an international treaty and as such, signatories have to comply with its regulations

YES: Nations like the United States and the United Kingdom have tried to facilitate the working of the treaty by establishing support agencies or by passing additional laws

NATIONAL SOVEREIGNTY
Should the Hague Convention take precedence over the national laws of individual countries?

SUPPORT
Has the convention received enough support from western nations?

NO: International laws cannot undermine national sovereignty; national laws and judicial process must take precedence

NO: Many western countries have been slow to educate their judiciary to apply the convention or to adapt their national laws

PART 2
TRADE AND THE ENVIRONMENT

INTRODUCTION

Regulations dealing with trade are one of the most important and also contentious areas of international law. While goods and services are bought and sold across borders every day, these transactions occur within a complex system of laws, regulations, and restrictions subject to both unilateral and international trade agreements.

The prosperity of most nations is predominantly based on their ability to be able to negotiate favorable trade agreements with other states. These relationships fall into three basic categories—bilateral ones such as the Canada-United States Free Trade Agreement, multilateral arrangements, such as the World Trade Organization (WTO), and regional agreements, such as the North American Free Trade Agreement.

Globalization and the promotion of trade liberalization as endorsed by organizations such as the WTO have, some observers believe, facilitated international trade and helped many economies grow. Critics counter that agreements like NAFTA greatly advantage already wealthy nations, while working to the detriment of developing nations.

The United States
The fundamental approaches to trade throughout U.S. history have been based on two opposing philosophies: free trade, as espoused by British economist Adam Smith, among others, and protectionism. The first seeks to allow business to be conducted without the imposition of restrictive tariffs or taxes in the belief that the laws of supply and demand and the workings of the marketplace will ensure the operation of an efficient economy. Protectionism, the more interventionist approach, is based on the use of regulations such as quotas that limit exports or imports; sometimes certain goods are banned to help protect domestic industry.

One of the great periods of protectionism in U.S. history came in the 1920s, at a time when the United States largely tried to isolate itself from the rest of the world following World War I (1914-1918). As the U.S. economy boomed, politicians became determined to isolate the economy from foreign competition by imposing tariffs on many imports. Other nations responded by adding reciprocal tariffs on U.S. imports. At the end of the decade this had the effect of both strangling international trade.

Economic orthodoxy at the start of the 21st century was dominated by free trade. International bodies such as the General Agreement on Tariffs and

Trade (GATT) or the WTO aim to remove all legal barriers to international trade. In theory countries concentrate on those areas of economic activity at which they are best and trade to gain access to those goods or services that they are not able to produce themselves. Critics of free trade claim, however, that in practice this does not benefit poor economies. It is all very well for the United States and leading western economies to advocate free trade, they say, since their economies are strong; but such nations can force smaller economies to accept imports. At the same time, they know that many cyberspace. Many countries have passed laws to encourage companies to act responsibly toward the environment, but globalization and the growth of transnational corporations—businesses that operate in more than one country—have led critics to lobby for more comprehensive environmental protection legislation. Some nations, however, object to restrictions on their business operations, viewing them as threats to their national sovereignty. The United States, for example, has attracted considerable criticism for its failure to ratify the Kyoto Protocol, an

---

"International law is that law which the wicked do not obey and the righteous do not enforce."
—ABBA EBAN (1915–2002), ISRAELI POLITICIAN

---

of these economies find it difficult to sell their own goods into more developed marketplaces. Observers also claim that the United States pays lip service to free trade: It is quick to impose quotas or tariffs on other countries' imports, such as on British steel in 2003, and this is hypocritical.

The environment

Another area of concern is making sure that business practices and international trade do not harm the environment. People have over the last 30 years or so become more concerned about protecting the planet and, by extension, ensuring the survival of humankind. International treaties exist to regulate everything from air pollution and carbon dioxide emissions to the oceans, outer space, and

international agreement that aims to limit the production of carbon monoxide and other harmful greenhouse gases. It has also been criticized for its lack of commitment to the environment through such practices as the drug eradication program, which allegedly includes environmentally harmful crop spraying.

Issues

The following topics look at a few key trade and environment issues. Topic 7 examines the often-voiced criticism that international trade law reflects the priorities of rich nations. Topic 8 discusses cyberspace and considers whether it should be subject to national or international law, and Topic 9 looks at the drug-crop eradication program from a legal perspective.

Topic 7

DO INTERNATIONAL TRADE LAWS FAVOR THE RICH?

YES

FROM "DIVIDE AND CONQUER: BILATERAL TRADE AGREEMENTS"
THE DOMINION, APRIL 6, 2004
YUILL HERBERT

NO

"BILATERAL DEALS ARE NO THREAT TO GLOBAL TRADE"
FINANCIAL TIMES, JULY 27, 2003
DANIEL GRISWOLD

INTRODUCTION

The sale of goods and services across national boundaries is subject to international laws established through trade agreements. Those agreements can be bilateral arrangements between two nations; regional agreements, such as the North American Free Trade Agreement (NAFTA), signed by the United States, Mexico, and Canada; or multilateral arrangements, such as the General Agreement on Tariffs and Trade (GATT) or agreements forged by its successor, the World Trade Organization (WTO).

Since the formation of GATT in 1948 multilateral agreements, and many bilateral and regional agreements, have sought to reduce restrictions on international trade, which often take the form of tariffs or limits (quotas) on imports. Neoclassical economic theory holds that global free trade is the most efficient way to foster growth. Each country specializes in producing the goods and services to which it is best

suited and trades them for what it cannot produce as competitively. Worldwide production would become more efficient, making better use of finite resources and maximizing growth in all nations. In such a view any laws that promote free trade do not favor one nation over another since their effect will benefit all.

Critics of free-trade agreements argue that opening markets to competition from abroad does not always generate development. In fact, it allows developed nations to dominate the economies of poorer nations by, for example, using cheap imports to undermine domestic manufacturing.

For such critics international trade is inherently unequal, and the legislation that governs it reflects the interests of the world's richest nations and the corporations that dominate their economies. They maintain, for example, that NAFTA has increased the number of Mexicans living in poverty by anything from 8 to 19 million. Supporters, however, counter that Mexico's international trade has trebled since NAFTA was implemented in 1994, and that up to a quarter of the Mexican population may have benefited from increased wages. Neoclassical economic theory argues that although unemployment may occur in some sectors of an economy following liberalization, it is short-term. Once labor and resources are redeployed to more competitive industries, the theory states, the full benefits of free trade are realized.

> *"No nation
> was ever ruined
> by trade."*
> —BENJAMIN FRANKLIN
> (1706–1790), POLITICIAN

Global economic organizations such as the International Monetary Fund (IMF) promote trade liberalization. The IMF argues that no modern economy has raised living standards without being open to trade. Restrictions on trade foster inefficiency, discourage foreign investment, reduce productivity, and stifle growth.

As evidence the IMF highlights the rapid rise in incomes in countries such as India, China, Korea, and Singapore, which have entered trade agreements and embraced free trade to varying degrees. This compares favorably to countries in Africa and the Middle East, where markets remain partly protected and still depend on the production and export of traditional commodities.

Critics of international trade laws cite another problem, however—that free trade is not equally free. Richer nations, such as the United States and the members of the European Union (EU), profess to support free trade but then use agricultural subsidies and other trade barriers to prevent poor countries from gaining access to lucrative markets. At the same time, they force developing nations to open up their own markets to U.S. and EU exports.

This contradiction has become a critical problem in WTO negotiations. Developing nations walked out of WTO talks in Cancún, Mexico, in 2003 in protest at the refusal of richer nations to reduce their subsidies on agricultural products and labor-intensive manufactures such as clothing and textiles. These are sectors in which poorer nations have a comparative advantage—that is, they can produce them more efficiently than other nations. When richer nations subsidize their own domestic sectors, they cancel out that advantage. The United States spends $4 billion a year subsidizing cotton production, for example. This depresses the world price of cotton, hurting farmers in Latin America, Africa, and Asia. The EU, meanwhile, spends around 2.7 billion euros each year making sugar profitable for its farmers to produce. This also effectively shuts EU markets to low-cost imports from the developing world. Critics argue that the negative effects of subsidies outweigh the benefits of any free-trade agreement for poor nations. Supporters counter that such subsidies are a commonsense form of welfare that cushion vital domestic economic sectors during times of hardship.

The articles that follow examine some of these issues.

DIVIDE AND CONQUER: BILATERAL TRADE AGREEMENTS
Yuill Herbert

Yuill Herbert is a founder of Environs: The Student Journal of Environmental Studies (see http://www.mta.ca/faculty /socsci/environs/ info.htm). This article appeared in April 2004.

See Volume 3, Economics, Topic 11 Is the World Trade Organization fair to poor countries?

Why might the presidents of Brazil and Venezuela be eager to limit the scope of a free-trade agreement? What have they got to lose?

Global Trade Watch is an organization that campaigns against corporate globalization. CAFTA, concluded in December 2003, will create a free-trade agreement between the United States and five Central American states: Honduras, Guatemala, El Salvador, Costa Rica, and Nicaragua.

YES

✓ Last September saw the spectacular collapse of World Trade Organization treaty talks in Cancun, Mexico. Joseph Stiglitz, former Chair of Clinton's council of economic advisors and Nobel Prize winner described the talks as "the usual: hard bargaining, extreme positions, last-minute concessions, arm twisting, peer pressure, tacit threats of cutting off development assistance and other benefits, and secret meetings among a small number of participants are all designed to extract concessions from the weakest".

Negotiators from the "Group of 21" developing nations walked out of the summit, vowing not to return to the table until the US and Europe reversed their stance on agricultural subsidies....

The collapse of the Cancun WTO meeting resulted in heightened political pressure on the US to achieve a result in Miami at the ministerial of the Free Trade Agreement of the Americas (FTAA). Faced with strong opposition to a NAFTA-style trade accord by both Brazil's Lula and Venezuela's Chavez due to their concerns about potential wide-ranging impacts, the United States was forced to accept either an "a la carte" agreement or nothing at all.... In response to the prospect of a limited FTAA, Franklin J. Vargo of the National Association of Manufacturers remarked to *The Washington Post*, "We want full benefits out of Brazil."

A bilateral strategy

It is in this context that the US has been vigorously pursuing trade agreements bi-laterally, or one country at a time, an approach that is proving more successful. Lori Wallach, Director of Public Citizen's Global Trade Watch, bluntly describes US efforts with the recently concluded, but as yet un-ratified, Central American Free Trade Agreement (CAFTA). "After ten years of terrible real life effects, the NAFTA model is in such ill repute that its Bush Administration boosters struck out at the WTO in Cancun, were forced to shrink the FTAA in Miami and now have to rely on bullying a few relatively weak Central American countries into accepting the NAFTA poison through the proposed CAFTA."

In the past two years, the US has initiated comprehensive free trade negotiations with 19 countries, a market representing an estimated US $2.5 trillion worth of opportunities to American business. Simultaneously, however, these agreements open the American market, exposing, in particular, US industries dependent on sweat labour that cannot compete with low labour costs in poorer countries around the world. The difference is that the US has the resources to diffuse the pain of the transition, amounting to support of US$1.8 billion in 2003, while developing countries simply suffer.

Each of these trade agreements is based on the NAFTA model, further refined in more recent bi-lateral agreements with Chile and Singapore. These agreements are binding and contain enforcement mechanisms. According to Zoellick, "[foreign countries] keep our products out, they illegally copy our technology, and they block us from providing services. We want to make sure our products and services get a fair chance to compete, and to be vigilant and active in enforcing our trade agreements so that American workers have a level playing field".

Can you think of an industry in which the United States has lost jobs to cheaper labor overseas? Is that an acceptable price for Americans to pay as part of the movement toward global free trade?

Robert B. Zoellick was appointed U.S. trade representative by George W. Bush in 2001. Go to www.ustr.gov for information on free-trade negotiations from the Office of the United States Trade Representative.

U.S. access

In reality, bilateral agreements give US companies and investors un-equalled access to foreign markets. They open up service sectors, including health and education, to US companies. And they give corporations the right to sue for damages if past, present or future investments are jeopardised by legislation. Presently, this new corporate–national relationship is playing out in Costa Rica at this moment. In 1994, as part of a structural adjustment program sponsored by the International Monetary Fund, Costa Rica granted concessions for oil exploration. Harken Energy, an oil company that is reported to have close ties to President Bush, acquired exploration rights to pristine sections of the Caribbean coast. When Costa Rican environmental impact legislation prevented Harken's drilling plans, the company sued the country for US$57 billion, more than three times Costa Rica's GDP, through the World Bank…. On March 11, the government announced that it does not have to pay Harken anything as it has the jurisdiction to protect its natural resources. However, that may all change if CAFTA is ratified by government, as it includes the investor state mechanism….

Should Costa Rica be able to impose legislation to protect its own environment? Why do you think the author mentions Harken's connection to George W. Bush?

Further, governments at all levels lose the ability to give preferential treatment to companies in order to boost local employment or meet other qualitative objectives. Governments cannot support specific sectors such as agriculture or industry in order to meet social objectives. And protection of intellectual property rights is guaranteed for up to 30 years, an increase over the period of 20 years outlined in the World Trade Organisation, minimising options for low-cost drugs and protecting companies who patent biological resources. In summary, bilateral trade agreements significantly constrain decision-making in what has traditionally been considered the realm of public, democratically-elected governments.

In Cancun, a core group of developing nations, centred around Brazil, demonstrated that they would not accept the neo-liberal agenda of the economic superpowers, effectively halting the WTO negotiations. However, such solidarity is not possible in the bilateral negotiations that are currently the focus of US efforts. Faced with the overwhelming resources and shear economic might of the US, the agreements are driven by the US agenda. In a speech in 2001, Zoellick remarked, "economic strength—at home and abroad—is the foundation of America's hard and soft power.... Trade is about more than economic efficiency. It promotes the values at the heart of this protracted struggle." Exactly what "protracted struggle" Zoellick is referring to is not clear, but to developing countries, his words are ominous.

The case of Bolivia

Take Bolivia, which is likely to begin negotiations with the US sometime this year as part of the Andean Free Trade Agreement (AFTA). Bolivia will be bargaining from an impossible position. Each year, Bolivia receives US$107 million in social and economic aid from the US, as well as US$59 million for the police and military. Its GDP is US$7 billion and its debt is US$4.5 billion. At US$800 million, external assistance from governments, the International Monetary Fund and World Bank equals ten percent of the GDP—one third of public expenditure. The US strategy of negotiating the AFTA one country at a time means two things—a previous treaty with Chile, and most likely one with Columbia, will set the standard for the scope of the agreement and secondly, there is no opportunity for solidarity in the negotiations. Combine Bolivia's economic desperation with technical and legal inexperience and the impoverished country is in no position to negotiate favourable terms.

See Volume 14, International Development, Topic 12 Do patents lead to higher-priced drugs?

"Hard" power is the U.S. ability to tell other countries what to do; "soft" power refers to less direct forms of international influence.

AFTA was first created in 1991. It abolished or reduced duty on imports to the United States from Bolivia, Colombia, Ecuador, and Peru. The agreement expired in 2001. In 2003 the United States began negotiations to create a new AFTA with Colombia and Peru, with plans to incorporate Bolivia and Ecuador at a later date.

The only card left to play is the strength of the social movements within Bolivia, battle-hardened from recent upheavals over water privatization, which are certain to resist new trade agreements.

Further, the negotiations surrounding CAFTA illustrate the manner in which these agreements are being concluded. The entire process took less than a year, making the possibility of meaningful analysis by government or civil society groups extremely limited. At the beginning of negotiations the US demanded that all parties sign a confidentiality agreement, classifying the texts as national security. According to the agreement, negotiators could not reveal even the agenda of meetings without the unanimous consent of all negotiating teams—giving any one country a veto over what information was released....

Should any business conducted by the U.S. government be confidential? Do citizens have a right to know what is being done in their name? Or might confidentiality protect national interests?

A failure to deliver

There is increasing evidence that the trade and investment theories are not delivering for the poor countries. United Nations Conference on Trade and Development (UNCTAD)'s 2002 Trade and Development Report stated that developing countries have not garnered rapid and sustainable income gains from trade and investment. "With the exception of a few East Asian first-tier newly industrializing economies (NIEs), with a significant industrial base already closely integrated into the world trading system, developing-country exports are still concentrated on products derived essentially from the exploitation of natural resources and the use of unskilled labour which have limited prospects for productivity growth and lack dynamism in world markets. The statistics showing a considerable expansion of technology-intensive, supply-dynamic, high-value-added exports from developing countries are misleading," observes UNCTAD.

UNDP's Human Development Report in 2003 indicated that 54 developing countries suffered average income *declines* over the course of the decade.... But perhaps the most staggering indicator is 2004 *Forbes* magazine report that lists a record 587 individuals and family units worth $1 billion or more, an increase from 476 in 2003. The combined wealth of this year's billionaires also reached record levels—a staggering $1.9 trillion, an increase of $500 billion in just one year. The wealth of these few hundred people exceeds the gross domestic product of the world's 170 poorest countries combined. Such data makes it clear who is gaining and who is losing from these powerful trade agreements....

What does the number of billionaires in the world have to do with trade agreements? Is it inevitable that some people are very rich while others are very poor? Or do you think that personal wealth and international wealth are connected?

BILATERAL DEALS ARE NO THREAT TO GLOBAL TRADE
Daniel Griswold

Daniel Griswold is associate director of the Center for Trade Policy Studies at the Cato Institute, an organization dedicated to free trade and libertarianism. This article was published in the British newspaper the Financial Times in July 2003.

NO

The belated efforts of the US to sign bilateral agreements with Chile, Singapore and a few other small partners threaten, we are told, to destroy the entire trading system. A "selfish hegemon", as Jagdish Bhagwati and Arvind Panagariya call it ("Bilateral trade treaties are a sham", *Financial Times*, July 14), is conspiring with special interests to distort the global system. Such arguments themselves distort reality.

To begin, the US is hardly treading on new ground. The multilateral system makes room for free-trade areas through Article 24 of the General Agreement on Tariffs and Trade. The World Trade Organisation's charter allows customs unions or free-trade agreements between members, recognising "the desirability of increasing freedom of trade by the development, through voluntary agreements, of closer integration between the economies of [those] countries". More than 250 such agreements have been negotiated; if the Chile and Singapore agreements become law, the US will be party to exactly five.

The Chile and Singapore FTAs were approved by the House in July 2003 and became law in December 2003. Since then the United States has also begun or concluded FTAs with other countries, including Bahrain and Australia.

Benefits of FTAs

Beyond their economic impact, free-trade agreements of the sort the US is pursuing can benefit the parties involved, the global trading system, and the world at large in many ways.

First, FTAs provide an important safety valve if multilateral negotiations become stuck—an all-too-real possibility. Since the Kennedy Round concluded in 1967, only two other comprehensive multilateral agreements have been reached: the Tokyo Round in 1979 and Uruguay Round in 1994. And because of the need for consensus, it takes only one of the 146 nations in the WTO to scuttle a new agreement. Given the history of multilateral negotiations, it would be unwise to put all of our eggs in the Doha Round basket.

The Doha Round of WTO talks began in Geneva in early 2002.

Fears that FTAs will divert attention from the multilateral track are unfounded. The US government signed pacts with Israel, Canada and Mexico during the Uruguay Round negotiations from 1986 to 1994 without reducing its

President George W. Bush (2001–) has signed many bilateral trade agreements. Supporters claim that such agreements are beneficial not only to the parties involved but also to global trade as a whole.

COMMENTARY: GATT Article 24

The promotion of free-trade areas and of other bilateral free-trade agreements (FTA) is covered by Article 24 of the General Agreement on Tariffs and Trade (GATT). The article recognizes "the desirability of increasing freedom of trade by the development, through voluntary agreements, of closer integration between the economies of countries parties to such agreements." There is a proviso, however, that the creation of a free-trade area should not result in unduly high tariffs or restrictions placed on trade with other GATT members. In 1994 an understanding was added to the article to clarify its definitions, yet there remains considerable debate about what is actually covered by FTAs. The article states that duties and restrictions should be eliminated on "substantially all the trade" in a free-trade area. However, there is no agreement on what this phrase means. Critics of FTAs argue that developed economies such as the United States thus often exclude politically sensitive sectors of the economy from FTAs. One of the main such exclusions is agriculture: Numerous types of agricultural produce are excluded from NAFTA, for example, which introduced free trade among the United States, Canada, and Mexico.

commitment to a final multilateral agreement. Robert Zoellick, US trade representative, is leading the Doha Round with proposals to liberalise global trade in manufactured goods, agricultural products and services.

FTAs can also level the playing field for US exporters put at a disadvantage by free-trade agreements that exclude the US. In Chile, for example, US exporters of wheat, soya beans, corn, paper products, plastics and heating and construction equipment have lost market share since its government began in 1997 to aggressively pursue free-trade agreements with its non-US trading partners. FTAs can also help less-developed countries lock in economic reforms. A signed agreement prevents nations backsliding in times of economic or political duress, assuring foreign investors that reforms mark a permanent commitment to liberalisation. So FTAs can serve as carrots to encourage the spread of political and economic freedom abroad.

> Does Griswold's claim that FTAs encourage political freedom seem a bit far-fetched?

Negotiation and consensus

Moreover, FTAs can provide useful templates for broader negotiations. As membership of the WTO grows, reaching consensus becomes more difficult. Negotiators can be forced to consider only the lowest common denominator. Negotiating with one nation or a small group of like-minded countries can allow more meaningful liberalisation in areas such as sanitary and regulations, technical barriers to trade, service trade and investment, electronic commerce, customs facilitation, labour and environmental standards and market access for politically sensitive sectors. Those talks can blaze a trail for wider regional and multilateral negotiations.

If the United States only negotiates with "like-minded" nations, will it ever be able to benefit the poorest countries in the world?

FTAs and Article 24

Finally, FTAs can spur the economic reform and consolidation within member states cited in Article 24. By encouraging regional integration, they increase economies of scale and create a more integrated production process. Consolidation may be most pronounced in more heavily protected service sectors such as telecommunications, financial services and transportation. More efficient industries and infrastructure can yield dynamic gains year after year, boosting growth, investment, and demand for imports from FTA partners and the rest of the world. NAFTA is one reason why North America has been an engine of global growth in the past decade. For all those reasons, the Bush administration's FTA agenda is worth pursuing. Despite their peculiarities and incremental nature, the agreements can serve the cause of freedom and development by breaking down barriers to trade between nations.

Consolidation is a process of streamlining and strengthening economic organization to avoid, for example, unnecessary competition.

Do you think that NAFTA has helped economic growth? Was North America an engine of global growth before NAFTA existed?

Summary

Both articles consider the issues surrounding trade laws by considering bilateral trade agreements between the United States and other countries. In the first article Canadian student and journalist Yuill Herbert argues that rich countries are forced into concessions by the threat from rich countries to withdraw economic and social aid. He cites Bolivia as coming under pressure of this kind from the United States in the creation of a free-trade agreement. He claims that weaker nations that enter bilateral trade agreements are more vulnerable because they are unable to draw on the support of other nations during negotiations. Herbert also shows how FTAs benefit transnational corporations. He cites an example in which a U.S. oil firm, Haken, tried to sue Costa Rica for not permitting it to explore for oil. Under future trade agreements, Herbert argues, such suits might have a chance of victory. He concludes with further evidence that while the poor lose out under international trade laws, rich individuals are being further empowered.

By contrast, Daniel Griswold believes that bilateral free-trade agreements (FTAs) are beneficial both to the parties to the agreement and international trade more generally. He argues that FTAs can help undeveloped and developing nations "lock in economic reforms" in the face of political and other pressures; this in turn can attract foreign investors. Griswold also uses standard economic theory to back up his argument. He proposes that FTAs can increase economies of scale and also serve as an incentive to make production more efficient. These factors will boost economic growth and investment, as well as demand for the poor nation's imports.

FURTHER INFORMATION:

Books:

Orme, William A., Jr., *Understanding NAFTA: Mexico, Free Trade, and the New North America*. Austin, TX: University of Texas Press, 1996.

Vizentini, Paulo, and Marianne Wiesebron (eds.), *Free Trade for the Americas? The United States' Push for the FTAA Agreement*. New York: Zed Books, 2004.

Useful websites:

http://www.globalpolicy.org/globaliz/econ/2003/0714rta.htm
"Bilteral trade treaties are a sham" by Jagdish Bhagwati and Arvind Panagariya.

http://www.worldgameofeconomics.com/Vietnam_US_TradeAgreement.htm
Essay examining the benefits of the trade agreement signed by the United States and Vietnam in 2000.

The following debates in the Pro/Con series may also be of interest:

In this volume:

 Part 2: Trade and the environment, pages 84–85

In *Economics*:

 Topic 11 Is the World Trade Organization fair to poor countries?

In *Commerce and Trade*:

Part 4: The United States

DO INTERNATIONAL TRADE LAWS FAVOR THE RICH?

YES: Completely free trade exists only in theory. In practice inbuilt inequalities in the global economy mean that liberalization comes at a cost of increased poverty in poor countries.

YES: Although the United States and the European Union preach free trade, they use, for example, subsidies to help domestic sectors such as agriculture compete with imports

ECONOMIC THEORY
Does trade liberalization benefit only a minority in the long term?

IMBALANCE OF TRADE
Are rich nations being hypocritical when they urge poorer nations to liberalize markets?

NO: Free trade promotes the development of competitive advantage. It also encourages economic efficiency, growth, and long-term poverty reduction; it works to the advantage of the global economy.

NO: Article 24 of GATT implicitly recognizes nations' ability to protect certain sectors of their economies. It is the overall thrust of legislation that is important, not the detail.

DO INTERNATIONAL TRADE LAWS FAVOR THE RICH?
KEY POINTS

YES: It is inevitable that larger, stronger, and richer countries will endeavor to achieve maximum advantage from trade for the sake of their citizens

YES: Trade is based on resources such as materials or labor: Some countries simply have more such resources than others

POWER RELATIONS
Is trade inherently unequal?

NO: Economic theory argues that free trade will allow nations to specialize in goods in which they have a comparative advantage. This is the same for all nations.

NO: The laws on which international trade is based are binding only on those nations that voluntarily sign up to them. Those laws neither advantage nor disadvantage individual nations.

Topic 8
SHOULD CYBERSPACE BE TREATED AS INTERNATIONAL SPACE?

YES
FROM "THE CYBERSPACE REVOLUTION"
KEYNOTE ADDRESS, COMPUTER POLICY AND LAW CONFERENCE,
CORNELL UNIVERSITY, JULY 9, 1997
DAVID G. POST

NO
"THE HOT NEW FIELD OF CYBERLAW IS JUST HOKUM, SKEPTICS ARGUE"
BOOMTOWN COLUMN, *THE WALL STREET JOURNAL*, JULY 1, 2002
LEE GOMES

INTRODUCTION

Cyberspace—a term first coined by U.S. sci-fi writer William Gibson in 1984—is the virtual environment created by a huge international network of computers and internet service providers (ISP). Among other things, it contains vast amounts of information, and it facilitates both global, fast contact and transactions between people and businesses living and operating in different parts of the world.

At the start of the 21st century almost half a billion people worldwide had Internet access, and some estimate that cyberspace will generate more than $7 trillion in international trade in 2004. Statisticians also forecast that by 2010 over half of the world's population will use cyberspace, creating a vast global market for goods, services, and entertainment.

While many advocates have heralded the possibilities that cyberspace has opened up, creating a truly democratic

space and a "global village," critics believe that it has also created all kinds of problems. Cyberspace enables people to access information on practically any subject, often within seconds, but that also means that it is difficult to monitor access to or to prevent certain types of material from being available to the masses. Governments and law-enforcement agencies are, for example, concerned about easy access to pornography—especially involving children. They are similarly disturbed by far-right groups that have used the Net to promote racism and homophobia, for example, and they are worried by terrorist groups that have used cyberspace to disseminate their ideas, to recruit new members, and also to organize operations. Some observers subsequently argue that the Internet as a global entity undermines national sovereignty and the laws of nation-states that serve both to protect vulnerable groups from exploitation and to protect national and also international security.

One of the main problems that the Internet raises is that it does not operate within specific geographical boundaries: It is a global space. Some commentators therefore state that it cannot be subject to national laws, and it must be treated as international space, subject to international law. The problem, however, with this rationale is that nations vary as to what is acceptable within law. For example, while the U.S. First Amendment guarantees the right to free expression, no such guarantee exists in many other nations; their governments may wish to restrict the kind of information their citizens can get. It would thus be difficult, some experts argue, to persuade certain nations to accept international laws that undermine their own cultural or societal standards.

> *"In cyberspace, the First Amendment is a local ordinance."*
>
> —JOHN PERRY BARLOW (1947–), CYBER-RIGHTS PIONEER

China is an example of one state that has tried to regulate and control the content of, and access to, cyberspace. It has introduced strict laws that prevent antigovernment media. Government has also created its own national Internet, which is separated from the global Internet by a firewall—a filter used to block undesirable electronic communications. However, this has not stopped opposition groups from flouting the system: Chinese dissidents have been able to find ways around the "great firewall of China" by such means as routing information through apparently innocuous sites.

Other countries have also passed legislation to force nationally based ISPs to monitor and regulate the content they make available to their subscribers. Australia, for example, passed a law in 1999 that required national ISPs to block or remove adult content. Civil rights organizations immediately objected: Electronic Frontiers Australia accused the government of making Australia the "global village idiot." In 2000 a French judge also ruled that the U.S. ISP Yahoo should prevent French users accessing online auctions of Nazi memorabilia. Yahoo's lawyers subsequently appealed the ruling to a U.S. court. They claimed that France could not have jurisdiction over a U.S. ISP (see box on page 106).

Such arguments have led some observers to conclude that the only way to regulate cyberspace is to treat it in the the same way as the law of the seas—by making it international space regulated by international conventions. Cyberspace should be ruled by international "cyberlaws," they claim. Some scholars, however, counter that this is unnecessary. They believe that cyberspace may have created a global village but that it is the responsibility of national governments to protect their own citizens. They claim existing national and international protocols offer adequate protection.

The following articles examine the question of whether cyberspace should be treated as international space.

THE CYBERSPACE REVOLUTION
David G. Post

David Post is a lecturer in law at Temple University, PA, and is one of America's leading commentators on law and the Internet. This is the text of a speech he gave in 1997.

YES

✓ ... The world, I think, can be divided into 2 kinds of people: ... those who think the Internet and the new communications technologies herald a revolution calling for radical rethinking of our basic notions of law and politics and society, and those who think it does not ...

There are lots of things I could talk about, but let me focus on two: first, the Net challenges and will ultimately warp beyond recognition existing notions of sovereignty, and second, it is at its most powerful in destroying existing hierarchies around which we organize political, social, and commercial life.

Sovereignty

There's a strong form and a weak form of my argument, but the latter is sufficient for my purposes here: that the new information technologies, of which the Net is the most dramatic but by no means the only example, render territorial boundaries far less significant; that sovereign power is fundamentally tied to the existence of those territorial boundaries; and that therefore the power of sovereign states to constrain conduct in this context is dramatically weakened....

Writing in ... *Foreign Policy*, Stephen Kobrin wrote:

[W]e face not the end of the state, but rather the diminished efficacy of political and economic governance that is rooted in geographic sovereignty and in mutually exclusive territorial jurisdiction. Questions such as, Where did the transaction take place? ... and Whose law applies? will lose meaning.

I think Kobrin is right, because the existing legal system *cannot* answer the question "what rules govern my conduct?" in a coherent or intelligible way. Let me explain briefly.

The central legal issue on the Net ... is: who makes the law?

I get a lot of questions of the form: "is it a violation of copyright to [fill in the blank—frame a web page? link to infringing material? etc.]" But to answer that, you have to first answer the necessarily antecedent question: what law governs? What version of copyright law applies to the

Many people see a parallel between the Internet's overcoming of national boundaries and the spread of international commerce and culture, known as globalization. Do you think they are both evidence of a decline in the importance of the territorial nation-state?

Using personal examples can be an effective way of elaborating your argument.

conduct at issue? We can pretend this is a manageable problem by giving it a name—choice of law, or conflict of laws—but that just masks the fact that it is a profound and in many ways an unanswerable question.

Ordinarily, we answer this choice of law question by looking, fundamentally, to physical geography: *where* does an event or transaction take place, and *where* are the effects of that transaction felt? But the "where" question is indeterminate and fundamentally irrelevant on this global network, which was designed precisely to make geography irrelevant and indeterminate. Machines … on the Internet have a "location," an address, but it is an address that is not tied to physical location in any way. So we can ask "where does a transaction take place," but it is only meaningful with respect to this network address, this virtual location, not to the physical location of the machine....

Do you think that Post is overlooking the fact that even though computer addresses are not physical locations, the computer itself is in a physical place? Is there any reason why it should not count as the country in which the transaction actually takes place?

And as to the question "where are the effects of this Net transaction felt?," the answer, of course, is that the effects are felt equally *everywhere*.

Gambling in Costa Rica

An example might be useful here. I was recently contacted by a business that was looking to open up a Web-based gambling operation using a server located in Costa Rica. Who has a legitimate claim to set the rules for this conduct? … Perhaps the law of Costa Rica should govern, since the activity "takes place" there. But that's trivial—Costa Rica was chosen precisely because there's no prohibition.... What about the laws of the United States? Aren't the effects of this conduct felt in Missouri and Minnesota? Doesn't that give Missouri and Minnesota a legitimate claim on this conduct?

Should web operators have the right to take advantage of differences between national laws as bankers and savers do, for example? See Topic 11 Should tax havens be made illegal? for more information.

The answer is, of course, "yes"—these jurisdictions are affected by the conduct in Costa Rica and may therefore assert a legitimate claim on the activity taking place there. But the same holds for any sovereign—all have, by this reasoning, an equal claim to set the rules for this behavior. The answer to the question "is this wrongful conduct?" is thus a resounding "it depends …". What kind of a legal system is this, that cannot give a coherent answer to this question?

This is disorienting, to be sure; the sovereign state has served us well for a long time, and it is not easy to imagine a world in which law emanates from some other place. But imagine it we must; the Net calls on us to develop not just a new law of copyright, but a new *kind* of law of copyright, one that does not look to the entity in control of physical territory for its justification....

See Volume 18, Commerce and Trade, Topic 12 Does the Internet make it difficult to enforce copyright law?

Disintegration of hierarchy

Go to http://www. copyright.gov/fls/fl 102.html for an explanation of "fair use." Do you think cyberspace makes it difficult to apply?

We live in a world that is organized in more or less predictable, and hierarchical, ways.… [M]uch of our law makes sense only within the context of these hierarchies. Consider the "fair use" doctrine in copyright law; we all know that it makes no sense to say that my decision about whether to hand a Dilbert cartoon out to my class should be based on a delicate balancing of four statutory factors (… the purpose of the use, the nature of the copyrighted work, the amount of the work taken, and the effect of the copying activity on the market for the original), and we know that there are thousands, probably millions, of violations each day of the fair use principles.

But we don't really care about that very much, because the existing hierarchies allow us to give meaning to the doctrine, provided that the key intermediary institutions—the libraries, copy shops, educational institutions, and the like—libraries understand their obligations.

Some estimates argue that only about 40 percent of information on the Internet is reliable. Might the development of new laws make it easier to determine what sites are more reliable than others? What kind of information would help?

But the Net … upsets these ordered relationships.… We are entering a networked, and not a hierarchical, world; … as far as the Net is concerned, my newsletter site is the same as the *Wall Street Journal*'s or the *New York Times*'.…

So formal rules (derived from long-standing notions of sovereignty) and informal relationships of all kinds organized into relatively predictable hierarchical structures are in total flux and challenged on all sides.…

A revolution in progress

In his book *The Radicalism of the American Revolution* … [Gordon Wood] argues that the well-known political revolution of 1776 was embedded in, and inextricably linked to, a social revolution, a revolution in the way people interacted with one another and constructed a map of their social universe. And the echoes for what is happening in cyberspace are truly remarkable, I think. Wood writes:

Gordon S. Wood is a leading historian of the American Revolution. The book from which this quote comes was published in 1992.

The American Revolution was as radical and social as any revolution in history.… By the early years of the nineteenth century the Revolution had created a society fundamentally different from the colonial society of the eighteenth century.… The Revolution did not merely create a political and legal environment conducive to economic expansion; it also released powerful popular entrepreneurial and commercial energies that few realized existed and transformed the economic landscape of the country.…

What is so interesting to me about this is that new conceptions of *sovereignty* were at the heart of this political revolution, and helped to bring about, and were in turn fed by, new social structures that challenged, fatally, the established hierarchical orderings of pre-revolutionary colonial life.…

On the pivotal question of sovereignty, which is the question of the nature and location of the ultimate power in the state, American thinkers attempted to depart sharply from one of the most firmly fixed points in 18th century political thought.

Developing notions both of popular sovereignty—that the only undivided power that is subject to no law and is literally a law unto itself rests in the People—and … divided sovereignty—that there need not be one absolute sovereign but that the attributes of governmental sovereignty may be divided and distributed among different levels of institutions—became central to the republican creed. And this new conception of political sovereignty—of the legitimacy of the law-maker—helped to bring about the total collapse of the hierarchical social order of the colonial world.…

The Net and the law

What does all this have to do with cyberspace? We are again facing a fundamental challenge to notions of how laws are legitimately made, at the same time as the structure of the society within which law has been made and applied is changing dramatically. The net is forcing us to ask the most basic question of all in law: Who is the law-maker? What is the process by which rules of conduct get made? How do we express the notion of "popular sovereignty" today? That we don't have the answer to the question "What law governs?" is the *good* news.…

Somehow we have come to view the law as something made "out there," and we look to the "experts" to tell us whether or not we're doing something wrongful. We have in some sense forgotten that the law is not something imposed from above by the sovereign, but are rules that *we* are ultimately responsible for. The net *demands* that we take another look at this.… We are engaged—whether we know it or not—in a gigantic, worldwide conversation about sovereignty, about the source of rules for conduct, and, though I have ideas about where this conversation may lead us, none of us can say what new conception of sovereignty lies around the bend.…

Post argues that simply because something is well established or accepted doctrine does not mean that it will always be so. Do you think that the Internet will help people think about matters in different ways through easy access to different ideas, traditions, and cultures?

The United States has its own system for making laws and reviewing their legality. Do you think that accepting that cyberspace is subject to international laws would undermine national sovereignty? Go to Topic 14 Does the United States have too much influence on international law?

Laws are highly complex. Should they be left in the hands of experts who understand precedent and other legal principles?

THE HOT NEW FIELD OF CYBERLAW IS JUST HOKUM, SKEPTICS ARGUE
Lee Gomes

Lee Gomes is a reporter on The Wall Street Journal, a respected business newspaper. This article was published in July 2002.

NO

Is there really a cyberspace full of "cybercitizens" who need only be accountable to their own "cyberlaws"? A loose-knit group of law professors is bucking one of the big fads in the legal field by calling that whole idea "cybersilly."

Law involving the online world is hot right now. Law schools trying to stay current have courses in it, which tend to be popular with a generation of law students reared on Wired magazine and Napster. Experts in so-called cyberlaw typically have technology-friendly legal views, and are thus frequent guests at the tech world's many conferences. They're also quoted all the time in media accounts of online legal disputes.

Cyberskeptics

There is, though, a much less well-known but equally determined group of legal experts—let's call them the "cyberskeptics"—who are deeply troubled by just about everything about this trend. The skeptics start by questioning the very existence of cyberspace, which they say is no more real than a "phone space" involving all the people on the telephone at a given time. They go on to argue that something happening online shouldn't be treated any differently by the law than if it occurred on Main Street.

Is it unrealistic to compare the Internet to the telephone system? Does that seem outdated to you?

You can usually find the skeptics in law journals rather than at tech conferences. Orin S. Kerr, of George Washington University Law School, for example, is wary of courts looking at Internet legal issues from the perspective of users, who may indeed think of themselves as cavorting about in cyberspace. A more productive approach, he says, might be to look at what is happening in the real world, where one usually simply finds a group of computers connected to each other and passing along data.

Although advocates claim that cyberspace is a new world, it is still a commercial venture for many profit-making firms. Does this imply that cyberspace has to be treated as part of the real world?

Timothy Wu, a professor at the University of Virginia School of Law, writes that there is no single Internet, but instead, many different Internet applications that all need to be discussed differently.

Richard Clarke is special adviser to the president on cyberspace security.

COMMENTARY: Yahoo and Nazi memorabilia

The issue of how to protect and preserve certain standards in cyberspace has led to much heated debate. In 2000 a French court case involving the U.S. ISP Yahoo focused public attention on a number of legal issues involving cyberspace and national sovereignty. In April 2000 LICRA, the Paris-based International League against Racism and Anti-Semitism, and the Union of French Jewish Students (UEJF) announced that they were launching a joint action against Yahoo to prevent it hosting online auctions of Nazi memorabilia. LICRA argued that "This sale of symbols of the greatest ever crime against humanity trivializes Nazism in the extreme." France has strict laws against selling anything that might incite racism, including Nazi memorabilia. Although Yahoo's French site did not sell any Nazi-related material, around 1,000 items of memorabilia were offered for sale daily on its U.S. site, which was accessible by users in France.

The verdict and its implications

In May 2000 Judge Jean-Jacques Gomez found that Yahoo had offended France's "collective memory" He ordered Yahoo to pay fines of up to 400,000 euros (around $360,000) per day to both LICRA and UEJF. Yahoo's lawyer, however, argued: "The question put before this court is whether a French jurisdiction can make a decision on the English content of an American site, run by an American company ... for the sole reason that French users have access via the Internet." Yahoo in the United States also claimed that closing the offending sites would contravene the First Amendment's guarantee of free speech.

Yahoo eventually decided that it was impossible to prevent French users from accessing certain sites: It therefore banned the sale of Nazi memorabilia from all of its websites—a decision applauded by many observers. However, it also appealed against the French ruling. It filed an appeal in California to ask a federal judge to rule on whether French courts had jurisdiction in the United States. The judge agreed that the French ruling may indeed have infringed on the right to free speech. This opened the doors, many believe, for Yahoo to appeal the original decision.

Angry with the decision, three other French rights groups launched a second attack, this time against Yahoo's former president Tim Koogle, accusing him of "justifying war crimes and crimes against humanity." In February 2003, however, a Paris court ruled that this was not true.

Jack Goldsmith, of the University of Chicago law school, defends a decision two years ago by a French judge who said that Yahoo couldn't sell Nazi memorabilia in France, which bans the material. Netizens pounced on the ruling as an affront to their brave new digital world. But Prof.

Goldsmith says that Yahoo, since it has a subsidiary in France, should no more be immune to French laws than General Motors is.

More importantly, he says, the French judge went through with the ruling only after determining that it was feasible, through various screening technologies, for Yahoo to prevent its French visitors from seeing the ads but still display them to others.

> Other Internet companies also use screening filters to regulate their commerce: eBay, for example, has software that recognizes French-language browsers.

While the skeptics emphasize different points, they all have as a core principle a rejection of the notion of "Internet exceptionalism," or the idea that the Internet is a new, unique thing that requires its own special laws. "The steam engine … probably transformed American law, but the 'law of the steam engine' never existed," writes Joseph H. Sommer, counsel at the Federal Reserve Bank of New York, in a law review article called "Against Cyberlaw." He also fretted that the cyberbuffs are afflicted with "insufficient perspective, disdain for history, unnecessary futurology and technophilia."

> Go to http://www.law.berkeley.edu/journals/btlj/articles/vol15/sommer.html to read this article in full.

The skeptics have no particular beef with computer and Internet technology. Most, in fact, are avid users. They just think that it shouldn't be pandered to. And they certainly deride the ideas behind the "Declaration of Independence of Cyberspace," which is posted on many Web sites and poses a "hands off" challenge to government.

> The Declaration of Independence of Cyberspace was written by John Perry Barlow in 1996. Barlow calls himself a "cognitive dissident" and is cofounder of the Electronic Frontier Foundation. Go to http://www.missouri.edu/~rhetnet/barlow/barlow_declaration.html to read the declaration.

Character of a skeptic

The dispute between the buffs and the skeptics doesn't have the usual left–right overlay to it. The skeptics tend to be Republican but come from both sides of the spectrum.

A better question, perhaps, involves the politics of the cyberspacians—not their defenders in law schools as much as the cyberactivists themselves. Many observers assume them to be politically progressive, beyond their obvious libertarianism.

But are they really? Prof. Wu thinks not, calling them deeply technocratic and elitist despite their populist rhetoric. And most of the activists continue to see the Internet as a utopian ideal—despite the fact that many progressives are beginning to worry that the Web is really just a very efficient way for companies to move white-collar U.S. jobs overseas.

Prof. Goldsmith says that most law professors are becoming increasingly wary of the legal claims being made for cyberspace. But what about his students? Well, he concedes, they're another matter. Many of them, with the passion of youth, are still enthralled with the whole idea of a separate universe, one they can call their own.

> Do you think that the debate about cyberspace is really a debate between the young and the old?

Summary

Although the writers of the two articles agree that the Internet is an important new technology, and that it requires a degree of regulation, they disagree about whether that regulation would require the development of a new area of international law.

Law professor David Post, the author of the first article, argues that the Net challenges existing notions of national sovereignty and restructures the hierarchies around which we organize society. In particular, questions regarding geographical location lose their meaning since cyberspace makes them irrelevant. Moreover, traditional relations between elements of society are completely transformed in a networked, not hierarchical, world. Therefore the Net demands that we take another look at political sovereignty. The question for Post is not only what laws apply but also who will make these laws—this is the subject, he says, of an ongoing global debate.

Journalist Lee Gomes, author of the second article, asks whether there really is a cyberspace full of "cybercitizens" who are accountable to their own "cyberlaws." He claims that although advocates of cyberspace might be more visible at conferences, law journals are full of "cyberskeptics" who maintain that cyberspace is no different than "phone space." Online traffic should therefore be dealt with by the same laws as the rest of society. To support the case, he quotes a lawyer as arguing that "the steam engine probably transformed American law, but the law of the steam engine never existed." Gomes finishes by citing law professors who see "cyberactivists" as youthful idealists, technophiles, and elitists.

FURTHER INFORMATION:

Books:

Lessing, Lawrence, *Code and Other Laws of Cyberspace*. New York: Basic Books, 1999.

Spinello, Richard A., *Cyberethics: Morality and Law in Cyberspace* (2nd edition). Boston, MA: Jones and Bartlett Publishers, 2003.

Useful websites:

http://www.economist.com/printedition/displayStory.cfm?Story_ID=471742
Article about government regulation of the Internet from *The Economist* magazine.

http://mockingbird.creighton.edu/srp/govern.htm
"How to Govern Cyberspace: Frontier Justice or Legal Precedent?" by Carl S. Kaplan.

http://www.temple.edu/lawschool/dpost/writings.html
Essays on the law of cyberspace by David Post.

The following debates in the Pro/Con series may also be of interest:

In this volume:
 Part 2: Trade and the environment, pages 84–85

In Media:
 Part 3: The new media

In *Commerce and Trade*:
 Topic 12 Does the Internet make it difficult to enforce copyright law?

SHOULD CYBERSPACE BE TREATED AS INTERNATIONAL SPACE?

YES: Cyberspace does away with national frontiers and thus makes irrelevant all laws based on old-fashioned ideas of national sovereignty

YES: Companies and institutions will have to share information that may currently be protected by national data-protection or privacy laws, thus helping agencies police cyberspace

LAWS
Is it unfeasible to apply existing laws to cyberspace?

POLICING CYBERSPACE
Would making it an international space make it easier to police?

NO: Like the telephone system, for example, cyberspace is really a network of physical machines and connections, and can thus be subject to national and international laws

NO: Countries could still invoke national laws if they felt that international laws or law-enforcement agencies were infringing on national-sovereignty or security issues

SHOULD CYBERSPACE BE TREATED AS INTERNATIONAL SPACE?
KEY POINTS

YES: The Internet allows—and even facilitates, some critics believe—the abuse of copyright. International cyberlaws would help prevent this from happening.

YES: Cyberspace has helped created a "global village" and a democratic space in which people have the right to express themselves freely. Cyberspace laws will just enshrine this right.

COPYRIGHT
Are international cyberlaws necessary to protect copyright holders?

FREE SPEECH
Will cyberspace laws help enforce free speech?

NO: There are always ways to circumvent copyright restrictions; introducing cyberlaws will not prevent abuses from happening

NO: Many countries do not have a guaranteed right to free speech. They will just refuse to ratify any such agreements or, like China, may set up their own national Internet.

Topic 9
DOES THE PROGRAM FOR ERADICATING ILLICIT CROPS VIOLATE HUMAN RIGHTS?

YES
"WOLA DELEGATION IN PUTUMAYO TOLD: 'STOP THE FUMIGATION!'"
COLOMBIA UPDATE, WINTER 2000/SPRING 2001
JOE ELDRIDGE

NO
FROM "AERIAL ERADICATION OF ILLICIT CROPS: FREQUENTLY ASKED QUESTIONS"
FACT SHEET, MARCH 24, 2003
BUREAU FOR INTERNATIONAL NARCOTICS AND LAW ENFORCEMENT AFFAIRS

INTRODUCTION

Many of the world's most powerful narcotics come from plants, including heroin from the opium poppy and cocaine from the coca plant. Illegal growing of the plant sources of banned drugs is, however, most often concentrated in poor countries with corrupt or weak law-enforcement capacity and ineffectual governments.

Opium poppies and coca have long been grown as commercial crops by low-income rural farming communities—the former predominantly in Southeast Asia, Afghanistan, and parts of Latin America, the latter in Colombia, Bolivia, and Peru. While some people may grow such plants for their own use, the majority of farmers cultivate them because they are high-yielding cash crops that earn more revenue for the growers than other legal crops. A Colombian farmer, some estimates suggest, can earn up to $800 for the harvested coca leaf required to produce a kilogram of coca paste,

which is refined in illegal laboratories into pure cocaine hydrochloride powder. Colombia produces more than 80 percent of the world's cocaine, much of which ends up in the United States: In 2001 the U.S. authorities confiscated 111 metric tons of cocaine, worth around one billion dollars on the illegal market.

Governments around the world have made a concerted effort to eliminate the drug trade—to varying degrees of success. Strategies include encouraging farmers to grow licit crops and controversial measures such as controlled crop spraying to prevent illicit plants from growing. Crop spraying has been heavily criticized by rights protection groups; they claim that governments and law-enforcement agencies have committed human rights abuses while trying to eliminate the drug trade.

As part of the effort to control drugs, President Bill Clinton's administration

(1993–2001) launched Plan Colombia, which under his successor George W. Bush (2001–) was broadened into the Andean Regional Initiative. The plan provides U.S. finance and military hardware to Colombia, among other areas in the region, to tackle drug production at source. As part of the strategy, aircraft provided by the United States spray illegal coca fields with the herbicide glyphosate, one of the most widely used agricultural chemicals in the world. It is meant to kill plants without damaging the soil.

"We have no birds or butterflies."

—RESIDENT OF

PUTAMAYO, COLOMBIA

Supporters claim that only illegal drugs are damaged since the Colombian National Police helps to carefully identify targets for spraying. Satellite technology also warns pilots if they deviate by more than three feet from the proscribed line of spraying, and this helps minimize environmental damage. U.S.-backed initiatives also support eradication with more positive programs, such as using financial inducements to persuade farmers to promote the substitution of coca with other crops.

The spraying operations have also generated negative comments in both the United States and Colombia. The major criticism of the spraying program is that it hurts poor farming communities while actually doing little to stop the drug trade. Critics believe that many low-income farmers have had legitimate crops, such as plantain and cassava, destroyed during the aerial operations since the spraying is not as precise as its advocates claim. The glyphosate also not only kills food crops indiscriminately but also seeps into the soil, contaminating water sources and killing fish. Some observers believe that destroying the farmer's only source of income without replacing it breaches their basic right to earn a living, although critics have countered that this only occurs in cases in which farmers have planted their crops alongside or among illicit coca fields. Some activists have also claimed that people have become ill—or even in extreme cases died—after exposure to aerial spraying. Symptoms are alleged to vary from shortness of breath and skin irritations to renal failure and death, although experts state that glyphosate has been tested and does not cause such reactions.

Some people also believe that farmers raise these crops because there is no other option. Officials, however, say that farmers are offered economic assistance as part of the program to eradicate illicit drugs and as an incentive to cultivate legal crops. They acknowledge that there have been delays in providing this assistance but claim that this does not undermine the legitimacy of the entire program. Another reason why farmers continue to grow drug crops, critics claim, is that they are forced to do so by local drug cartels or by the antigovernment left-wing guerillas of the Revolutionary Armed Forces of Colombia (FARC), who raise funds from taxing drug operations in their territories. Others claim that paramilitaries and the regular army are also complicit in the drug trade.

The following articles examine the topic further.

WOLA DELEGATION IN PUTUMAYO TOLD: "STOP THE FUMIGATION!"
Joe Eldridge

Joe Eldridge is chaplain at the Kay Spiritual Life Center at American University, Washington, D.C. He visited Colombia in 2000 with a delegation from the Washington Office on Latin America (WOLA), which monitors human rights throughout the region.

YES

Fifteen mayors from Putumayo cannot have it wrong, especially when their views are echoed by other local officials, health care workers, human rights defenders and small farmers. During a recent visit to the region organized by WOLA (which included two members of Congress), dozens of local government officials, human rights and health workers, small farmers and community organizers gathered in Puerto Asís to vehemently deliver a message which they hoped would reach Washington: Stop the campaign of aerial fumigation!

The U.S. strike

Without warning on December 19 of last year the US launched a massive aerial strike on coca cultivation. Thousands of hectares of coca have been destroyed, but according to many small growers collateral damage to food crops has been extensive. Indiscriminate fumigation has defoliated forests, killed cassava and plantain crops and threatened to pollute watersheds. The spraying also targeted farms of many who had signed an agreement with the government for manual eradication. According to procedures established by the Pastrana government, coca farmers participating in the government plan would be spared bombardment with toxic chemicals and receive technical and economic assistance. These social contracts have been ignored in the haste of the eradication efforts....

Andres Pastrana was president of Colombia from 1998 until 2002.

The delegation heard moving testimonies about the growing costs of the aerial fumigation. In the municipality of San Miguel, the town had agreed to voluntary destruction of the coca plants, yet endured a month of defoliants dumped on their forests, rivers, farms and homes. The border with Ecuador, inhabited by indigenous tribes, and which had been declared off limits by the government, has had more than 90% of its land sprayed. The massive use of defoliants has disrupted thousands of poor families, destroyed farms and left a residue of potentially serious health consequences.

Do you think that indigenous peoples are likely to receive as much protection from governments as other members of society?

A farmer harvests coca leaves. Between 1995 and 2001 the area of Colombia used to grow coca nearly quadrupled, to around 420,000 acres. Plan Colombia aims to reverse that trend.

Both the Revolutionary Armed Forces of Colombia (Farc) and the paramilitary forces, now competing for control of the region, have at least theoretically agreed with the universal call for manual eradication. However the 24th Army Brigade, garrisoned in Putumayo, has been blocking manual eradication. The brigade also stands accused of human rights violations which has led to a suspension of cooperation with the United States. (The Leahy amendment to the Appropriations bill forbids U.S. military aid to units accused of human rights violations.) An investigation is under way and a renewal of Pentagon support is pending.

Community leaders, aware of the perils inherent in the cocaine industry, seemed genuinely interested in finding an economically viable alternative to coca. According to the governor of Putumayo, Ivan Gerardo Guerrero, the peasant farmers are fearful of both the paramilitaries and the Farc guerrillas. According to Guerrero, if peasants denounce the paramilitaries they will wind up dead—same with the Farc. The growers are caught in the middle, fearful of becoming the latest statistic in the escalating conflict between "paras" and guerrillas or between the military and the guerrillas.

All the voices from Putumayo were unanimous about Washington's reliance on force. Huey and Blackhawk helicopters are not the answer. The citizens of Putumayo believe that reliance on the Colombian military as a strategic ally in the fight against drugs will yield only more violence and death.

Regrettably not only is the lion's share of US aid directed toward the military and the police, but that is the only aid in yet in evidence in Putumayo—or elsewhere. The economic assistance is lagging far behind—to date not one farmer reported having seen any economic or development aid.

A single-resource community

Virtually everyone in Putumayo is sustained by coca. At present the growers have no incentives to move from the illicit to the licit economy. Without an accelerated and comprehensive approach to crop substitution and financial help, peasant farmers will have no choice but to move to other areas to resume cultivation of coca. While USAID is considering alternatives such as rubber, extensive cattle grazing, fish, medicinal plants, much more consultation and research will be required to determine both feasibility and sustainability.

Meanwhile the violence continues to escalate. Over the last several months the paramilitary armies have seized control of

Should the United States work with foreign troops with poor human rights records? If not, what other options might there be for finding local allies in the war against drugs?

Are military force and the deaths of Colombians a price worth paying to stop the spread of drugs in the United States?

USAID, the U.S. Agency for International Development, was established in 1961 to encourage economic growth, physical health, and democratic government around the world. Visit www.usaid.gov for more details.

many of the productive areas of coca cultivation, by challenging the Farc. Like the Farc, the paramilitaries tax the cultivation, the processing and the marketing of coca products. On the other hand, sometimes they find it more efficient and profitable to vertically integrate, simply seizing control of all levels of production and trafficking. When asked about assigning blame for human rights violations, human rights workers (both governmental and nongovernmental) were quick to assert that the paramilitaries had become the most notorious offenders.

As more people are displaced from their farms and deprived of their livelihoods, they provide a recruiting bonanza for both the paramilitaries and the Farc. While many are conscripted against their will, hunger drives others into the ranks of the armed groups.

The heart and soul of Plan Colombia is the coca eradication effort in Putumayo. If the last several months are indicative, it is off to a rocky start.

Unless there is a major policy adjustment, it is doomed to failure. The failure will not only be measured by grams of cocaine on U.S. streets. It will be measured by the number of innocent lives claimed in Colombia.

If the result of Plan Colombia is to create more paramilitaries, might it weaken the ability of the Colombian government to deal with the drug problem? Or does the role of the United States mean that the Colombian government is not important in the process?

The author concludes with a pair of striking sentences that crystallize the thrust of his argument.

AERIAL ERADICATION OF ILLICIT CROPS: FREQUENTLY ASKED QUESTIONS
Bureau for International Narcotics and Law Enforcement Affairs

This fact sheet was published by the Bureau for International Narcotics and Law Enforcement Affairs in March 2003. The bureau is part of the State Department. Visit http://www.state.gov/g/inl/ to find out more.

NO

Q: What is the aerial eradication program?
A: The aerial eradication program in Colombia is a program of the Antinarcotics Directorate of the Colombian National Police (DIRAN-CNP), supported by the Narcotics Affairs Section (NAS) of the U.S. Embassy in Bogota. This program uses aircraft to spray a glyphosate-based herbicide mixture on fields of coca and opium poppy, which are illegal in Colombia and are the vital ingredients of the cocaine and heroin trades.

Q: How are spray targets selected?
A: The Government of Colombia (GOC) chooses the areas to be sprayed through an interagency process. The DIRAN reviews information from a variety of sources and flies over growing regions on a regular basis to search for new coca and opium poppy growth and to generate estimates of the illicit crops. These flights target the areas identified by the Colombian National Police in their estimates of illicit crops. An aircraft-mounted global positioning computer system identifies the precise geographical coordinates where those crops are being grown. A computer program then sets up precise flight lines (the width of a spray swath) within that area....

Most coca fields are planted in areas of cleared woodland. Do you think that aerial identification is likely to be accurate enough in such circumstances?

Q: What chemicals are being used in Colombia for the eradication of illicit crops?
A: The only herbicide used for aerial eradication is a formulation of glyphosate, the most widely used agricultural chemical in the world. It is commercially available under many different brands in Colombia and worldwide....

Q: Has glyphosate been tested for environmental safety?
A: Yes. Glyphosate has been extensively tested and evaluated in Colombia, in the United States, and in other countries around the globe. Worldwide, it is among the most widely

used herbicides by volume and is currently employed in over 100 countries for a variety of agricultural purposes....

Q: Is glyphosate harmful to human beings?
A: There are no risks of concern for glyphosate by itself, from dermal or inhalation routes of exposure, since toxicity is very low. Scientific studies have demonstrated that glyphosate is non-carcinogenic and has no effects on reproductive ability or developmental capacity ...

However, due to the presence and quantity of an inert (pesticide inactive) ingredient in the formulated glyphosate product concentrate, which was used through most of 2002, there is concern for acute eye irritation. Program workers who handled (mix and load) this product concentrate before it was diluted to make the spray solution would have had the greatest potential for exposure and risk of eye irritation. At the end of 2002, use of this product was discontinued and the program began using a different glyphosate product formulation....

Does the fact that a pesticide is widely used mean that it must be safe? In 1972 the pesticide DDT was banned after over 30 years of widespread use; government tests showed that it was a health risk.

Effects of glyphosate

Q: Does glyphosate destroy the soil and prevent plant growth?
A: Glyphosate enters a plant through contact with its leaves and only kills plants that are above ground at the time of spraying. In the soil, glyphosate is quickly broken down by microorganisms into naturally occurring compounds such as carbon dioxide. Thus the rejuvenation of plant growth ... can begin immediately after spraying....

Opponents of spraying argue that glyphosate does damage the soil. Is there any way in which both arguments can be right?

Q: Don't legal crops and other plant life get sprayed, too?
A: Legal crops are not deliberately sprayed unless they are interspersed with illegal crops. Pilots release the spray only after they have visually identified coca in the flight line.... Food crops do not get sprayed unless they are intermingled with coca....

Does the use of the word "deliberately" here mean that this assertion does not include accidental spraying?

Q: Does glyphosate contaminate the water...?
A: No. Glyphosate bonds tightly to the soil particles and thus is unlikely to leach into groundwater or contaminate drinking water. Colombia's aerial eradication operations avoid spraying bodies of water directly....

Q: If glyphosate is so benign, why are there complaints...?
A: Many of these reports are based on unverified accounts by growers whose illicit crops have been sprayed. Because

Do you think the U.S. government gives "objective" information about the program? Is it in its best interests to give out negative information concerning the program?

their illegal livelihoods have been affected by the spraying, these persons do not offer objective information about the program. Illegal armed groups are the source of other complaints, since they derive much of their incomes from illicit crops and have a significant interest in fomenting opposition to the spray program.... Despite numerous investigations, not a single claim of harm to human health as a result of the spray program has ever been substantiated. These health problems are more likely to be caused by bacteria, parasites, and infections endemic in the remote rural areas where illicit cultivation takes place. Many are also likely caused by exposure to the other pesticides and processing chemicals used by growers of illicit crops or by diseases endemic to the regions.

Q: How are complaints about glyphosate investigated?
A: The Government of Colombia has implemented procedures for a more rapid, efficient process for investigating citizens' complaints that legal crops were sprayed in error. Under the new process, complaints will first be examined to determine whether computer flight records indicate that spraying indeed took place in the vicinity on the specified date. This initial check eliminates many of the claims and the rest are investigated in the field.... Although the spray pilots are experienced and well trained, occasional technical and human errors are unavoidable, so this compensation process is needed to provide a fair, rapid means by which Colombian citizens can seek compensation in these instances.

Forests cover about 49 percent of Colombia and are home to about 10 percent of global plant and animal species, making it the second most biodiverse country in the world. About 1.5 to 2.2 million acres of forest are destroyed each year. At such a rate the forests will be gone in around 40 years.

Q: Is spraying contributing to the deforestation of Colombia?
A: Damage from deforestation is wrought by drug cultivators who must cut down up to four hectares of forest for each hectare of coca planted, two-and-a-half hectares of forest for each hectare of opium poppy. Coca and poppy growers then poison the surrounding streams and soil with the chemicals used in coca cultivation and narcotics processing. Deforestation is increasing at an alarming rate. It threatens Colombia's rich biodiversity and sustainable agriculture and is increasing the potential for natural disasters such as landslides and floods....

Q: Why doesn't the United States Government fund alternative development programs in Colombia...?
A: The U.S. Government is the largest donor to alternative development programs in Colombia, including crop

substitution where appropriate, infrastructure construction, environmentally responsible agro-forestry initiatives. Alternative development is an essential part of the solution to the world's illegal drug problem and the U.S. is working closely with Colombia's national plan for alternative development (PNDA). Because democracy and human rights protection are necessary for peace and economic development in Colombia, USAID assistance also includes, among other things, funding for houses of justice (casas de justicia) and assistance to Internally Displaced Persons (IDPs), people forced to leave their homes for other areas of Colombia because of armed conflict. In all, USAID assistance to Colombia in FY02 came to $105 million.

Critics accuse the Colombian military, which is an ally of the United States, of violating human rights. In such circumstances does this make U.S. funding for other human rights initiatives hypocritical?

Q: Doesn't the spray program hurt the small farmer who has no other way of earning a living?
A: Most coca cultivation in Colombia takes place on a large-scale basis, but smaller fields are often financed by narcotraffickers and are equally illegal. Many Colombians presently suffer from severe economic hardship. This unfortunate fact should not be used by anybody as an excuse to pursue a livelihood that is unlawful, environmentally destructive, and causes further harm to the nation of Colombia. Colombian coca growers are not simply innocent farmers who produce an agricultural product that somebody far away turns into a deadly drug; they are in fact actively engaged in drug production at field-side processing laboratories.

Furthermore, the illegal drug trade contributes to economic destabilization in Colombia by supporting the terrorist groups that cause great harm to the country and development in rural zones in particular.

Does the problem of drugs in the United States give the U.S. government the right to decide what is good or bad for other nations? Is this an infringement of other nations' national sovereignty? Go to Volume 8, U.S. Foreign Policy, Topic 12 Does the War on Drugs give the United States the right to intervene in other countries' affairs?

Summary

Joe Eldridge, who visited Colombia as part of a human rights monitoring survey, reports Colombian complaints about U.S.-sponsored fumigation, or aerial spraying. Although the spraying is intended to eradicate illicit drug plantations, he says that it is being implemented in an indiscriminate way. Contrary to procedures established by the Colombian government, aircraft have sprayed both the fields of coca-growers who had joined a popular government program for manual destruction of illicit crops and areas inhabited by indigenous tribes. He argues that massive use of defoliants is jeopardizing the livelihoods of rural communities and driving more Colombians to support left- and right-wing paramilitary groups that both encourage the drugs trade and create a climate of political violence.

The factsheet issued by the Bureau for International Narcotics and Law Enforcement Affairs maintains that defoliation is carefully targeted to avoid legal crops unless they are grown among illicit crops. It argues that the defoliant used, glyphosate, is widely used around the world. It has been tested and proven to be safe for the environment—it does not harm soil or water supplies—and for people. The factsheet questions the reliability of complaints about spraying, arguing that they are made by people involved in the drug trade. It says that poverty is no excuse for turning to illegal activity.

FURTHER INFORMATION:

Books:

Rabasa, A., and P. Chalk, *Colombian Labyrinth: The Synergy of Drugs and Insurgency and Its Implications for Regional Stability*. Santa Monica, CA: RAND, 2001.

Useful websites:

http://antiwar.com/lobe/?articleid=2055
Article arguing that crop eradication is harmful to Colombia.
http://news.bbc.co.uk/1/hi/world/americas/891289.stm
Looks at Plan Colombia to tackle drugs, including spraying of crops.
http://www.stanford.edu/class/e297c/war_peace/u_s_policy_in_central_and_south_america/szuniga.html
An analysis of the working and effectiveness of Plan Colombia.
http://usinfo.state.gov/regional/ar/colombia/
Looks at U.S.–Colombian relations. Focuses on drugs, Plan Colombia, and money laundering, among other things.

The following debates in the Pro/Con series may also be of interest:

In this volume:
Topic 15 Is the United States the ultimate defender of international human rights?

In *U.S. Foreign Policy*:
Topic 10 Has the United States exploited Latin America?

Topic 12 Does the War on Drugs give the United States the right to intervene in other countries' affairs?

DOES THE PROGRAM FOR ERADICATING ILLICIT CROPS VIOLATE HUMAN RIGHTS?

YES: Many farmers have no choice but to grow their crops near coca fields. Spraying has damaged food crops such as plantain and yucca.

YES: There are numerous reports of, for example, glyphosate contaminating water supplies and killing fish in rivers

LIVELIHOOD
Are legitimate farms being harmed?

ENVIRONMENT
Is this program harming the environment?

NO: Spraying is carefully targeted to affect only crops identified by the Colombian police and visually confirmed by the pilots of the airplanes

NO: Glyphosate has been heavily tested and is widely used around the world. It kills only plants above the ground and does not harm the soil or groundwater.

DOES THE PROGRAM FOR ERADICATING ILLICIT CROPS VIOLATE HUMAN RIGHTS?

KEY POINTS

YES: The dominance of drug traffickers and their paramilitary allies means that farmers could not break out of coca-growing even if they wanted to. No other crop is so profitable.

YES: It is unfair to penalize people who are simply exercising their right to make a living in the best way possible without giving them another viable way of earning income

ALTERNATIVE
Do Colombians grow coca because they have no alternative?

BALANCE
Are poor farmers being treated unfairly in the War on Drugs?

NO: Programs such as those promoted and funded by USAID offer farmers incentives to adopt alternatives such as rubber production

NO: Poverty is no excuse for breaking the law. Coca cultivation is illegal in Colombia, and farmers are receiving economic assistance in order to grow other crops.

IMPROVING YOUR MEMORY

"Memory, of all the powers of the mind,
is the most delicate and frail."

—BEN JONSON, ENGLISH DRAMATIST (1572–1637)

The ability to remember information on a wide range of subjects in different situations is important in all areas of life. School and college students need to memorize vital facts, dates, and other information— whether for an exam, a class assignment, or during a debate—and the capacity to recall details accurately is practically a requirement for success in many careers. But what if you have difficulty remembering facts? Are there ways to improve your memory?

Good memory, great brain?

In 2002 the British Institute of Neurology published a study on memory and brainpower. It stated that good memory did not equate to superior brainpower and concluded that people with good memories had trained certain parts of their brain to store and retrieve information.

Memory improvement is a multimillion-dollar business. Certain "smart" drugs and nutritional supplements are said to enhance memory, and there is no shortage of audiovisual material and websites dedicated to techniques for improving memory. There are, however, a few fundamental factors that may influence how much information you are able to retain and recall on any one day. Concentration is central to how much you are able to listen to, learn, or remember at any one time (see Volume 24, *Work and the Workplace, Improving your concentration*, pages 150–151), and factors such as stress, lack of sleep, or a bad diet may negatively affect your ability to recall information (see Volume 21, *U.S. Judiciary, Stress management*, pages 124–125).

Unless you have a photographic memory, it is simply impossible to memorize everything you are taught. There are numerous different techniques you can use to help improve your memory, however, some of which are listed below

1. Mnemonics

Mnemonics are a widely practiced technique for improving memory. They involve the use of rhymes, limericks, and mental associations such as images or letters to remember certain facts. There are three basic principles underlying the use of mnemonics—association, imagination, and location. You link, or associate, what you need to remember with something else to help you remember it—for example, by merging images or by linking them to a certain color, smell, or letter. You use your imagination to create the associations that will develop the best mnemonic for you. Finally, location gives you a context into which you can place the information and a way of separating one mnemonic from another. The following methods are all examples of mnemonics.

- Acronyms: These are formed by grouping the first letter of a series of words together to form a new, often much shorter word. The word "laser," for example, stands for "Light Amplification by Stimulated Emission of Radiation." Many acronyms are used in everyday language.
- Sentences and acrostics: Like acronyms the first letter of each word is used to aid memory, but instead of making a new word, the letters are used to form a sentence or a string of words that use familiar images or associations to prompt memory recall. For example, the colors of the spectrum are red, orange, yellow, green, blue, indigo, and violet. In the sentence "Richard Of York Gained Battles In Vain" the initial letters of the sentence represent each color in order as it appears in the spectrum.
- Rhymes and songs: The reason why people often remember pop songs is because the use of rhythm, repetition, and melody can help improve memory. We are taught from a very young age to use music, rhyme, and repetition to memorize numbers, colors, and the alphabet. This is a simple, fun, and very effective way to remember things.
- Method of loci (Latin for "places"): This technique uses visual memory, association, and organization skills to prompt memory. You visualize a familiar location, such as a house or a street, and place the objects or ideas that you need to remember in landmark positions in this space. You can then mentally walk around the space, visualizing—and so remembering—the objects or ideas you have put there.

2. Chunking

Usually used to recall numbers, chunking is based on the idea that the brain can in the short term easily remember digits in groups of five to nine. Phone numbers are easy to memorize since there are usually fewer than nine digits, but remembering groups of more than nine figures becomes more difficult. To make large amounts of figures easier to remember, break them up into chunks of fewer than nine digits. You can use a similar method for factual information—try breaking the text or lesson down into key points to help ensure you recall only the essential facts.

3. Repetition and recitation

Practice makes perfect, and repetition is a very good way of improving memory. Reciting material aloud over and over again—such as multiplication tables—will help you retain the information in your long-term memory.

Application

While these techniques may help you improve your memory, it is very important to recognize that memorizing and recalling something are not the same as understanding it. Using memory techniques such as mnemonics may prompt you into recalling certain facts or ideas, but they will not necessarily be of much help if you do not comprehend the material or know how to apply it.

PART 3
CRIME

For many people terrorist action taken in the United States in September 11, 2001, in Bali in 2002, and in Spain and Russia in 2004, among others, have highlighted the importance of international law in fighting both terrorism and crime.

An easy task?

On the face of things crime should be one of the more straightforward aspects of international law. Nations have many differences about politics, economic organization, trade, and environmental policies that sometimes prevent them from agreeing on laws that apply to such areas. It would seem likely, however, that virtually all nations would agree on what constitutes a crime in terms of theft, for example, or violent crimes against the person. Criminals have, however, long taken advantage of differences or loopholes in legal codes between different nations. Movies such as *The Thomas Crown Affair* (1968, 1999) have even capitalized on this, creating the villain-as-romantic hero role, in which the protagonist commits a crime in one country but is then able to flee to another nation where he or she cannot be prosecuted.

The differences between countries in terms of criminal law usually have less to do with definitions of what does or does not constitute a crime and more to do with jurisdiction. There are many complex relations and agreements governing whether the justice system in different countries can be used to prosecute illegal acts committed in other states even if they are accepted crimes in both places. There are also various questions that affect the practical application of the law. Police forces, for example, are not usually allowed to operate in other nations' sovereign territory. Many countries also prefer to try their own citizens wherever possible, rather than have them be subject to other legal codes, even an internationally applied one.

Reciprocal agreements

Unlike some parts of international law, crime and the treatment of criminals are usually not subject to general agreements or conventions that apply equally to all nations. Each state has the ability to define its own crimes and to specify the appropriate punishment.

While many U.S. states retain the death penalty for murder, western Europe does not. Such variations in law between America and other countries can hinder international cooperation to fight crime, which usually takes the form of reciprocal agreements between countries dealing with specific crimes.

At the same time, however, felonies are becoming increasingly international in scope. Criminals use legal loopholes, the Internet, and differences in banking procedures to avoid detection and to hide their often ill-gotten gains.

Extradition, tax, and immunity

Extradition is the process by which one country can request another to detain an individual suspected of a crime and surrender him or her to the requesting country for trial. It has long been used to prevent wanted criminals from finding sanctuary in countries different from those in which they committed their crime. There is no common law of extradition, however. Governments strike specific treaties with other countries—the United States has treaties in place with more than 100 countries—to specify what offenses are extraditable. Topic 10 asks whether

believe that this is an accounting trick that amounts to deception, others argue that tax havens are important in encouraging international trade.

Tax havens and the banking secrecy that tends to go with them are also alleged to make it easier for criminals to launder money. Criminals exploit international banking procedures to move around the proceeds of crime from account to account until the money's provenance cannot be traced. They can then spend it without fear of detection. Critics believe that money laundering is too easy, and various international initiatives are addressing

---

"It is crucial that law-enforcement authorities around the world assist each other by sharing information and evidence. The challenge comes without compromising either national sovereignty or the privacy rights of law-abiding citizens."
—DANIEL J. MITCHELL, THE HERITAGE FOUNDATION (2001)

---

extradition breaches a suspect's human rights, for example, by sending him or her for trial in countries with harsher punishments or less rigorous legal systems than the country from which they are being extradited.

Another area of considerable interest is that of tax havens—countries with low rates of tax or no tax at all— where registered residents or businesses avoid paying tax on their income or profits. Americans keep around $5 trillion in tax havens such as Bermuda or the Cayman Islands. They therefore avoid paying taxes on this money to the Internal Revenue Service (IRS), thus decreasing federal revenues in the United States. While some people

the problem. However, the secrecy traditionally involved in banking and criminals' sophisticated accounting procedures make preventing international money laundering a difficult problem. Topics 11 and 12 look at tax havens and money laundering respectively.

The last debate in this section examines another contentious issue often raised when discussing international crime—whether diplomatic immunity should be retained. It is traditionally extended to official representatives of other governments, who cannot be punished for anything but very serious crimes. This has caused heated debate.

Topic 10

DO EXTRADITION TREATIES VIOLATE HUMAN RIGHTS?

YES

"ACLU LETTER TO THE SENATE FOREIGN RELATIONS COMMITTEE URGING OPPOSITION TO RATIFICATION OF THE REVISED UNITED STATES–UNITED KINGDOM EXTRADITION TREATY SIGNED BY ATTORNEY GENERAL JOHN ASHCROFT AND HOME SECRETARY DAVID BLUNKETT"
ACLU LETTER, DECEMBER 18, 2003
AMERICAN CIVIL LIBERTIES UNION

NO

"KILLING OF INNOCENT CIVILIAN NOT 'POLITICAL' CRIME"
METROPOLITAN NEWS-ENTERPRISE, MARCH 11, 2004
KENNETH OFGANG

INTRODUCTION

Extradition is the surrender of wanted criminals by one nation to another country where they are accused of a criminal offense. There is no general international law of extradition. Most extradition treaties are reciprocal agreements between two countries to deport wanted persons to each other on request, provided that stipulated criteria are met, which are often laid down in international law.

The United States has extradition treaties with more than 100 countries; the specific terms of each treaty may vary in what offenses are extraditable. Extradition can only be considered in the case of crimes specifically mentioned in each respective treaty. Although some nations, including Germany, France, and the Netherlands, refuse to extradite their own citizens, many others, including the United States, do not impose such limitations.

All treaties include provisions designed to protect the right of citizens to a fair trial. That right is guaranteed under the Sixth Amendment to the U.S. Constitution, which begins: "In all criminal prosecutions, the accused shall enjoy the right to a speedy and public trial, by an impartial jury of the State and district wherein the crime shall have been committed...." Within the United States arrangements also allow for the extradition of suspects from one state to another.

The principles of extradition treaties are often based on what is known as "double criminality." An extraditable act must be illegal in both countries. In 1949, for example, the United Kingdom turned down a U.S. request to extradite a suspect because the act of which he was accused—perjury by lying on an application to leave the country—did not qualify as perjury under UK law.

In most countries extradition requests are examined by a court to establish that there are reasonable grounds for a trial. This ensures that a court case cannot be based on evidence that would not justify a trial in the United States, for example. Many countries also refuse to extradite fugitives if they believe that they would face harsher punishments abroad. When the United States concluded an extradition treaty with the European Union (EU) in 2003, for example, EU countries insisted on the right to refuse extradition if a suspect faced the death penalty. No EU countries have the death penalty. Observers state that another safeguard is the principle of speciality: A person can only be tried on the specific charge for which he or she has been extradited, not for a different crime.

"The more corrupt the state, the more numerous the laws."

—TACITUS (ABOUT A.D. 55–120), ROMAN HISTORIAN

Some experts argue that people are protected against unfair treatment through the long-standing exclusion of political offenses from extradition treaties. Such offenses are defined as those that take place to further a political movement or during a move to take control of the government of a state; they usually do not include offenses that are also felonies, such as murder or terrorism. People cannot be extradited to face charges of disagreeing with a government, for example. The United States can grant such dissidents asylum.

Some commentators believe that the terrorist action taken by Al Qaeda against the United States on September 11, 2001, and the subsequent War on Terrorism have, however, brought into question whether existing extradition treaties go far enough. Many politicians, particularly in the United States, have advocated easier extradition procedures in order to help them bring terrorists to trial. Critics claim that most extradition treaties are tried and tested—the first was introduced by Belgium in 1833— and have proved sufficient until now. Why, they ask, should procedures be revised? Opponents have fought any procedural changes that might undermine or challenge the basic human rights of citizens. There was, for example, much opposition to the original Anglo-American treaty, which proposed that the United States extradite anyone suspected of being "anti-British" or opposed to British conduct in Northern Ireland, on the grounds that it threatened the right to free speech.

The United States has also come under heavy criticism from even its allies for its detention without charge or trial of around 600 prisoners captured during the conflict in Afghanistan in 2002. This may have the effect of making other countries more reluctant to allow the extradition of terrorist suspects to the United States if they believe that they would also be denied the right to a trial. Some may also resist sending suspects for trial by military tribunals, which have the power to pass the death sentence.

The following articles discuss this subject further.

ACLU LETTER TO THE SENATE FOREIGN RELATIONS COMMITTEE …
American Civil Liberties Union

This letter was sent to Senators Richard G. Lugar and Joseph R. Biden, respectively chairman and ranking member on the Senate Foreign Relations Committee, in December 2003.

The separation of powers is a basic principle of the Constitution. Do you think that the government is in a better position than the judiciary to judge what is in the nation's best interest?

Supporters of the new arrangements argue that they are necessary to guarantee security from terrorists. Is neutrality or security more important?

The ACLU (American Civil Liberties Union) was founded in 1920. It exists to protect and defend the rights of citizens.

YES

Dear Senators Lugar and Biden,

On behalf of the American Civil Liberties Union and its more than 400,000 members, we urge you to oppose ratification of the new extradition treaty between the United States and the United Kingdom that was signed by Attorney General John Ashcroft and Home Secretary David Blunkett on March 31, 2003.

The treaty contains alarming court-stripping provisions, which threaten the fundamental due process rights of Americans and others accused of crimes by the British government. Most troubling, article 4(3) eliminates the American judiciary's role in determining whether an extradition request should be denied on the basis of the political offense exception. Under the treaty, the Executive Branch, i.e., the Department of Justice, is given sole discretion to determine whether this exception applies.

The political offense exception to extradition has a centuries-old pedigree that protects Americans and others from political, religious or other impermissible persecution. The exception ensures that the United States does not unwittingly become the agent of punishment for a government's political opponents and dissidents. The exception also ensures the interests of the United States by safeguarding its neutrality in the political affairs of other countries. The exception is a general bar on extradition of alleged offenders who are sought for protected political activity, regardless of their ideology.

Dealing with terrorism

The ACLU agrees that terrorists and others who use violence against innocent civilians should find no haven in the United States. However, eliminating judicial review of the political offense exception is not necessary to ensure the extradition of suspected terrorists. American and international law provide that those who commit war crimes, crimes against humanity or who aid or commit terrorist acts against innocent civilians for political or ideological ends do not enjoy the benefits of the political offense exception.

Senator Richard G. Lugar is the chairman of the U.S. Senate Foreign Relations Committee. Civil rights activists contacted Lugar to protest about the proposed extradition treaty between the United States and the United Kingdom. They claimed that it infringed on certain human rights.

Many Irish Americans sympathize with the wish of Catholics in Northern Ireland, a Protestant-majority part of the United Kingdom, for union with neighboring Ireland. From the 1960s to the 1990s both Catholic and Protestant paramilitary groups used terrorism to promote their cause, including shootings and bombings, among other things, in Northern Ireland and the rest of Britain.

Are there any differences between Britain's "War on Terror" in Northern Ireland and that launched by President George W. Bush in September 2001? Go to www.bbc.co.uk and www.cnn.com respectively to look up relevant articles. Should the United States expect British help if it makes it difficult to extradite people the British want to put on trial?

The current extradition treaty with the United Kingdom, adopted in 1972, was amended by a Supplemental Treaty, ratified in 1986, that narrowed the political offense exception. The Supplemental Treaty, as originally proposed in 1985, would have eliminated any judicial role for determining whether any offense was a political offense. A firestorm of criticism greeted that proposal as opening the door to wholesale harassment of Irish American and other critics of British government policies, and the Senate refused to ratify it. Instead, a Supplemental Treaty was negotiated that excluded serious violent crimes from the political offense exception while ensuring judicial review to allow consideration of whether the accused would receive a fair trial in the United Kingdom.

The Senate Foreign Relations Committee described the 1986 Supplement Treaty as a successful "effort to balance anti-terrorism concerns and the right of due process for individuals." Senator Biden explained, in a colloquy with Senators Kerry and Lugar that was adopted in the report accompanying the treaty, that the Senate intended the Supplemental Treaty to allow for broader judicial review:

[T]he defendant will have an opportunity in Federal court to introduce evidence that he or she would personally, because of their race, religion, nationality or political opinion, not be able to get a fair trial because of the court system or any other aspect of the judicial system in a requesting country, or that the person's extradition has been requested with a view to try or punish them on account of their race, their religion, nationality or political opinion.

The consequences of the new treaty

The new treaty would undo this compromise by eliminating this review. If the new treaty were ratified, an American who opposed British policy—for example, an investigative journalist who wrote of police abuses in Northern Ireland for an Irish American newspaper—could face arrest and extradition without having any ability to challenge, in an American court, whether the criminal charges are really a pretext for the punishment on account of race, religion, nationality or political opinion.

While the treaty preserves the courts' role in reviewing whether there is probable cause that the accused committed the crime, the "probable cause" standard is a low one and depends on information supplied by the foreign government. Such information may be difficult for the accused to rebut. For an extradition hearing to be meaningful, the accused must also be able to submit information about the improper political motivation of the extradition request, and an American judge must be free to consider such evidence.

Preservation of the political offense exception is an important bulwark for freedom in the world. Since the time of Thomas Jefferson, the United States has refused extradition requests for political offenses. Indeed, in the Declaration of Independence, the colonists accused King George of "transporting us beyond Seas to be tried for pretended offences." That principle applies with equal force today, no less than in 1776. No one in America should be sent to face trial in any foreign country without meaningful judicial review of all aspects relevant to extradition.

The treaty contains other deeply troubling provisions. These include provisions which eliminate the statute of limitations as a defense to extradition (article 6), allow for "provisional arrests" for as long as sixty days with no formal extradition request providing supporting details (article 12), and which allow for the treaty to be applied retroactively (article 22).

Wider influence?

While the United Kingdom is a close ally and democratic country, Attorney General Ashcoft announced at the signing ceremony that the new treaty "should serve as a model to the world" and could lead to revising other extradition treaties. As a result, Senate approval of this treaty could encourage the Administration to pursue treaties with other nations that diminish due process and meaningful judicial review.

Without a meaningful political offense exception as a part of our extradition laws, the United States could well lose its place as a haven for the persecuted. In the early days of the Cuban revolution—before the United States broke off diplomatic relations with Fidel Castro—the political offense exception prevented the return of Cuban dissidents to face criminal charges by the Castro regime. The political offense exception also sheltered a Greek public official from being sent back to face corruption allegations that resulted from his opposition to the takeover of his town by a Communist party government.

The Senate should stand in favor of meaningful judicial review of political offenses, and should reject this treaty.

Sincerely,
Laura W. Murphy, Director, Washington Legislative Office
Timothy H. Edgar, Legislative Counsel

Do you think that the United States takes political freedom too seriously because of its origins? Is political freedom always a good thing?

Do you think that this is a violation of human rights? Or do people who commit inhumane acts, such as murder or terrorism, give up such rights?

Both the examples the authors cite reflect general U.S. opposition to communism. Do you think that the political offense exception should also be used to offer a "haven" to communists themselves, say, or to Muslim fundamentalists?

KILLING OF INNOCENT CIVILIAN NOT "POLITICAL" CRIME
Kenneth Ofgang

Kenneth Ofgang is a staff writer on Metropolitan News-Enterprise, a daily Los Angeles newspaper that specializes in legal and social policy issues. Go to www.metnews.com to look at the online edition.

NO

A person accused of killing a civilian bystander in the course of anti-government activity cannot claim the benefit of the "political offense" exception under an extradition treaty, the Ninth U.S. Circuit Court of Appeals ruled yesterday.

"In nations where democratic institutions and the ballot box provide a peaceful means for evolutionary change, it is unacceptable to circumvent the system and to pursue political or other goals by unlawfully raining down violence on a society and its citizens," Judge Stephen Trott wrote for the panel.

Such violence, the judges said, cannot be held "incidental" to efforts for political change and thus cannot fit within the exception.

The ruling affirms a 2002 decision by U.S. District Judge Oliver Wanger of the Eastern District of California that the government may extradite Kulvir Singh Barapind to India to face charges related to clashes between government forces and Sikh separatists in the 1980s and early 1990s.

India's 14 million Sikhs make up only 2 percent of its population. India is 80 percent Hindu. Clashes flared between Indian government forces and Sikhs in the state of Punjab who were campaigning for a separate Sikh state, Khalistan.

Wife shot

Barapind, according to testimony, was at one time a popular leader of a Sikh student movement in the state of Punjab. One of the charges is that he was one of a group of men who invaded a residence shared by several Sikhs who had allegedly collaborated with the government and shot dead the wife of one of them.

The violence escalated dramatically following the "Golden Temple Massacre" of June 1984.

The 16th-century Golden Temple in the city of Amritsar is the spiritual center of Sikhism. Go to Volume 20, Religion and Morality, page 160 for more information.

The government launched an all-out attack on rebels who had taken refuge in the Golden Temple, the Sikhs' holiest shrine. The temple was badly damaged, at least 500 people were killed, and many civilians were caught in the crossfire.

The assassination of Prime Minister Indira Gandhi by two Sikh bodyguards the following October was said to be an act of revenge for what happened at the temple. In the next

Following the Golden Temple massacre in 1984, many people took to the streets in protest.

10 years, between 30,000 and 100,000 people are estimated to have been killed in related violence.

Barapind was a college student in Punjab and a Sikh activist accused of having been involved in a series of violent activities in 1991 and 1992. An Indian magistrate issued warrants for his arrest in connection with 11 alleged incidents of murder, attempted murder and robbery.

Barapind arrived in the United States in 1993, traveling under a passport bearing another name. He was detained by the INS [Immigration and Naturalization Service] and later asked for asylum.

He was in detention in Bakersfield when the Indian government asked for his extradition pursuant to the 1931

> *In international law asylum is protection offered by a state to protect an individual from his or her own state. It is usually used to protect people accused of political offenses, such as treason.*

133

extradition treaty between the United States and Great Britain, which was made applicable to India in 1942 and continues to govern offenses committed before the U.S.-India extradition treaty was entered into in 1997.

The Board of Immigration Appeals ruled over Barapind's objection that his asylum application would be held in abeyance until the extradition proceedings were completed, a ruling that the Ninth Circuit upheld.

After six days of hearings, Wanger ruled that five of the incidents fell within the treaty's exception for political offenses. Such offenses are not defined in the treaty but have been defined in past federal cases to be crimes "committed in furtherance of a political uprising, movement or rebellion" in the country where the crimes allegedly occurred.

If practices such as torture and coercion are already connected with the case, is there a likelihood that they might be used against Barapind if he is returned to India?

As for the other six incidents, Wanger ruled that evidence pertaining to three of them had been discredited by a showing that it had been obtained by torture, coercion, or extrajudicial detention. But he found Barapind to be deportable with regard to the other three incidents, including the murder of Kulwant Kaur.

According to affidavits submitted by Indian authorities, Kaur and her husband were in the home of his extended family when Barapind and three other men entered. Barapind, the witnesses said, shot and killed Kaur's brothers-in-law before the other men searched the house and found and killed Kaur and her husband.

While Kaur's husband may have been a collaborator, the judge ruled, there was no evidence that she had any connection to the dispute between the separatists and the government.

In June 2004 Barapind was still detained in the United States, but his application for asylum was still suspended. Does this seem fair? Go to www.google.com to look up articles on this case.

The exception, Wanger wrote, is "inapplicable to shield the knowing effort to kill or injure unarmed, uninvolved, innocent civilians who are non-combatants in the struggle."

Wanger found Barapind extraditable and remanded him to custody pending a final decision by the State Department, which has the last word in all foreign extradition cases.

The Ninth Circuit

In upholding that ruling, the Ninth Circuit rejected Barapind's argument that the Kaur murder should be deemed political, and that the case against him is so tainted by police misconduct he should not be extradited on any of the charges.

The latter argument fails, Trott explained, because the treaty incorporates the rule of specialty. Under that doctrine, if the country from which extradition is requested agrees to return the accused to face some but not all of the charges, the requesting country must agree to try the defendant only for the offenses specified.

It is up to the executive branch, not the judiciary, to enforce the rule, Trott said.

Political offenses—or not?

With regard to the Kaur murder, Trott rejected dicta in an earlier Ninth Circuit opinion suggesting that crimes against innocent persons could, at least in some cases, be classified as political offenses if committed with a political objective.

The suggestion that tactics are "simply irrelevant," Trott insisted, was wrong.

"This overindulgent approach indiscriminately and unwisely delegates to the Timothy McVeighs, the John Wilkes Booths, and the Mohammed Attas of the world the final legal decision as to what conduct is cognizable under the 'incidental to' test pursuant to treaties recognizing the political offense exception," the judge wrote.

Trott's opinion was joined by Ninth Circuit Senior Judge Jerome Farris and visiting Senior Judge Charles R. Weiner of the Eastern District of Pennsylvania.

The case is *Barapind v. Enomoto*, 02-16944.

The Indian courts argued that Barapind was implicated in 52 killings. Should he be protected by the principle of specialty?

Timothy McVeigh was executed for killing 168 people by bombing a federal building in Oklahoma City in 1995; John Wilkes Booth assassinated President Abraham Lincoln in 1865; Mohammad Atta was the suspected leader of the 9/11 terrorist attacks in the United States.

Go to http://caselaw.lp.findlaw.com/scripts/getcase.pl?court=9th&navby=year&year=2004-3 to read about this case.

Summary

In the first article the American Civil Liberties Union (ACLU) appeals to the Senate Foreign Relations Committee to oppose revisions to the extradition treaty between the United States and Britain. The ACLU argues that the proposed new version of the treaty would deprive the U.S. judiciary of any say in determining whether a fugitive's alleged offense was political and therefore excluded from extradition arrangements. That power would rest with the executive branch of government in the shape of the State Department. The authors claim that this would be against U.S. interests: The "political offense" exception in extradition cases is a cornerstone of liberty. They argue that scrapping existing provisions is not necessary to help the War on Terrorism, because terrorists can already be brought to justice under U.S. and international law. Although the ACLU admits that Britain is unlikely to abuse the extradition process, it argues that there is a danger that the new treaty might set a precedent for relations with less reliable nations.

The second article is a report of a case in which the U.S. Ninth Circuit Court of Appeals upheld a decision to extradite a Sikh to India to face terrorist charges. The judge found that some of the offenses for which the fugitive was wanted were political within the terms established by federal case law, and that others were based on statements obtained under duress. However, he rejected claims that one murder with which the Sikh was charged was political and found that the victim was an innocent bystander. Despite the doubts about the validity of the other charges, the court therefore allowed extradition.

FURTHER INFORMATION:

 Books:

Nicholls, Clive, Clare Montgomery, and Julian B. Knowles, *The Law of Extradition and Mutual Assistance: International Criminal Law, Practice and Procedure*. London, England: Cameron May, 2002.

Useful websites:

http://www.insightmag.com/news/2003/ 08/19/National/Treaties.Challenge.U.Sovereignty-449587.shtml
August 2003 article by Paul Rush examining whether extradition treaties challenge national sovereignty.
http://www.useu.be/TransAtlantic/US-EU%20Summits/ June2503WashingtonSummit/JUne2503USEU SummitExtradition.html
United States Mission to the European Union press release examining agreements in 2003 to help combat terrorism.

The following debates in the Pro/Con series may also be of interest:

In this volume:
 Part 3: Crime, pages 124–125

 Topic 9 Does the program for eradicating illicit crops violate human rights?

 Topic 12 Is money laundering too easy?

 Topic 13 Should diplomatic immunity be retained?

DO EXTRADITION TREATIES VIOLATE HUMAN RIGHTS?

YES: *There is no way to guarantee the treatment of defendants if they are returned to a country such as India, which has been criticized for its human rights record*

YES: *The detention of prisoners at Guantanamo Bay without trial is a clear breach of human rights. Many countries also believe that the death penalty contravenes human rights.*

INADEQUACY
Does existing extradition law inadequately protect people's human rights?

U.S. JUSTICE
Are the rights violated of people extradited to the United States?

NO: *Procedures ensure that the charges faced by the accused would merit a trial in the United States, and that the trial will be fair*

NO: *People extradited to the United States are entitled to a fair trial under the provisions of the Sixth Amendment to the Constitution*

DO EXTRADITION TREATIES VIOLATE HUMAN RIGHTS?
KEY POINTS

YES: *If the decision is left to the executive branch of government, it may reflect national policy and priorities more than justice. The separation of powers is essential to guarantee justice.*

YES: *The United States has one of the world's outstanding legal systems. It is morally obliged to protect people from systems with lower standards.*

POLITICAL OFFENSE
Should the judiciary be involved in judging whether or not an offense is political?

HOME IS BEST
Should extradition be disallowed to states with court systems different from that of America?

NO: *In the War on Terrorism only the executive has control of all the facts, which are sometimes secret. That makes it better equipped to make decisions for the good of the country.*

NO: *There is nothing particularly superior about the American justice system. Every nation has the right to apply its own laws in its own way.*

Topic 11

SHOULD TAX HAVENS BE MADE ILLEGAL?

YES
FROM "TAX HAVENS: RELEASING THE HIDDEN BILLIONS FOR POVERTY ERADICATION"
EXECUTIVE SUMMARY, JUNE 2000
OXFAM UNITED KINGDOM

NO
FROM "THE MORAL CASE FOR TAX HAVENS"
WWW.LEWROCKWELL.COM, OCTOBER 30, 2002
ROBERT STEWART

INTRODUCTION

A "tax haven" is the name popularly given to a country with low taxation where overseas investors can keep their money to avoid paying higher taxes in their home country. According to a recent survey by the Internal Revenue Service (IRS), around $5 trillion of U.S. money is kept overseas in offshore financial centers (OFCs). These centers, including Belize, Bermuda, and the Cayman Islands, attract business through banking secrecy and minimal taxation. Such policies are highly controversial. They allow the wealthy to avoid paying taxes on much of their earnings in their countries of origin, thus, critics believe, raising the tax burden on the rest of society. Moreover, law-enforcement agencies claim that banking-secrecy laws hamper their efforts to track criminal activities such as terrorist funding.

In 2004, 30 nations in Europe, North America, and Australasia threatened to adopt "defensive measures" against countries with "harmful tax practices." Through the multinational Organization for Economic Cooperation and Development (OECD) they drew up a list of places where they believed banking and tax laws should be changed. The list grades tax havens as either "cooperative" or "uncooperative," depending on whether they make commitments to improving banking openness with tax and police agencies from other countries. Uncooperative tax havens, such as Andorra, Liberia, and Monaco, are liable to international sanctions, which include extra taxes on earnings taken out of them and the termination of tax treaties.

Historically tax havens first became important in international commerce about 50 years ago. After World War II (1939–1945) countries in Europe and North America adopted higher taxes to help pay for reconstruction among other things. Tax rates were as high as 75 percent for the wealthy. At the same time, as former colonies struggled to become independent, they set out to attract business through beneficial tax legislation. Since many such countries had English as an official language, they became convenient places to which to move funds and conduct business. They grew into today's major OFCs. Although tax rates have broadly fallen around the world since then, other factors have encouraged their continued use— including the easy movement of money through e-commerce. Even moderately wealthy Americans, such as lawyers and stockbrokers, can now use tax havens.

> *"We don't pay taxes. Only the little people pay taxes."*
> —LEONA HELMSLEY (1920–),
> BUSINESSWOMAN

Using OFCs to avoid paying taxes is in many cases legal. For example, a multinational business may manufacture products in a high-tax country but route its invoicing and finances through an OFC to minimize its overall tax bill. Companies claim that this tactic, which is known as "tax planning," allows them to remain profitable and offer lower prices for their products. However, other businesses and individuals exploit practices such as banking secrecy to illegally conceal their earnings from the IRS. The United States is estimated to lose around $70 billion a year to this sort of tax evasion.

Advocates of tax havens, including their governments, banks, and financial advisers, point to the benefits that banking privacy, a low-tax economy, and offshore status offer world commerce. Such "tax-neutral" regimes may encourage collaboration between companies from different countries by removing conflicts between domestic tax systems. Banking secrecy can encourage joint commercial ventures by concealing them from competitors. Advocates of the system also argue that nations have a sovereign right to decide on their own banking laws and set their own tax rates— and that wealthy individuals or corporations have a right to do what they like with their money.

Critics of tax havens, who include the IRS and the FBI, claim that their laws make it very difficult to track illegal activity such as tax evasion or money laundering. They protect, for example, the bank records of suspected fraudsters or drug traffickers. The international community represented by the OECD, meanwhile, says that tax havens benefit their residents and savers at the expense of other countries. While tax havens have the right to set their own laws, the OECD argues, other countries can take defensive measures against the effects of those economies, which often offer sanctuary to corrupt regimes, terrorist organizations, and drug barons among others. Critics believe that wealthy taxpayers have a moral obligation to contribute to the maintenance of the society that allows them to make their money by paying taxes to fund essential services that benefit the disadvantaged and vulnerable members of society, including investment in education or welfare-assistance programs.

The following two articles discuss tax havens from opposing viewpoints.

TAX HAVENS: RELEASING THE HIDDEN BILLIONS FOR POVERTY ERADICATION
Oxfam United Kingdom

Oxfam is a UK-based charity dedicated to famine relief in the developing world. This paper was published in June 2000.

Does it matter that there are no accurate figures at the heart of the debate?

If countries are so poor that they need financial aid, where is the money coming from that is being put into tax havens? Are developing nations more likely to have corrupt governments?

YES

Tax havens and offshore financial centres (OFCs) have seldom figured as prominently in media coverage of economic affairs as they do today. Interest has focussed on the concerns of northern governments and the interests of powerful transnational corporations (TNCs). The main actors in the debate are revenue authorities, corporate lawyers, tax accountants and financial journalists. By contrast, the world's poorest countries are conspicuous by their absence. This is unfortunate because offshore tax havens represent an increasingly important obstacle to poverty reduction. They are depriving governments in developing countries of the revenues they need to sustain investment in basic services and the economic infrastructure upon which broad-based economic growth depends....

It is impossible to calculate the financial losses to developing countries associated with offshore activity. Secrecy, electronic commerce and the growing mobility of capital have left all governments facing problems in revenue collection. The borderline between tax evasion and tax avoidance is becoming increasingly blurred. But at a conservative estimate, tax havens have contributed to revenue losses for developing countries of at least US$50 billion a year. To put this figure in context, it is roughly equivalent to annual aid flows to developing countries. We stress that the estimate is a conservative one. It is derived from the effects of tax competition and the non-payment of tax on flight capital. It does not take into account outright tax evasion, corporate practices such as transfer pricing, or the use of havens to under-report profit.

A wider context

Revenue losses associated with tax havens and offshore centres cannot be considered in isolation. They interact with problems of unsustainable debt, deteriorating terms of trade, and declining aid. But there is no doubt the implied human development costs of tax havens are large. The US$50 billion loss is equivalent to six times the estimated annual costs of achieving universal primary education, and almost three times the cost of universal primary health coverage. Of course, ending the diversion of resources from governments into corporate profit margins and offshore bank accounts provides no guarantee that the funds released will be used for poverty reduction purposes. This will depend on governments developing effective poverty reduction strategies. But allowing current practices to continue will undermine the successful implementation of such strategies.

The extent of offshore financial activity is not widely appreciated. The globalisation of capital markets has massively increased the scope for offshore activity. It is estimated that the equivalent of one-third of total global GDP is now held in financial havens. Much of this money is undisclosed and untaxed—and the rest is under-taxed. Governments everywhere have become increasingly concerned at the implications. In Britain, the government's efforts to prevent the use of tax havens to under-report profit (and hence tax liability), has brought it into conflict with powerful transnational companies. At least one major corporation has responded by threatening to relocate their investments from Britain. Such problems have lead to a proliferation of initiatives designed to tackle various aspects of the problem. The OECD is leading an initiative to crackdown on harmful tax competition, UN agencies are trying to curb money laundering, and the Financial Stability Forum (FSF) is examining the impact of the offshore system on global financial stability.

Gross Domestic Product (GDP) is a measure of how much a country generates through goods and services in a year.

The Financial Stability Forum is an international group created in 1999 by national bank and government representatives to promote the exchange of information and cooperation in financial surveillance.

View from the South

These initiatives are useful up to a point, but they primarily reflect the concerns of northern governments. Ironically, these governments are in a far stronger position than their counterparts in developing countries. If revenue authorities in Britain and Germany feel threatened by offshore activity, how much more severe are the problems facing countries with weak systems of tax administration? And if governments in rich countries see tax havens as a threat to their capacity to finance basic services, how much more serious are the threats facing poor countries? After all, these are countries in which 1.2 billion people have no access to a health facility, in which 125 million primary school age children are not in school, and in which one out of every five people live below the poverty line.

Lack of attention to poverty is only one part of the problem with current initiatives. Another is their lack of balance. Some

Is there any way for poor countries to finance such services other than through taxation? Look at Volume 14, International Development, and Volume 23, Poverty and Wealth, for further information.

Do you think the authors make a convincing connection between offshore activity and what happens in major financial centers? What sort of activity might they be referring to?

developing country havens justifiably see the actions of northern governments as being unbalanced and partial. Financial havens are part of a much wider problem that extends beyond the 'offshore' activity of small island states to 'onshore' activity in major economies such as the City of London and New York. Yet OECD efforts to address harmful tax competition have involved a crackdown on small state financial havens, while a far more light-handed approach has been applied to member countries engaging in harmful tax practices.

Undermining poor countries

Tax havens may seem far removed from the problem of poverty, but they are intimately connected. There are three major ways in which offshore centres undermine the interests of poor countries.

• Tax competition and tax escape. Tax havens and harmful tax practices provide big business and wealthy individuals with opportunities to escape their tax obligations. This limits the capacity of countries to raise revenue through taxation, both on their own residents and on foreign-owned capital. This can seriously undermine the ability of governments in poor countries to make the vital investments in social services and economic infrastructure upon which human welfare and sustainable economic development depends. It also gives those TNCs that are prepared to make use of international tax avoidance opportunities an unfair competitive advantage over domestic competitors and small and medium size enterprises. Tax competition, and the implied threat of relocation, has forced developing countries to progressively lower corporate tax rates on foreign investors. Ten years ago, these rates were typically in the range of 30–35 per cent—broadly equivalent to the prevailing rate in most OECD countries. Today, few developing countries apply corporate tax rates in excess of 20 per cent.… If developing countries were applying OECD corporate tax rates their revenues would be at least US$50 billion higher. If used effectively, funds siphoned through tax loopholes into offshore financial centres could be used to finance vital investments in health and education.…

If transnational corporations (TNCs) can force countries to change their taxation levels by threatening to relocate, does that mean that corporations are now more powerful than governments? Go to Volume 18, Commerce and Trade, Topic 8 Do transnational corporations have more influence on the world economy than national governments?

• Money laundering. The offshore world provides a safe haven for the proceeds of political corruption, illicit arms dealing, illegal diamond trafficking, and the global drugs trade. While some havens, such as the Channel Islands and the Cayman Islands, have introduced anti-money laundering legislation, the problem remains widespread. Havens facilitate

The Channel Islands are a British possession in the English Channel between Britain and France. They include the islands of Guernsey and Jersey.

the plunder of public funds by corrupt elites in poor countries, which can represent a major barrier to economic and social development. It has been estimated that around US$55 billion was looted from Nigerian public funds during the Abacha dictatorship. To put the figure in perspective, the country is today blighted by an external debt burden of US$31 billion....

• Financial instability. The offshore system has contributed to the rising incidence of financial crises that have destroyed livelihoods in poor countries. Tax havens and OFCs are now thought to be central to the operation of global financial markets. Currency instability and rapid surges and reversals of capital flows around the world became defining features of the global financial system during the 1990s. The financial crisis that ravaged east Asia in the late 1990s was at least partly a result of these volatile global markets. Following the Asian crisis, the Indonesian economy underwent a severe contraction and the number of people living in poverty doubled to 40 million. In Thailand, the health budget was cut by almost one-third....

Do you agree? Are other factors important? Go to www.economist. com, and look at articles relating to the subject.

Policy options

The following policy options could be considered by the international community to help poor countries stem tax evasion and reduce the negative impact of tax havens:

• A multilateral approach on common standards to define the tax base to minimise avoidance opportunities for both TNCs and international investors.

Go to Volume 23, Poverty and Wealth, Topic 15 Have transnational corporations helped eradicate poverty?

• A multilateral agreement to allow states to tax multinationals on a global unitary basis, with appropriate mechanisms to allocate tax revenues internationally.

• A global tax authority could be set up with the prime objective of ensuring that national tax systems do not have negative global implications.

• Support for the proposal for an International Convention to facilitate the recovery and repatriation of funds illegally appropriated from national treasuries of poor countries.

• Standards on payment of taxation in host countries should join environmental and labour standards as part of the corporate responsibility agenda. Standards requiring TNCs to refrain from harmful tax avoidance and evasion should be factored into official and voluntary codes of conduct for TNCs and for the tax planning industry.

• A multilateral agreement to share information on tax administration to help countries, especially poorer ones, to stem tax evasion.

THE MORAL CASE FOR TAX HAVENS
Robert Stewart

Robert Stewart is an executive, company director, and financial author who lives in Bermuda. This paper was published in October 2002.

NO

X   … Bermuda has a terrible reputation with foreign government elites. It is a mid-Atlantic affront to the American and European governments who believe they have a right to tell the rest of the world how to live and what their tax laws should be. The guts of the problem is, that Bermudians do not pay income tax on their earnings, capital gains taxes, or corporate taxes on profits…. Many politicians wish to close down, or at least hobble, the activities of pirate countries like Bermuda, The Bahamas, The Cook Islands, Switzerland, and about 35 other financial pygmies that are mere dots on the map of the world.

Over the past ten years or so, governments (and other quasi governmental organisations such as the OECD) in the United States and Western Europe have been throwing … rotten arguments at the so-called tax havens like Bermuda and the Cayman Islands on the grounds that they siphon off legitimate tax revenues. This has been described as "harmful tax competition" (an oxymoron), or has been categorized as illegal tax evasion. The clients of tax havens, wealthy individuals and multi-national corporations, are, it is said, dodging their legitimate tax obligations to their countries of domicile and as a result those who are left at home are unfairly compelled to pay higher taxes. Spending on social programs such as education and pensions is reduced and many high-powered and high-paid lawyers and accountants expend time and effort in tax dodging when they could usefully be engaged in more productive tasks.

An oxymoron is a phrase whose parts contradict one another, such as "a silent scream."

Cost of government

For years, orthodox economics has condemned tax avoidance as unproductive, as well as being unfair to other taxpayers. Yet public expenditures in almost every country one can name (including Bermuda) are unproductive and have risen steadily, absorbing over 50% of GDP in many countries. Most thoughtful people now belatedly understand to their horror that government bureaucracies (often employing about a fifth of the labor force) are not staffed by disinterested philosopher kings who somehow magically understand what the people want and impose taxes accordingly. It is not

In the United States in 2003 public expenditure was around $2 trillion from a GDP of around $10.5 trillion, a rate of around 20 percent.

overstating the case, to say that many public employees arrived at their desks with the objective of doing good, but somewhere along the way, they ended up doing very well for themselves.

Why should the activities of tax havens be put in the spotlight of public distaste in North America and Europe? One reason is that the success of Bermuda and other tax efficient countries feed the fantasies of pro-government and anti-business fanatics—after all Enron established a few off balance sheet entities in the Cayman Islands, the fabled numbered bank accounts in Switzerland have long been accused of facilitating money-laundering and linked to drug trafficking, and, more recently, low-tax jurisdictions are a bogey-man of anti-terrorists. A more important reason is that high-spending Western governments desperately need lost revenues to keep the state machine ticking over whilst taxpayers resent the grasping mitt of government on their wallets. When governments grab over 40 percent of a country's income in taxes a natural resistance to having incomes and wealth confiscated builds up in the minds of productive citizens.

History of taxation

We need to remind ourselves that until the early 20th century, governments tended to restrict their activities to maintaining an army against foreign aggression, a police force to protect law-abiding citizens against robbers and thieves, and a limited number of social activities such as public health and education. In most countries, less than ten percent of incomes were taken in taxation. All of this changed because of the costs of fighting two world wars and innumerable other small conflicts, a desire to redistribute incomes from the rich to the poor, and the recognition that governments by spending huge amounts on social programs could effectively bribe voters with their own money to vote high spending politicians into office....

Perceptive voters recognised that government looting of their private property, incomes, and wealth impeded the production of goods and services, and was being abused by hyper-active and incompetent governments. From the end of the Second World War, in 1945, a few wealthy individuals and corporations decided to take remedial action to protect their assets from the plundering activities of government....

As the burden of taxation and other nefarious activities of governments increased, largely because of military spending and the creation of massive welfare states in Europe and the

Do you agree with Stewart that he is not "overstating the case"? Do you share his view that public employees are out to do well for themselves?

Stewart mentions some of the arguments against tax havens. Would his argument be further validated if he spent more time discussing them?

For the financial year ending in April 2005, the highest U.S. tax rate was 35 percent for individuals earning over $319,101 a year. Does that seem fair to you?

Do you think that people should have a right to citizenship or residence in a country to which they do not pay any taxes?

United States, the activities of a few tax freedom-fighters mushroomed into something of a major cottage industry. There are now something like 40 or so tax havens, and even countries like Hungary are getting into the business of preserving the assets and incomes of those who find that tax authorities (representatives of the looting class) were penalizing relatively minor economic figures like dentists in Belgium, tennis players in Germany, or movie stars and writers in UK. Such people, pilloried by politicians as being unpatriotic, were simply people who loved their countries but feared the plundering and economically counter-productive activities of their governments....

Once the government bite on individual incomes reaches 30 percent or thereabouts a silent tax revolt takes place. People either stop working (hence the huge numbers of the underclass that simply mooch around most of the day), they cheat on their tax returns, or they shift assets and commercial activities abroad to countries where the tax regime is less hostile to earnings and the preservation of capital. Just as the exploited and victimised left Europe in the 18th and 19th centuries for the freedom of the United States and elsewhere, the wealthy also vote, not with their feet as did "the huddled masses yearning to breathe free" but with their bank balances and intellectual capital. They are heirs to a time-honoured custom of free people of telling overbearing government to take a hike....

Moral issue

There is a huge morally important point at stake. Government taking is usually justified by the fact that it performs good works and provides endless benefits to its citizens. The State is somehow more important than the individual, and he should willingly stump up his share because of all the benefits showered on him by benevolent rulers. Others, like the American Founding Fathers, argue that the individual takes precedence over government and there are inalienable rights to privacy, life, liberty, and property and that the compulsory sequestration of the individual's property through taxation makes the rights of man dependent on the goodwill of the state.... Once income taxes were imposed on the citizen, the level of earnings he was allowed to keep became dependent on the goodwill of the government; and how much he was allowed to keep varied with the size of the government jackboot.

Those who value individual freedom over government benevolence (or should that be malevolence) seek to protect

How much do you think that high taxation has to do with the creation of an economic underclass in the United States? Go to Volume 23, Poverty and Wealth, Topic 7 Are income taxes an effective way of redistributing wealth?

Does Stewart's reading of the Framers' intentions mean that the government should not collect any taxes? What changes might that make to life in the United States? Who would finance public services?

their assets and their privacy from prying eyes, but they are usually portrayed as greedy selfish barons who neglect their responsibilities to those at home. Whilst most of the tax avoiders do not act from altruistic motives, it is relevant to recall that Joseph Schumpeter in his essay "The Fiscal State" pointed out that one of the consequences of the unlimited power of governments to tax their citizens would be a misallocation of resources away from wealth producing investments and into largely non-productive public spending designed to redistribute income or the building of public monuments....

> Joseph A. Schumpeter (1883–1950) was one of the 20th century's leading economists. He advanced the ideas of the business cycle and the dynamism of capitalism among other theories.

Tax haven vs. tax efficient

The most important activity of the misnamed tax havens is to avoid governmental unproductive spending and to allow entrepreneurs freely to invest and produce the goods and services needed for the world to prosper. Tax efficient countries like Bermuda therefore enable resources to be used for the purposes of increasing the standard of living of everyone including the poor. Left to politicians, assets would be used for non-productive purposes and living standards would improve less rapidly. Time and time again, it has been shown that much of government expenditure is wasted on such things as huge public buildings, subsidies, national airlines, futile redistribution of wealth programmes, armaments, or just simple corruption of public officials. Modern government has become a gigantic slot-machine that uses the political process to take from everyone and give to some, the major objective being its own preservation.

> Among other things, taxation funds schools. Could this be classed as "nonproductive"?

Tax-efficient countries provide a mechanism for restricting the ability of governments to impose onerous tax burdens on their citizens, and assist in compelling governments to provide an economic climate more receptive to the peaceful activities of business. Without the safety valve of tax havens, taxpayers in North America and Europe would be milked even more vigorously by the looting class than they are at present. Far from cheating citizens of North America and Europe tax havens provide an essential escape route that enables capital to be preserved for productive purposes. In addition, it buttresses what is a core value of the West, namely freedom....

> Most people who use tax havens are wealthy. Do you think they would use this money for "productive purposes"? What might they be?

Can there be a more moral case for tax havens, than tax efficiency, restraints on government power to grab the income of its citizens, the preservation of capital to increase prosperity, and freedom to enjoy private property? I think not.

Summary

The writers of the two articles have completely opposing views on the merits of tax havens. In particular, they disagree about whether the international community should take steps against offshore financial centers.

The Oxfam report argues that tax havens are part of the global poverty problem and must therefore be brought onto the reform agenda. Their main effects are: to decrease government revenues in developing countries by at least $50 billion per year, to facilitate money laundering, which encourages political corruption, illicit arms dealing, and the global drugs trade, and to increase global financial instability, such as that experienced by east Asian economies in the late 1990s. Oxfam suggests a series of new policies that the international community should adopt to help poor countries reduce both tax evasion and the negative effect of tax havens.

In the second article Robert Stewart proposes a moral case for keeping tax havens. He discusses how the tax burden increased after World War II and argues that it caused a laudable tax revolt as people realized that governments were wasting their money. People stopped working, faked their tax returns, or shifted their assets to less hostile tax regimes. This last option is a moral choice for those who value individual freedom over government interference, he argues. Moreover, it puts pressure on governments to be more efficient. Tax havens, he claims, restrain a government's power to grab the personal income of its citizens and preserve capital for increased prosperity.

FURTHER INFORMATION:

Books:

Azzara, Thomas, *Tax Havens of the World* (8th edition). New Providence, NJ: New Providence Press, 2003.

Neal, Terry, L., *The Offshore Solution*. New York: Mastermind Media Publishing Company, 2001.

Useful websites:

http://www.free-market.net/spotlight/taxhavens/ Article that argues tax havens provide refuge for the oppressed.

http://www.libertyhaven.com/doityourself/offhaven.shtml Article by Adam Starchild on using tax havens legitimately, published on the libertyhaven site.

http://www.oecd.org/document/19/0,2340,en_2649_ 37427_1903251_1_1_1_37427,00.html Organization for Economic Cooperation and Development (OECD) site on tax havens. Contains recent news, legislation, and articles.

The following debates in the Pro/Con series may also be of interest:

In this volume:

Part 3: Crime, pages 124–125

Topic 12 Is money laundering too easy?

In *Commerce and Trade*:
Topic 8 Do transnational corporations have more influence on the world economy than national governments?

SHOULD TAX HAVENS BE MADE ILLEGAL?

YES: People have a duty to pay back something to the society that enabled them to become wealthy

YES: The ease of money laundering encourages political corruption, illicit arms dealing, and the global drug trade

PERSONAL FREEDOM
Should individuals be prevented from moving their wealth from high-tax regimes?

CORRUPTION AND CRIME
Will stopping the banking secrecy of tax havens prevent corruption and crime?

NO: An individual's money is his or her own property. People should have the freedom to do with it as they wish.

NO: This is a breach of personal privacy and may be subject to abuse and misuse by governments and federal agencies

SHOULD TAX HAVENS BE MADE ILLEGAL?

KEY POINTS

YES: Tax havens provide a safe place for often illegally obtained funds. These could be put to use in loans and aid to poor nations, which would help the global economy.

YES: Employees who work in the offshore financial sector are well trained and likely to find alternative employment

GLOBAL TRADE
Would the world economy cope well if tax havens were closed?

LOCAL ECONOMY
Will the local economies of tax havens recover from the loss of their financial status?

NO: Increased taxation on companies would make prices skyrocket, decreasing living standards, and possibly causing an economic recession

NO: Most offshore centers are based in small states with few other possible areas for wealth generation

Topic 12
IS MONEY LAUNDERING TOO EASY?

YES
"U.S. SENATORS SEEK CRACKDOWN ON MONEY LAUNDERING"
HTTP://RUSSIANLAW.ORG/REUTERS080301.HTM
ANDREW CLARK

NO
"U.S., COLOMBIA, CANADA AND UNITED KINGDOM JOINTLY ANNOUNCE DISMANTLING
OF MASSIVE INTERNATIONAL MONEY-LAUNDERING RING"
PRESS RELEASE, MAY 4, 2004
DRUG ENFORCEMENT ADMINISTRATION

INTRODUCTION

Money laundering is the processing of income earned from crime or dishonest practices in order to disguise its origins —making it appear "clean" when it is really "dirty." It normally occurs in three stages. *Placement* is getting money into the global financial system, for instance, by buying money orders or bonds or by depositing it in banks in small amounts to avoid attention. *Layering* comprises passing money through various bank accounts or other financial systems to obscure its provenance, or moving it to places where it will not attract notice, such as a country whose banking systemis protected by secrecy laws. Finally comes *integration*—spending the money on legitimate purposes such as real estate or stocks and shares.

At the end of the 20th century estimates of global money laundering were between $590 billion and $1.5 trillion—around 2 to 5 percent of the world's gross domestic product. Most states have legislation in place to prevent money laundering, which is seen as an essential part of the fight against organized crime and, for example, international drug trafficking. Since the U.S. declaration of the War on Terrorism in 2001, anti–money-laundering techniques have also become important in tracing terrorist funding. However, money laundering still remains a serious problem.

Countries such as the United States require banks to monitor and report unusual activity, including deposits of more than $10,000 or suspected money laundering. There are more than 170 federal money-laundering offenses, many of which were introduced by the Money Laundering Control Act of 1986 and the Money Laundering Suppression Act of 1994. However, banks are also restricted in some of the action they can take by legislation designed to protect individual privacy, such as the

Privacy Act of 1974. The government's move in the 2001 USA PATRIOT Act to give the Treasury Department greater powers in monitoring banking activity drew condemnation from rights groups concerned about individual freedom and privacy. There is also an argument that reporting customers goes against a bank's primary objective, which is to increase business and profits. Running constant checks on transactions is also expensive and time-consuming.

"The need to launder money has led organized crime to avail itself of the full range of banking services...."
—PRESIDENTIAL COMMISSION ON ORGANIZED CRIME (1988)

For critics of current anti–money-laundering legislation the problems lie not only within the United States but also on an international level. There are many places where secrecy laws protect banking systems from being investigated. They include well-known offshore financial centers such as the Cayman Islands or the Pacific island of Nauru, which has only a few thousand inhabitants but more than 400 registered banks. Even large banking centers such as New York and London have offshore businesses where people can enjoy more secrecy. Many criminals favor dealing with the world's larger banks if possible.

People who believe that current initiatives against money laundering are

sufficient point to numerous examples of increased international cooperation between governments and international law-enforcement agencies, such as Interpol, to tackle the problem. In 1989, for example, the G-7 group of the world's leading economies created the Financial Action Task Force on Money Laundering (FATF) to coordinate an international response. The FATF, which includes the major financial centers of Europe, the Americas, and Asia, drew up 40 recommended measures for national governments to implement anti–money-laundering programs. There are also regional organizations, such as the Caribbean Financial Action Task Force and the Asia/Pacific Group on Money Laundering. In 1996 these organizations and the FATF created the International Money Laundering Information Network (IMoLIN), a website for sharing resources. It includes model laws on which countries can base legislation.

Critics argue that detection of money laundering still remains too difficult. It is by its nature highly sophisticated and complex. It benefits not only from variations in banking regulations in different countries but also from various national laws that protect the privacy of individuals. In large parts of the world, moreover, it can take advantage of traditional systems of money transfer, such as *hawala* in India, *hundi* in Afghanistan and Pakistan, and *chop* in China, which do not create traceable records. Such systems are largely legitimate, but they may easily be exploited by criminals or terrorists.

The following two articles examine further whether more could be done under international law to make money laundering more difficult.

U.S. SENATORS SEEK CRACKDOWN ON MONEY LAUNDERING
Andrew Clark

Andrew Clark is a business writer for the news agency Reuters. This piece was written in August 2001.

YES

A bipartisan group of senators on Friday introduced legislation to try to crack down on money laundering by corrupt foreign officials and stem the growing flow of dirty cash into the U.S. financial system.

The effort follows embarrassing revelations in recent years that major U.S. banks have been used to channel billions of dollars linked to drug trafficking, fraud and organized crime. Money laundering involves moving such funds through a series of banks or bank accounts to disguise their origin and ownership.

Is preventing money laundering the job of the government? Or can banks be trusted to police their own affairs?

"Estimates are that $500 billion is being laundered through U.S. banks each year," said the bill's chief sponsor, Michigan Democrat Carl Levin, who chairs the Senate Permanent Subcommittee on Investigations. "Our anti-money laundering laws are out-of-date and inadequate to counter this threat…."

High-profile cases

Among other things, [the bill] would add foreign corruption offenses, such as bribery and theft of government funds, to the list of crimes that can trigger a U.S. money laundering prosecution, bar U.S. banks from dealing with shadowy foreign "shell" banks, and require closer review of large U.S. bank accounts opened for overseas customers.

In the past three years, Levin's subcommittee has conducted a series of probes into money-laundering vulnerabilities in U.S. banks' private banking operations and so-called "correspondent" relationships—which allow foreign banks to use them for services like wire transfers and check clearing.

Carlos Salinas was president of Mexico from 1988 to 1994. Raul Salinas was accused of receiving money from Colombian and Mexican drug cartels. He was imprisoned in Mexico while investigators traced the origins of more than $100 million deposited in Swiss bank accounts.

In a 1999 report, it criticized Citigroup Inc. for helping Raul Salinas, brother of the former Mexican president, move $100 million in alleged drug money out of Mexico and for its dealings with the family of former Nigerian dictator Sani Abacha, who has been accused of embezzling some $3 billion [see box on "Nigeria's missing millions" on page 154].

General Sani Abacha (1943–1998) was a military officer and Nigerian head of state from 1993 until his death. During that time he is alleged to have siphoned off billions of dollars to offshore accounts.

COMMENTARY: Nigeria's missing billions

One of the recent cases that threw light onto the murky world of money laundering is that of former Nigerian military dictator Sani Abacha (1943–1998). During his five-year rule of the West African nation Abacha siphoned off billions of dollars from the country. Those who spoke out against Abacha were imprisoned or, in some cases, executed. Abacha died suddenly in June 1998. Presidential elections the following year brought to power Olusegun Obasanjo (1937–), a former military ruler of the country remembered for handing power back to the Nigerian people.

Hunting the money

Obasanjo made it a priority to track down and recover the money stolen by Abacha, which he said amounted to $4.3 billion. The total comprised $2.3 billion taken directly from the national treasury, $1 billion awarded in phoney contracts to front companies, and $1 billion Abacha had extorted in bribes from foreign contractors. The money had been transferred out of Nigeria into bank accounts in the names of Abacha's family and associates. The banks were in many countries, including Switzerland, the United Kingdom, Liechtenstein, Luxembourg, France, and the United States.

The Nigerian government requested government assistance to recover the cash. In December 1999 the Swiss authorities froze $550 million in more than 120 accounts in a dozen banks while they investigated possible money laundering. In 2002 they ordered Swiss banks to return about $1 billion held in accounts both in Switzerland and around the world, after an alleged deal between Obasanjo and Abacha's family under which they would be allowed to keep $100 million. In return for Switzerland lifting its secrecy laws to help Nigerian investigations, Nigeria guaranteed the Abacha family's human rights in the event of any criminal proceedings. However, the Swiss authorities were embarrassed in November 2002 when Achaba's son Mohammed, himself a convicted money launderer, refused to sign documents releasing the money from Swiss banks. He claimed that the money was the result of legitimate business deals. Although Nigeria had received nearly $100 million from the Swiss by the end of 2003, the remaining money was still outstanding.

Investigators faced similar problems in other countries: Tracing the cash was one thing, but recovering it was another. In the United Kingdom the High Court allowed the government to investigate 23 London banks—including branches of the U.S. giants Goldman Sachs, Merrill Lynch, and Citibank—that handled up to $1.3 billion belonging to Abacha and his associates. The case led to severe criticism of UK money-laundering controls. The Financial Services Authority condemned 15 banks for "significant control weaknesses" in their monitoring of accounts. However, the Nigerians were still negotiating for the return of any funds in 2004.

United States "can't have it both ways"

"After all, America can't have it both ways," Levin said. "We can't condemn corruption abroad, be it officials taking bribes or looting their treasuries, and then tolerate American banks profiting off that corruption."

Earlier this year, the panel cited major U.S. banks, including Citibank, Bank of America, Chase Manhattan and Bank of New York, for being too quick to open accounts for offshore banks, too lax in monitoring them and too slow to close them down when problems became apparent.

In response, the legislation proposes a wide array of measures, including:

- Requiring banks to keep a record of the identity of foreign owners of U.S. bank accounts.
- Barring U.S. banks from opening correspondent accounts for shell banks, which have no physical presence anywhere.
- Requiring enhanced reviews before opening private bank accounts of $1 million or more for foreigners or correspondent accounts for banks located in offshore financial havens.
- Modifying forfeiture rules to allow the government to seize funds linked to money laundering that are held in foreign banks' U.S. correspondent accounts.
- Expanding U.S. courts' jurisdiction over foreign banks involved in money laundering in the United States.

While an aide said Levin was "optimistic" about the bill's chances in the Senate, its further prospects remain unclear. Bank groups have opposed new curbs, saying current laws are tough enough and new ones would be costly and burdensome.

And the Bush administration is widely seen as having sent mixed messages on the topic, saying it is committed to aggressive enforcement of existing laws but would like to see a better return on the money being spent to combat the problem.

Many people abroad accuse the United States of double standards in its attitudes to subjects such as corruption. But is it mainly foreigners who deserve criticism, while the U.S. system prevents corruption?

"Shell" banks exist only on paper. They have no staff, branches, or other physical holdings. They are common in offshore financial centers (OFCs). See Topic 11 Should tax havens be made illegal?

Is it reasonable for the government to apply the same value-for-money criteria to anticrime initiatives as to other areas of funding? Is fighting crime more important than worrying about dollars and cents?

U.S., COLOMBIA, CANADA AND UK …
DISMANTLING … INTERNATIONAL
MONEY-LAUNDERING RING
Press release, Drug Enforcement Administration

NO

David N. Kelley, the United States Attorney for the Southern District of New York, Anthony Placido, the Special Agent in Charge of the United States Drug Enforcement Administration ("DEA") in New York, Raymond W. Kelley, the Commissioner of the New York City Police Department, Michael J. Thomas, the Special Agent in Charge of the United States Internal Revenue Service, Criminal Investigation Division ("IRS-CID") in New York, Luis Carlos Barragan Samper, the Director General of Operations for the Colombian Departamento Administrativo De Seguridad ("DAS") in Bogota, Colombia, Michael Cabana, the Inspector with the Royal Canadian Mounted Police ("RCMP") in Montreal, Canada, and Jim Gamble, the Assistant Chief Constable of the National Crime Squad in London, England, announced today the coordinated dismantling of a massive international money-laundering ring that laundered millions of Colombian drug dollars in the United States, Canada and the United Kingdom through the Colombian Black Market Peso Exchange System.

The United States Attorney announced (a) the unsealing of an Indictment against 34 members of the money-laundering ring located in the United States, Canada and Colombia, (b) the forfeiture to the United States of $20 million in laundered funds, and (c) the issuance of seizure warrants for more than $1 million in additional laundered funds.

Black market exchange
The Indictment charges that the defendants participated in the Colombian Black Market Peso Exchange (the "BMPE"). The BMPE is an informal currency exchange system in which one or more "peso brokers" serve as middle-men between, on one hand, narcotics traffickers who control massive quantities of drug money in cash in the United States, and, on the other,

Attorney General John Ashcroft heads the Justice Department, which seeks to track down the laundered profits of drug cartels.

Informal money exchange systems exist in many countries. Does the international community have any right to interfere with such national traditions?

companies and individuals in Colombia who wish to purchase U.S. dollars outside the legitimate Colombian banking system so that they can, among other things, avoid the payment of taxes, import duties and transaction fees owed to the Colombian government.

The BMPE system involves three-steps. First, narcotics traffickers enter into contracts with peso brokers in which the broker delivers pesos in Colombia in return for cash drug money in the United States and Canada. Second, the peso broker uses accounts in the United States or other countries outside Colombia to place the narcotics proceeds into the international banking system. Finally, the peso broker enters into contracts with Colombian companies or individuals who deliver pesos to the broker in Colombia in exchange for a wire transfer of dollars. Both transactions are verbal, without any paper trail, and the disconnection between the peso transactions (which generally all occur in Colombia) and the dollar transactions (which generally all occur outside Colombia), make discovery of the money laundering by international law enforcement extremely difficult. Because of these inherent advantages, the BMPE system has become one of the primary methods by which Colombian narcotics traffickers launder their illicit funds.

Can you suggest any ways in which transactions can be traced if there are no written records?

Operation White Dollar

"Operation White Dollar," a two-year joint Organized Crime Drug Enforcement Task Force ("OCDETF") investigation involving the United States Attorney's Office for the Southern District of New York, the DEA, the NYPD, the IRS, the Office of the Special Narcotics Prosecutor for the City of New York, the Manhattan District Attorney's Office, and the South Florida Money Laundering Strike Force in Miami, Florida, as well as the National Crime Squad, the RCMP, and the DAS, targeted the BMPE system from top to bottom, from the peso brokers dealing directly with narcotics traffickers right down to the Colombian companies and individuals who facilitate the system by purchasing dollars in the system. According to the Indictment, 34 individuals and companies were involved in a BMPE conspiracy centered in Bogota, Colombia. Among others, the indictment charges 5 defendants alleged to be "First-Tier Peso Brokers," who make contracts directly with narcotics trafficking organizations; 2 defendants alleged to be "Second-Tier Peso Brokers," who concentrate on arranging for the pickup of street-level cash narcotics proceeds and placing those funds into the banking system; and 9 defendants alleged to be "Third-Tier Peso

The investigation included authorities from Canada and Colombia. Can international crime only be fought by an international police force? Go to www.interpol.int to learn about current international policing initiatives.

Brokers," who make contracts directly with the Colombian dollar purchasers.

In addition to announcing charges against the 34 members of the Colombian money-laundering organization, the United States Attorney today announced that Jose Douer-Ambar, a prominent Colombian industrialist who repeatedly purchased millions of dollars in the BMPE system over a period of years, has agreed to a deferred prosecution agreement in connection with which he has agreed to forfeit to the United States $20 million of BMPE proceeds, constituting the dollars that he purchased from the indicted peso brokers. In addition, the United States Attorney announced the issuance of seizure warrants authorizing seizure of, in aggregate, more than $1 million from more than 20 separate bank accounts.

Is it right for the U.S. Attorney to make deals with people who might be involved in drug running? What benefits might such deals bring?

Attacking the profits

United States Attorney General John Ashcroft stated:

"Today's arrests highlight the Justice Department's strategy to attack these drug cartels where it hurts most—on the money side. Those who choose to help hide the proceeds of illicit drug trafficking are as much a part of the problem as those who bring the drugs into this country, and they will be dealt with accordingly. We will not let these organizations keep their illgotten profits and continuously pump them into the drug pipeline."

Is money laundering really as serious as actual drug trafficking? Are the people who make and sell the drugs the real criminals, not the accountants and businesspeople?

If convicted, the … defendants face a maximum sentence of 20 years' imprisonment on each of the moneylaundering charges. In addition, various defendants face an additional maximum sentence of 5 years' imprisonment on illegal money-remitting and conspiracy charges.

Mr. Kelley praised the investigative efforts of the DEA, the NYPD, the IRS, the Office of the Special Narcotics Prosecutor for the City of New York, the Manhattan District Attorney's Office, the South Florida Money Laundering Strike Force, OCDETF, the DAS, the RCMP and the National Crime Squad.

Assistant United States Attorneys Boyd M. Johnson III, David Berardinelli, and Kevin R. Puvalowski are in charge of the prosecution.

Summary

In the first article, written in 2001, author Andrew Clark reports the initiatives of American senators of both main parties to stem the flow into U.S. banks of money acquired abroad through crime and corruption. Their proposals are an attempt to eliminate money laundering, a growing problem in which some of the foremost U.S. banks have unwittingly become involved. Among the most important suggested measures are the requirement for banks to record the identity of all account holders who are non-U.S. nationals and a complete ban on their dealing with shell banks that have no base anywhere. Although the legislation would give U.S. courts unprecedented jurisdiction over foreign banks, the main onus would be on the banks themselves. Many of them have protested the proposals on grounds of cost, and their misgivings seem to be shared by the administration of George W. Bush (2001–).

The second article is a press release announcing the breakup by the Drug Enforcement Administration (DEA) of an international crime syndicate that was exporting drugs from Colombia. The dollars generated by sales in the United States and Canada were passed by an informal money exchange system to Colombian businesses that wanted to avoid paying foreign trade tariffs. The latter deposited the money in bank accounts in various parts of the world. By the time the funds were transferred back to U.S. accounts, their origin was almost untraceable. The DEA bust resulted in the seizure of more than $20 million—evidence that the law-enforcement agencies can not only identify money laundering effectively but also act decisively to confiscate the takings of the perpetrators.

FURTHER INFORMATION:

 Books:

Rose-Ackerman, S., *Corruption and Government: Causes, Consequences and Reform*. Boston, MA: Cambridge University Press, 1999.

Stessens, G., *Money Laundering: A New International Law Enforcement Model*. Boston, MA: Cambridge University Press, 2000.

 Useful websites:

www.fatf-gafi.org
Financial Action Task Force on Money Laundering site.
www.imolin.org
International Money Laundering Information Network. Looks at international tools to prevent the crime.
http://www.state.gov/g/inl/rls/nrcrpt/2003/
International Narcotics Control Report, 2003, includes coverage regarding the prevention of money laundering.

The following debates in the Pro/Con series may also be of interest:

In this volume:

 Part 3: Crime, pages 124–125

 Topic 10 Do extradition treaties violate human rights?

 Topic 11 Should tax havens be made illegal?

IS MONEY LAUNDERING
TOO EASY?

YES: Recent scandals involving banks such as Citicorp show how easy it is for criminals and embezzlers to put funds into the United States

YES: It is too easy for bank officials to look the other way when huge sums of money are involved. Massive fines and prosecution would help deter them.

UNITED STATES
Do U.S. banking laws need tightening up?

DRUGS
Should banks that accept funds from drug cartels be fined?

NO: The United States is doing enough to deal with problems. Various sting operations have helped recover illegal funds.

NO: It is unfair to make banks responsible for fighting crime. It would be impossible as well as expensive for them to check every transaction that goes through their systems.

IS MONEY LAUNDERING TOO EASY?

KEY POINTS

YES: As much as $1.5 trillion is laundered each year. That is the equivalent of the GDP of many small nation-states; it has a real effect on the international economy.

YES: The operations that terror organizations use to disguise their funds are essentially the same as those used by money launderers. Effective action against the latter would undoubtedly affect terrorism.

INTERNATIONAL
Is money laundering a significant problem?

TERROR
Will more effective blocks on money laundering deter terrorist activity?

NO: The problem is not the money laundering: It is the crime that produces these funds in the first place. The fight against crimes is therefore much more important.

NO: Terrorists are careful to deal in much smaller sums of money than money launderers, so their transactions are likely to fall through the net

Topic 13

SHOULD DIPLOMATIC IMMUNITY BE RETAINED?

YES

FROM "PRIVILEGE OF DIPLOMATIC IMMUNITY FACING CHALLENGES FROM ALL SIDES"
THE WASHINGTON DIPLOMAT, MARCH 2002
JOHN SHAW

NO

"DIPLOMATIC IMMUNITY SHOULD END"
THE GUARDIAN, JULY 9, 1999
GEOFFREY ROBERTSON

INTRODUCTION

Diplomatic immunity, also known as extraterritoriality, is the legal principle that ambassadors and other officials of a foreign state are not subject to the jurisdiction of the country in which they are present. It extends not only to diplomats but also to foreign heads of state, troops in passage, and other categories of national representative. Following reports of diplomats being involved in illegal activities, including drug trafficking, murder, and even terrorism, many people are questioning whether diplomatic immunity should be retained.

The principles of diplomatic immunity are covered in various international agreements. The form of immunity varies, however, according to the precise status of the foreign representative and according to specific national laws or agreements between countries. There are more than 100,000 representatives of foreign governments, including their families, in the United States. They range from ambassadors to office staff. Many such people are entitled to a degree of immunity from U.S. law. That immunity covers both professional and personal actions, but it is not the same thing as a license to commit crimes. People whom it covers are still obliged to obey local laws, and the police investigate alleged criminal misconduct. If the State Department decides that someone with immunity should be prosecuted, it applies to his or her state to waive the immunity. If the state refuses, then the person is forced to leave the country and not allowed to return.

Diplomatic immunity has a long history. It was recognized in ancient cultures such as Egypt, Greece, and Rome that official representatives in other states could potentially have their activities curtailed by the host state. A system emerged of reciprocal arrangements that guaranteed diplomats immunity in one state in return for the same privilege in the other. It was codified law in Great Britain in 1708, following a scandal involving the Russian ambassador. The United States enacted a similar act in 1790, giving absolute immunity to diplomats, their families and servants, and their diplomatic staff. The act remained in force until 1978, when the Diplomatic Relations Act reduced the immunity of many lower-ranking diplomats. The new law brought the United States into line with the international Convention on Diplomatic Relations, signed at the United Nations in 1961.

> *"An ambassador is not simply an agent; he is also a spectacle."*
> —WALTER BAGEHOT (1826–1877),
> BRITISH ECONOMIST

Supporters argue that diplomatic immunity is necessary to allow national representatives working in other countries to perform their job. Without it, they claim, embassy, consular, and mission staff in other countries could be subject to legal systems very different from their own. To allow such officials to operate in potentially hostile nations, it is also necessary for countries such as the United States to extend diplomatic immunity in return. Advocates maintain that the importance of guaranteeing the principle of diplomatic freedom far outweighs the abuses of immunity that take place. Those abuses are largely minor, they argue—the majority involve offenses such as illegal parking and

shoplifting—and there are procedures in place for more serious crimes. When a Georgian diplomat was accused of killing an American child in a traffic accident in 1997, for example, Georgia waived his immunity. The diplomat stood trial and was sent to jail.

Some commentators, however, point to a number of high-profile cases in which immunity has been used as a cover for serious crimes. In 1984 in London, for example, a British police officer was killed by a shot that came from the Libyan Embassy (see page 169). Although the police believed that they knew the identity of the killer, he used diplomatic immunity to leave the country without being prosecuted.

There are also examples of the principles of extraterritoriality being set aside. In 1998 the British arrested former Chilean dictator Augusto Pinochet in London, who was wanted in Spain for crimes against Spanish nationals while president of Chile. The move challenged the principle of immunity for foreign heads of state. Pinochet was finally deemed too ill to stand trial and returned to Chile.

In 1993 Belgium created controversy when it passed a law—enacted in 1999—allowing its courts to hear cases involving genocide and crimes against humanity that occur outside Belgium and do not involve Belgians. The law does not recognize immunity even for serving political leaders, who can potentially be arrested while on Belgian soil. However, the International Court of Justice in The Hague ruled that Belgium could not issue a warrant for the arrest of a Congolese diplomat who had diplomatic immunity at the time his alleged crimes were committed.

The following two articles look at this debate in greater detail.

PRIVILEGE OF DIPLOMATIC IMMUNITY FACING CHALLENGES FROM ALL SIDES
John Shaw

John Shaw is a journalist on The Washington Diplomat. *This article was published in March 2002.*

YES

Diplomatic immunity is an ancient concept that is facing a raft of contemporary challenges. The very idea … is being questioned by segments of the public as they read sensational—often sensationalized—accounts of diplomats brazenly ignoring the laws of their host nations and appearing to be unaccountable for their actions.

Not surprisingly, sometimes the media seize on the relatively rare diplomatic indiscretions and present them as if they are regular, everyday occurrences. And a truly tragic situation, such as the 1997 auto accident in which Gueorgui Makharadze, a Georgian diplomat, killed a 16-year-old girl, angered many Americans and persuaded people across the world that diplomatic immunity was being soundly abused. That anger was softened only slightly when the Georgian government waived Makharadze's immunity, and he was convicted and given a seven-to-21-year sentence. (Makharadze has served about 80 percent of his minimum sentence and is now up for parole in his home country, where he has been serving his sentence since 2000.)

Do you think people should be allowed to serve their jail sentence in their own country? What advantages might there be?

Diplomatic immunity is also being challenged, or at least complicated, by expansive interpretations of international law in which courts in some nations are willing to consider suits against diplomats and political leaders.

Immunity in the future

The convening of ad hoc criminal courts for Rwanda and the former Yugoslavia and the impending creation of the International Criminal Court have raised intriguing questions about how diplomatic immunity will work in the future.

Yasser Arafat (1929–) is leader of the Palestine Liberation Organization; Ariel Sharon (1928–) became prime minister of Israel in 2001; Saddam Hussein (1937–) was dictator of Iraq until the 2003 U.S. invasion; Fidel Castro (1926–) has been president of Cuba since 1959. Why should such leaders be held to account by courts in Belgium?

Analysts, for example, have pondered legal developments in Belgium where lawsuits alleging human rights violations have been filed against more than a dozen past and present foreign leaders, including Yasser Arafat, Ariel Sharon, Saddam Hussein and Fidel Castro.

A Belgian law, which was adopted in 1993 and expanded in 1999, allows the nation's courts to hear cases of certain alleged atrocities, including genocide and other crimes against humanity, that took place outside of Belgium and don't involve Belgians.

… Under the provisions of this law, Belgium doesn't recognize the immunity of foreign officials, even currently serving leaders. The Belgian government wants to amend this law so there is at least immunity for serving politicians.

However, the World Court recently ruled that Belgium could not issue an arrest warrant for a Congolese diplomat because he had immunity at the time his crimes were allegedly committed, but the court did not strike down a controversial law that allows local judges to prosecute current and former heads of states in Belgium and around the world.

Why do serving politicians need protection from prosecution? Who does this benefit?

A vital cornerstone

Bruce Laingen, president of the American Academy of Diplomacy and a former American diplomat, said diplomatic immunity is a vital cornerstone of international affairs:

The American Academy of Diplomacy was founded in Washington, D.C., in 1983 to encourage the effectiveness of U.S. diplomacy. Go to www.academy ofdiplomacy.org to find out more.

"Diplomatic immunity is a very important principal. It's been around for a long, long time, and it's as important now as it's ever been. In fact, it may even be more crucial given the threat of rampant terrorism…. Diplomatic immunity is important in ensuring that the processes of diplomacy are conducted appropriately. When it is not respected there should be an uproar and expressions of outrage," he added.

Edith Ssempala, Uganda's ambassador to the United States, said diplomatic immunity is a bedrock feature of international law and needs to be treated with care.

"Diplomatic immunity is an important privilege that should be protected. But it's also very important that diplomats and ambassadors respect this privilege and accept full responsibility," Ssempala said.

Diplomatic immunity is a concept that has been part of the fiber of international relations for thousands of years. In his classic book, *Diplomacy*, Sir Harold Nicholson said this protection extends to the days of pre-history when warring tribes wished to negotiate with each other—if only to indicate that they had enough of the day's battle and would like a pause to collect their wounded and bury their dead….

Thucydides (died about 401 B.C.) was an Athenian politician and historian who spent much of his life traveling among the city-states of ancient Greece.

Historians observe that Thucydides's writings show that by the fifth century B.C., the Greeks had elaborated a system of diplomatic relations and that members of diplomatic missions were accorded certain immunities and considerations.

With the passage of the centuries, the idea of diplomatic immunity was refined, becoming a staple of international affairs. "The inviolability of ambassadors is sacred and acknowledged as such by all civilized peoples," Julius Caesar wrote more than 2000 years ago.

Diplomacy as a system—and immunity as a core principal—evolved slowly over time. Nicholson pointed out that it was not until the 15th century that Italian states appointed permanent ambassadors and that diplomacy as a profession was established. And it was not until after the Congress of Vienna in 1815 that the status and rules of diplomacy were set by international agreement.

Chas W. Freeman Jr., a former American diplomat and author of several books on diplomacy, said that diplomatic immunity became a bedrock feature of international affairs for practical as well as lofty reasons.

"A wise government will treat the diplomats accredited to it well and protect them from harm. It will then be able to demand that foreign governments do the same for its diplomats," he wrote....

Legal ruling

In an important legal ruling on diplomatic immunity several years ago in the United States, U.S. District Judge T.S. Ellis III argued forcefully that diplomatic immunity is crucial to the United States and, by implication, to all nations.

"Diplomatic immunity is a valuable and integral feature of our relations with foreign nations. To protect United States diplomats from criminal and civil prosecution in foreign lands with differing cultural and legal norms as well as fluctuating political climates, the United States has bargained to offer that same protection to diplomats visiting this country," he wrote.

"Because not all countries provide the level of due process to which the United States citizens have become accustomed and because diplomats are particularly vulnerable to exploitation for political purposes, immunity for American diplomats abroad is essential. And understandably, reciprocity is the price paid for that immunity," he said....

Ellis observed that a certain amount of unfairness is inherent in the concept of diplomatic immunity: A diplomat may commit a serious and violent crime, yet be absolutely immune from prosecution in this country.

Diplomatic immunity was established in its modern form by the Vienna Convention on Diplomatic Relations in 1961. In 1952, the United Nations General Assembly requested that the International Law Commission codify international law on "diplomatic intercourse and immunities." The commission

The Congress of Vienna was held to discuss the shape of Europe following the abdication of the French emperor Napoleon and the collapse of his empire, which covered much of the continent.

The ruling was passed in 1996. You can read the full ruling at http://caselaw.lp.findlaw.com/cgi-bin/getcase.pl?court=4th&navby=case&no=951732p.

Why do you think that the judge believes that diplomats are vulnerable to exploitation? Is there any other answer to the problem apart from immunity?

prepared a draft text by 1957, received comments from 21 nations, and then presented a draft treaty to the General Assembly in 1958.

The UN Conference on Diplomatic Intercourse and Immunities convened in Vienna in 1961 ... adopted the Vienna Convention for ratification by the member nations. Forty nations initially signed the treaty. Since then, more than 150 nations have become party to the treaty.

"Peoples of all nations from ancient times have recognized the status of diplomatic agents," the treaty begins.

It adds that diplomatic immunities and privileges are important to "contribute to the development of friendly relations among nations." It asserts that the treaty's purpose "is not to benefit individuals but to ensure the efficient performance of the functions of diplomatic relations."

The objective of the Vienna Convention is to ensure that the staffs of diplomatic missions are afforded the highest level of privileges and immunities in the host country so they may effectively perform their duties....

Should the United States offer immunity to diplomats from countries that have not signed the Vienna Convention?

Limited immunity

A separate treaty, the Vienna Convention on Consular Relations in 1963, grants a very limited level of privileges and immunities to consular officials who work in offices that are located outside national capitals. There is a common misunderstanding that consular staffs have diplomatic status and are entitled to diplomatic immunity.

Under international law, consular officers have only official acts or functional immunity in respect to both criminal and civil matters, and their personal inviolability is quite limited. The property of consular officers is not inviolable....

Most staffs in international organizations in the United States enjoy only official-acts immunity and have no personal inviolability. In many cases, the senior executives of these staffs have been accorded privileges and immunities equal to those of diplomatic agents. This immunity, for example, is extended to the secretary-general of the UN, and senior officials of the International Monetary Fund, the World Bank and the Organization of American States.

Only governments—not individuals—can waive diplomatic immunity. The sending nation, in effect, owns these privileges and immunities. The U.S. State Department requests waivers of immunity in every case where the prosecutor advises that, except for the immunity, charges would be pursued. In serious cases, if a waiver is refused, the offender will be expelled from the United States.

This means that consular officials cannot be prosecuted for actions carried out as part of their job, but that they have very little immunity for their actions outside their work. Is this fair?

DIPLOMATIC IMMUNITY SHOULD END
Geoffrey Robertson

Geoffrey Robertson is one of Great Britain's leading trial lawyers. This article appeared in 1999.

Augusto Pinochet was arrested in London in 1998. Numerous states in Europe wanted him to be extradited to face charges of various crimes, but in the event, he was declared too sick to stand trial and sent back to Chile. See pages 34–35.

NO

Fifteen years ago, colleagues of PC Yvonne Fletcher were forced to protect her killer and his accomplices as they left the Libyan "People's Bureau" in St James Square en route to their heroes' welcome in Tripoli: the smoking gun used in the assassination was in their inviolable diplomatic baggage. This sickening spectacle was approved by the prime minister, Margaret Thatcher, on the same principle she now claims should protect a mass murderer, Augusto Pinochet. It is the principle of "sovereign immunity", a law which assists so much crime—from torture and drug running to shoplifting and unlawful parking—that its reform has become a moral and practical imperative.

Diplomatic immunity—the law which allowed the Libyan killers to escape with a police escort—is an offshoot of the theory that government members and agents are legally untouchable abroad for anything done during their term of office, even if it's a crime of private lust (like rape or child abuse). The Pinochet case is important because the law lords found one small loophole: it does not protect an ex-official of a state from prosecution for crimes against humanity, such as genocide or torture, where sovereign immunity is overridden by an international convention.

Does Robertson strengthen or weaken his case by comparing parking fines with serious crimes?

A license for crime

But this still leaves diplomats free to murder and rape and run up unpaid parking fines, because they are protected by a convention agreed in Vienna in 1961. It was drafted by government lawyers under orders to puff diplomats up with as much power as possible, so they bestowed upon them not just immunity but impunity, covering every crime and misdemeanour committed during foreign service, whether or not in the course of duty.

This may have been expedient during the cold war, to protect diplomats from being framed.... But it produced the result that foreign officials—and their spouses and children and chauffeurs—may fearlessly engage in serious crime, using their ... embassy premises and baggage for drug and gun-running and money laundering, or assist terrorists with whom their state is in political sympathy. The only thing that

COMMENTARY: The Libyan embassy siege

The siege that took place at the Libyan embassy in London in spring 1984 was one of numerous high-profile incidents that drew public attention to diplomatic immunity and its potential abuses. Libya is an Islamic state led by Colonel Muammar Qaddafi (1942–), whose internal policies have driven many of his opponents into exile around the world, including London. On April 17, 1984, pro- and anti-Qaddafi protestors were demonstrating peacefully outside the Libyan embassy in London's St. James's Square. A small group of London police were present to keep order. Without warning, someone fired a machine gun at the demonstration from an upper window in the embassy. The shots hit 11 people, including Police Constable Yvonne Fletcher, who later died of her wounds in the hospital.

The shooting created a dilemma for the British government. The public was outraged by the murder of an unarmed police officer in broad daylight. However, international law recognized the Libyan embassy as Libyan territory and prohibited the British police from entering its premises and arresting the killer. While the Libyan government denied any responsibility for the attack, angry mobs surrounded the British embassy in the Libyan capital of Tripoli. Meanwhile the British press demanded that Margaret Thatcher's (1979–1992) government take firm action against the Libyan embassy, which had been sealed off by police.

Tense standoff

Police negotiators opened discussions with the embassy, which was being run not by professional diplomats but by a group of officially sanctioned pro-Qaddafi student activists. The police sent in food to the embassy and assured the students that they would respect the immunity of the embassy, and that they would not storm the building. Such an attack had been successfully mounted against the Iranian embassy in London three years earlier, but only at the request of the Iranian government after a terrorist group had taken over the building and executed Iranian diplomats.

The British government demanded that the Libyan government waive its immunity temporarily to allow the police to search the embassy for evidence, arms, and explosives: The Libyans refused. A tense standoff lasted for several days until the British government decided that it had no option but to break diplomatic relations with Libya and expel the embassy staff from the country. There were no arrests, although the British police believed that they knew who was responsible. They photographed and fingerprinted all the embassy staff before they were sent back to Libya.

Some 20 years after the shooting Libya began to make diplomatic gestures toward western countries. As part of the process, in 1999 Libya accepted responsibility for the death of PC Fletcher. In 2004 British and Libyan police launched a joint investigation into the killing.

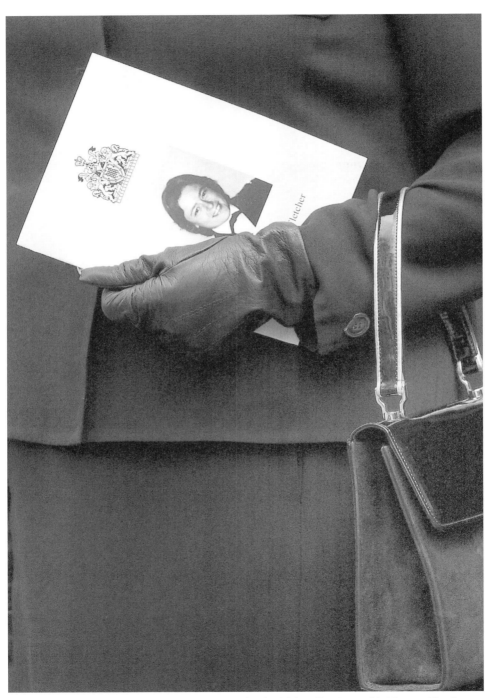

A mourner carries a program with a photograph of British Police Constable Yvonne Fletcher at the memorial service held in April 2004 to mark the 20th anniversary of the officer's shooting.

can happen is a declaration that they are persona non grata, followed by a police escort to the airport, unless their sending state waives immunity.

This law is obviously much wider than is necessary to protect the essential function of a diplomatic mission. The Libyan example ... is a singular outrage, but at street level in London abuse of diplomatic immunity is reflected in the city's unpaid parking tickets and unprosecutable offences of shoplifting. Some years ago, Scotland Yard reckoned that 40% of these unrequited crimes are committed by the vehicles or wives of foreign diplomats. (The US, plagued by more diplomats than any other country, has recently adopted a novel approach to their unpaid parking fines: it tallies the penalties incurred by every embassy and deducts the total from that country's foreign aid....).

Old-fashioned justification

The rationale for absolute immunity—that diplomatic missions keep open lines of communication between unfriendly states—is anachronistic in this age of email and video-conferencing. The fiction which sustains sovereignty—that state dignity would be lowered if its officials were prosecuted abroad—is absurd when states are headed by Saddam Hussein and Slobodan Milosevic. What sort of "respect" can accord impunity to ... the president of Equatorial Guinea who last year murdered his uncle?

When PC Fletcher was murdered, the Thatcher government lacked the confidence to declare a restriction on diplomatic immunity, namely that foreign officials would be put on trial if there was overwhelming evidence of their involvement in serious crime. Five years later, drug-running by diplomats became so serious that the UK at last threatened to sniff—and possibly to scan—inviolable baggage (although diplomats would not be prosecuted). The time has now come for the UK to state that foreign states will henceforth be expected to waive immunity for any ambassadorial official or family member accused of serious crime.

Robin Cook should begin by insisting on surrender by Libya of those diplomats suspected of involvement in the Yvonne Fletcher murder. It is not satisfactory merely for Libya to accept "general responsibility" for that outrage: the judgement at Nuremberg lays down that crimes are committed by individuals, not by states. When they are committed by diplomats with impunity, the notion of "restoring diplomatic relations" is oxymoronic.

Persona non grata is Latin for "unacceptable person." It refers to someone who is unwelcome or not in favor.

Even if diplomats have immunity, should it be extended to cover their spouses?

Slobodan Milosevic was president of Serbia during the Balkan wars of the early 1990s. In February 2002 he was put on trial for crimes against humanity for his part in the wars. See Volume 15, Human Rights, page 206 for information on the trial.

Robin Cook (1946–) was British foreign secretary from 1997 to 2001. In 2004 Libya began to cooperate with British police to investigate the killing of PC Fletcher. See the box on page 169.

Summary

The question of whether diplomatic immunity should be retained is a topical one. In the first article journalist John Shaw describes the history of diplomatic immunity. He says that it has fulfilled a necessary role in the relations between states since before written records began. He argues that the idea that the system is widely abused reflects journalistic exaggeration, and that a failure to recognize how well the existing system serves American interests reflects both shortsightedness and xenophobia. He also notes that some recent innovations that aim to extend the jurisdiction of national courts internationally are untried. He argues that they may damage the conduct of international affairs if they are implemented in a hasty fashion.

Trial lawyer Geoffrey Robertson, on the other hand, argues that legal immunity to prosecution is too extensive because it effectively places some individuals above the law. Diplomatic immunity may have had some valid basis in the past when diplomatic missions were the only way in which unfriendly states could keep open lines of communication between states that were in disagreement or even at war. This argument no longer applies, he argues, in a world with simple and rapid telecommunications. He uses the example of the shooting of a British policewoman by Libyan embassy staff to highlight the potential abuse of the system. Robertson goes on to argue that there is mounting evidence that individuals use diplomatic immunity and privileges into order to smuggle drugs and arms. The answer, he asserts, is for the British to demand that foreign governments waive all immunity for any of their representatives accused of a serious crime.

FURTHER INFORMATION:

Books:

Gordon, Philip, and Jeremy Shapiro, *Allies at War: America, Europe, and the Split over Iraq.* New York: McGraw-Hill, 2004.

Kissinger, Henry, *Diplomacy.* New York: Columbia University Press, 1989.

Useful websites:

http://ask.yahoo.com/ask/20020116.html
Explains what diplomatic immunity is.

http://www.canadianliberty.bc.ca/
liberty-vs-security/richard_sanders-bill-c35.html
Looks at the idea of extending immunity to terrorists.

http://www.state.gov/m/ds/immunities/c9118.htm/
State Department site. Includes information on the role of diplomats in the international arena. Has a useful chart on what diplomats have immunity from.

The following debates in the Pro/Con series may also be of interest:

In this volume:

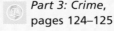
Topic 2 Should heads of state be prosecuted for crimes against humanity?

Augusto Pinochet: Patriot or war criminal?, pages 34–35

Part 3: Crime, pages 124–125

SHOULD DIPLOMATIC IMMUNITY BE RETAINED?

YES: Diplomats represent their own country's interests; they need protection from the host nation's laws, which might be used to constrain their activities

YES: The vast majority of diplomats comply with the laws of their host country. Sensationalist reporting is partly responsible for making abuse seem more widespread than it really is.

ABOVE THE LAW
Should diplomats be above national laws?

ABUSE
Are reports of diplomats abusing their privileges exaggerated?

NO: This is an old-fashioned attitude, and no one, not even a head of state, should now be allowed to violate accepted laws

NO: It is common for diplomats to use immunity to escape minor charges such as traffic offenses. Some also use immunity as a cover for more serious crimes, such as drug smuggling.

SHOULD DIPLOMATIC IMMUNITY BE RETAINED?

KEY POINTS

YES: Giving diplomats only partial immunity leaves them open to trumped-up charges about serious crimes

YES: Diplomats represent the best of their countries. Being deported is not only embarrassing but degrading for them and for the country they represent.

IMMUNITY FOR ALL CRIMES?
Should diplomats have protection from all crimes?

DEPORTATION
Does the threat of deportation help keep diplomats' behavior in check?

NO: Like everyone else, diplomats must be held responsible for serious crimes, such as terrorism, sexual crimes, or murder

NO: Deportation is not an effective deterrent if a diplomat's sending country condones rather than punishes his or her behavior

THE UNITED STATES AND INTERNATIONAL LAW

The position of the United States in international law is a complex one. It is complicated largely by the fact that the United States is the most powerful and influential nation in the world. That means both that it is expected to take the lead in the development and application of international law—which sometimes relies on the support of U.S. financial or military contributions—and that it is often exposed to more criticism than other nations because of its high profile and influence. These two factors have led to the evolution of an occasionally uneasy relationship between the United States and the rest of the world community. A notable expression of this uneasiness was the refusal of the government of George W. Bush in 2002 to ratify U.S. membership in the International Criminal Court (ICC). Established by the United Nations and endorsed by a majority of the world's nations, the ICC is intended to be the major forum for the prosecution of war crimes and crimes against humanity. It was endorsed by Bush's predecessor, Bill Clinton; but the Bush administration argued that the position of the United States and its involvement in international peace-keeping and other actions might leave American military and other personnel open to many malicious or politically motivated prosecutions.

Bush's reluctance to become part of the international legal system is far from unprecedented in U.S. history. At various times since the 1823 Monroe Doctrine rejected European interference in the Americas and precluded U.S. involvement in the Old World, the United States has been isolationist in its attitudes. At such times it has rejected both foreign interference in U.S. affairs and any international role for the United States. Such was the case after World War I (1914–1918), for example, when the United States Congress refused to ratify the League of Nations, the body set up largely at the behest of President Woodrow Wilson to resolve international disputes.

In other periods since World War I, however, the United States' impulse toward isolationism has proved incompatible with its widespread economic and strategic interests. America played a major role in trying to legislate limitations on the world's shipping in the 1920s, it was instrumental in setting up the international tribunals in Berlin and Tokyo at the end of World War II, and it has taken a leading role in UN peacekeeping operations.

However, while some countries applaud U.S. military interference in international affairs, others are more wary of it. They see U.S. military and financial superiority as an opportunity for U.S. abuse and bullying of other nations. They say that international law should limit rather than extend U.S. influence on world affairs.

War on Terrorism

Critics argue that the terrorist action taken against America on September 11, 2001, gave George W. Bush's administration more of an excuse to intervene in other nations' affairs. The United States gathered allies and wide support for its war in Afghanistan, which it suspected of harboring Al Qaeda terrorists. Its 2003 invasion of

political power is so great that its refusal to support a particular initiative virtually condemns it to fail. Some critics argue that the U.S. refusal to ratify the Kyoto Protocol—an international agreement aimed at reducing the production of harmful greenhouse gases around the world— and the International Criminal Court have hindered them. However, other observers believe that the United States is simply one member of the international community, and that its membership in organizations such as the UN means that its influence can be countered by that of other nations or

---

"The powerful do what they want anyway; treaties and systems of world order don't offer them any protection."
—NOAM CHOMSKY, POLITICAL COMMENTATOR (2004)

Iraq, however, drew widespread criticism at home and around the world. So, too, did its decision to detain prisoners from the Afghanistan conflict in Guantanamo Bay, Cuba, without putting them on trial or even giving them access to lawyers. In 2004 the U.S. Supreme Court declared that some 600 or so prisoners, who had been detained for over two years, were entitled to legal hearings and legal representation.

A complex relationship

The last three debates in this book all reflect the multifaceted nature of the United States' relationship with the rest of the world. Topic 14 asks whether America has too much influence on international law. In certain cases—as with the historical precedent of the League of Nations—U.S. economic and

international organizations. Topic 15 considers whether the United States is the ultimate defender of international human rights. For many people America's role in international affairs places it under moral obligation to protect and spread civil and human rights around the world. Others counter that U.S. economic interests often prevent the condemnation of human rights abuses; their evidence includes the U.S. decision to promote trade with China, for example, which has a poor human rights record.

The last topic in the volume looks specifically at the legal status of the War on Terrorism. While some people see the U.S. actions in Afghanistan and Iraq as a justified response to terrorism and threats to peace, others believe that America has broken international law.

Topic 14
DOES THE UNITED STATES HAVE TOO MUCH INFLUENCE ON INTERNATIONAL LAW?

YES
"SAVING KYOTO, IN NAME OR SUBSTANCE?"
SOUTH-NORTH DEVELOPMENT MONITOR, 2001
CHAKRAVARTHI RAGHAVAN

NO
"THE KYOTO KILLERS"
CATO INSTITUTE, AUGUST 2001
PATRICK J. MICHAELS

INTRODUCTION

The three main sources of international law are established custom, general principles of law, and international treaties. In recent years the last have proved the most controversial. Treaties are obligations that states accept voluntarily in association with other states. In the past decade the United States has refused to sign or to ratify a number of treaties and agreements that have been endorsed by many other countries. Some commentators believe that such a refusal exerts a damaging influence on international law.

In many situations involving international law, the United States ostensibly has no greater influence than any other country. In the General Assembly of the United Nations, for example—which laid the foundations for international law in 1945—it has the same voting rights as other countries. In practice, however, the economic strength of the United States gives it huge influence over other nations. The disapproval of the U.S. government can mean the loss of international aid, lucrative trade contracts, and other financial advantages.

One regularly cited example of U.S. influence over international law concerns the Kyoto Protocol of 1997. The protocol imposed legally binding targets on ratifying countries for the reduction of greenhouse gases, which are thought to contribute to global warming. President George W. Bush, who came to power after the protocol was signed, announced in 2001 that the United States would not ratify it as it stood, partly because countries such as India and China were excluded, and partly because it threatened to damage the U.S. economy. Critics argue that since the United States produces a large proportion of global greenhouse gas emissions—more than 30 percent of the total—this refusal has made the protocol largely ineffective, although it was supported by the majority of the world's nations.

Other key environmental treaties that the United States has yet to ratify include the International Standards Organization (ISO) greenhouse gas emissions standards and the UN Framework Convention on Biological Diversity. One concern is that U.S. refusal to ratify these agreements not only lessens their effectiveness but also encourages other nations to do the same. They are reluctant, for example, to put their industries at a disadvantage by imposing stricter environmental requirements on them than apply to their U.S. competitors.

"Unfortunately, our affluent society has also been an effluent society."
—HUBERT H. HUMPHREY
(1911–1978), POLITICIAN

Another area of international law in which U.S. attitudes seem to be counter to the international consensus is the treaty to establish the International Criminal Court (ICC), a permanent tribunal set up to try people accused of genocide, crimes against humanity, and war crimes. By 2002 the treaty had been signed by 138 governments, including that of the United States, and ratified by 66. Only 60 ratifications were required for the court's jurisdiction to begin. However, in May 2002 George W. Bush's administration effectively

withdrew the United States from the treaty. It was concerned that its military personnel could be brought before the court in politically motivated cases. Some observers saw the "unsigning" of a treaty as a worrying precedent that might encourage other governments to "unsign" treaties that no longer suit their purposes.

Supporters of the U.S. stance argue that it is not seeking to influence international law but rather to define its limits. National sovereignty, they argue, takes priority over international law. In other words, international courts have no jurisdiction over U.S. citizens. This is cited as a reason why, for example, the United States is one of only two members of the United Nations not to have ratified the 1989 Convention on the Rights of the Child. Although U.S. governments do not disagree with the principle of children's rights, they believe that the convention procedures would force the United States to account to the international community for its domestic policies. This is anathema to many Americans.

People who do not believe that the United States has too much influence in international law point to cases in which, they argue, other nations are influencing U.S. legislation. The United States, for example, faces near unanimous condemnation from its close allies about the continued use of the death penalty. That condemnation is beginning to have an effect on domestic law. The U.S. government has accepted, for example, that if it seeks the extradition of a terrorist suspect from a nation that does not have the death penalty, then the death penalty will not be able to apply in the case.

The following two articles address some of the issues in this debate.

SAVING KYOTO, IN NAME OR SUBSTANCE?
Chakravarthi Raghavan

Chakravarthi Raghavan is chief editor of the South–North Development Monitor, a publication founded by the International Foundation for Development Alternatives to provide information and analysis on global events from the perspective of the developing world.

Greenhouse gases, such as carbon dioxide and sulfur dioxide produced by burning fossil fuels, are thought to trap the sun's heat in earth's atmosphere. Many scientists believe that they contribute to global warming.

Is the state of the U.S. economy more important than preventing pollution and environmental abuses that might harm the whole planet?

YES

Ministers and diplomats from around the world are meeting over the next two weeks in Bonn at the Climate Conference, where there will be efforts to 'salvage' the Kyoto protocol—after the blow to its viability by the US President George Bush's refusal to endorse it, and with Japan now engaged in fence-straddling exercise between the US and the EU position.

The Bonn meeting is a resumption of the sixth session of the Conference of Parties to the convention (COP6), which was suspended last November in the Hague after negotiators failed to reach an agreement.

The COP has to finalise the rules for implementing the Kyoto protocol and spurring the industrial nations to achieve their targets, as also adopt measures to strengthen the financial and technical cooperation between developed and developing countries on climate friendly policies and technologies.

The protocol and George W. Bush

The Kyoto protocol (1997) set the targets for the industrialized nations to reduce their greenhouse gas emissions by at least 5% compared to their 1990 levels and to achieve this 2008–2012.

While setting these levels of commitments, the protocol left some of the rules and mechanisms to achieve this to be set by rules, and the COP had been engaged in this task when the decision of President Bush to withdraw the US backing has raised a whole range of issues.

Mr. Bush has argued that the targets set and the commitments to be undertaken by the US would affect the US economy, while the EU has been insisting that the industrial nations must take the steps to reverse the upward trends in man-made emissions of greenhouse gases held to be responsible for global warming.

Three working groups of the Inter-government panel on climate change (IPCC) have now come out with detailed assessments and estimations that show that the global

Many international companies are guilty of environmental abuses, including air pollution. The Kyoto Protocol would help reduce global carbon dioxide emissions.

warming if things remain unchanged would be much greater than originally forecast, and providing some estimations of the loss to the world, and to various regions, and the need for countries to take climate change mitigation actions.

Protocols and rules

At pre-conference press briefing here and in Amsterdam last week, the Executive Director of the UN Framework Convention on Climate Change, Mr. Michael Zammit Cutajar, suggested that after six years of arduous and complex negotiations, it was time "to finalize the system that will guide global action on climate change for the next two decades and beyond."

The United States has refused to be bound by the Kyoto targets, even though a previous administration signed the treaty. Should all countries have the right to pull out of treaties if their government changes? See pages 188–189.

The Kyoto protocol, he underlined, set out a framework for encouraging markets to work for emission targets, setting legally-binding targets and time tables supported by rigorous performance indicators, and a range of flexible options to achieve the targets at the lowest economic costs.

The protocol also provides incentives for emission-saving investments in developing countries.

"It would be a great waste to leave the rule-book for this massive undertaking unfinished, when we have already come so far," said Zammit Cutajar.

"Once the rules are finalized, governments will be in a better position to decide in what political context to apply them," he said. "I hope they will do so by bringing the protocol into force."

Ratification

For the protocol to come into force it needs 55 ratifications including that of the industrialized countries accounting for at least 55% of the total 1990 carbon dioxide emissions.

Transition economies are those developing free-market economies, such as China and the former states of the Soviet Union.

The US accounts for 31% and with Australia and Canada for 41.5%.

The EU, the transition economies, Switzerland, New Zealand and Russia account for 49.5% and Japan for 8.5%.

The protocol cannot come into force unless it is ratified by both the EU and Japan, and the latter as it goes into the Bonn meeting has made clear that while it backed the Kyoto protocol, it would not join with the EU in going ahead with ratification and isolating the US.

In any event, unless the US at some point or the other comes in and joins the protocol, attempts to forge ahead would not be very effective.

There has been some talk of 'amending' the Kyoto protocol. But an amendment is possible only after it enters into force. However, there is talk of working on an amendment that would bring in the US, and doing it in such a way that both could come into effect at the same time.

Fate of the protocol

While the fate of the Kyoto protocol is now tied to the three-way talks (US, EU and Japan), the developing countries are in effect sitting back and watching.

However there is a danger in their laid-back attitude.

Their commitments come into play only at the second stage, after the industrial nations have taken their steps, and have also provided financial assistance as well as technological help to developing countries to make the transition.

Among its objections to the Kyoto protocol, the US has argued that the developing countries, particularly the big countries like China, India and Brazil won't be taking any actions to reduce their own emissions.

So unless the developing countries watch out, any compromise that may be forged among the three (US, EU and Japan) may be promoted by trying to pressure the major developing countries to do their own share, but without any financial aid or technological help and transfer of technologies.

A major U.S. objection to the Kyoto Protocol is that its implementation will be expensive. That will increase the price of U.S. goods compared to those of competitors such as China that do not implement the Kyoto measures.

Developed vs. undeveloped world

In fact in the current round of new services talks, the US, Europe and Japan are trying to 'gain' the markets of the developing countries in terms of energy and other services— which would involve their enterprises gaining access to the markets of developing countries, through investments and 'technology' licensing accords. These, may well result in further outflows from the developing world, rather than their getting aid from the developed to meet the climate change problems, and the costs of mitigation.

It is not as if the developing countries are united.

A large number of island economies facing 'extinction' as a result of global warming and rise in sea levels are trying to get the major industrial nations to take actions, but at some point may join in putting some moral pressure on the major developing countries to do their share too.

The unfolding scenario is a very tricky one, and needs all the diplomatic skills and firm stands by the developing countries.

Sea levels are predicted to rise by around 3 feet during the 21st century due to global warming. That would endanger islands such as the Maldives and low-lying coastal nations such as Bangladesh. Go to http://www.earth-policy.org/Updates/Update2.htm to read about the effect of rising sea levels on the United States.

THE KYOTO KILLERS
Patrick J. Michaels

Patrick J. Michaels is a professor of environmental science at the University of Virginia. He is well known for his views on global warming, which he believes is a vastly overrated threat. This piece was written about a "Conference of the Parties" to Kyoto held in Bonn, Germany, in August 2001.

NO

Predictably, our European friends spent July 16 berating the United States for its refusal to go along with the infamous Kyoto Protocol on global warming. As most people know, Kyoto is an international agreement to reduce the emissions of greenhouse gases that, in reality, has no detectable influence on climate and costs a fortune.....

Chief among Monday's berators was Jürgen Trittin, Germany's Environment Minister, who thundered that, "We cannot allow the country with the biggest emissions of greenhouse gases to escape responsibility." That's us, because we have the world's biggest economy (which just happens to also be one of the most energy-efficient).

So who killed Kyoto? If any one person will be fingered by history, it will be Trittin himself. If any group of nations is to be singled out, it will be the EU, which has been out of step with the rest of the world on Kyoto since day one.

The last best chance

Kyoto's last best chance at adoption was last November, when the same people who are now berating us in Bonn met at The Hague, two weeks after Election Day. The Clinton-Gore team, struggling to find some economically defensible way of meeting Kyoto's totally unrealistic target—which would require a 33 percent reduction in total U.S. emissions (read: energy use)—proposed that we meet half of that target by planting trees, building up the organic content of our soils, and selling/giving clean power production technology to polluting, poor (the two are highly correlated) nations.

Would it be easier for the United States simply to cut its energy use rather than to adopt these other measures? What do you and your family do to try to reduce energy use? Are environmentally friendly policies emphasized enough?

Jürgen Trittin and the French Environment Minister, Dominique Voynet, said no. To them, speaking for the EU, the United States had to meet Kyoto by directly reducing energy use. Here they proved to even many radical American greens that Kyoto has nothing to do with climate and everything to do with hatred for the United States, very chic these days in Berlin, Paris and London.

Forests can help reduce atmospheric carbon dioxide, which trees convert to oxygen through their leaves.

So, the United States then proposed that it would only salt away 40 percent of its emissions in trees. No, said Trittin, Voynet and the EU. 30 percent? 20 percent? No. No. President Clinton gained the intercession of his friend, British PM Tony

COMMENTARY: Russia's key decision

Once the United States declared that it no longer intended to ratify the Kyoto Protocol, Russia's role in ratification became critical. Without Russian ratification the protocol is unlikely ever to come into force. It requires the participation of developed countries accounting for at least 55 percent of the world's 1990 emissions of carbon dioxide. By April 2004 the 122 ratifying nations represented just 44.2 percent of the required level of emissions. The participation of Russia, which produced 17 percent of world emissions in 1990, is crucial, therefore, if the protocol is ever to go ahead.

Strong position

Since the breakup of the Soviet Union in 1990 the economies of many of its separate states have collapsed, leading to a reduction in their level of greenhouse gas emissions. As a result, Russia should easily meet its commitments under the Kyoto Protocol should it decide to ratify the agreement. Since its emissions levels were well below the targets agreed on in 1997, it would likely benefit financially from selling "emissions credits" to other nations. Russia and other countries whose target limits were already above the emissions they produced in 1997 are entitled to sell parts of their entitlements to nations that are over their own target limits. The likely potential buyers are the Annex I (industrialized) nations bound by the protocol. Such "emissions trading"—which may generate millions of dollars—is intended to reward countries that meet or improve on their targets while also providing an incentive to other countries to meet their targets as soon as possible.

Mixed messages

Despite Russia's strong position and the general expectation that it would ratify the protocol, in September 2003 Russian President Vladimir Putin (2000–) declared his reluctance to commit. He cited a lack of faith by Russian scientists in the theory that global warming is largely caused by emissions of carbon dioxide. Putin declared that Russia would have to go through the treaty in detail before making a final decision.

The position became further confused at the end of 2003. One of Putin's top economic advisers announced that Russia had no intention of ratifying the treaty in its present form, only for a Russian government minister to insist the next day that no such decision had been made, and that the government continued to "move toward ratification" despite continuing reservations. The subject was discussed at a EU summit in May 2004, when Putin implied that he would proceed to ratification as soon as possible, making the full implementation of the Kyoto Protocol far more likely. However, in July 2004 Andrei Illarionov, a respected economist and Putin's adviser, said that Putin supported the Kyoto "process" but not the protocol.

Jürgen Tritten, Germany's environment minister, is a vocal advocate of the Kyoto Protocol.

Blair. Voynet then turned on him, saying that he "had conceded too much to America."

In disgust, the U.S. negotiation team packed its bags and left. As it later admitted to *USA Today*, the final proposals would have caused grave economic damage. On the way out, EU security guards sat on their hands, as green demonstrators assaulted U.S. negotiator Frank Loy with a pie in the face on world television.

Surely the EU knew that … there was a pretty good chance George Bush was going to be the next president. And not long after this happened, National Security Advisor Condoleeza Rice announced, "Kyoto is dead."

For that, we have been subject to incessant rants about the United States being a "pariah" and a "rogue state." So who's the pariah here? Kyoto doesn't apply to China, the world's most populous nation. Nor India, the second largest. Are people in Russia clamoring for its adoption? What about Indonesia, Pakistan, the Middle East? Africa has real fish to fry, like AIDS.

It is clear that the vast majority of the world's citizens either aren't bound by Kyoto or don't care anyway. The United States is merely siding with the majority against a vocal and radical European minority that supports an ineffectual and expensive treaty, which they say can only be implemented in a fashion that will cause us (and, ultimately, the rest of the world) grave harm. There is no way the U.S. Senate will ratify it, anyway.

A bad bet

Kyoto always was sickly. At its inception, in December 1997, the Europeans pressed for impossibly large emission reductions, agreeing to a cut to 8 percent below 1990 levels for a five-year period centered around 2010. At Kyoto in 1997, as in The Hague in 2000, the EU proved incapable of standing up to its most radical green elements. Nor has the EU learned from these mistakes. On July 16 in Bonn the 15 EU leaders issued a joint declaration promising to fulfill their treaty commitments, adding one final farce to this tragic comedy. Why anyone would engage in a failed effort to do something that everyone knows wouldn't even have a measurable effect on global climate remains a mystery.

So, who killed Kyoto? Not us. Bush was merely the coroner. Jurgen Trittin, now railing about holding the United States "responsible" for his own irresponsibility, was the perpetrator, and the EU, wildly out of step with the rest of the world, was the accomplice. But they're Not Guilty, by reason of insanity.

Michaels implies that European security guards deliberately did nothing to stop an attack on a U.S. representative. Does that sound realistic to you? What might have been the motives for such inaction?

Although China and India are the world's most populous nations, they produce respectively 12.7 percent and 4 percent of fuel-related carbon dioxide emissions. The United States produces around 31 percent. Do you think these figures strengthen or weaken Michaels's point?

If global warming is really such a threat, would it be better to try to reduce it, even if that effort cannot completely succeed?

Summary

If the Kyoto Protocol ever comes into force, its targets and timetables will be legally binding on all ratifying nations. Therefore, this treaty illustrates a situation in which the United States may (or may not) have too much influence on international law. In March 2001 President George W. Bush indicated that the United States did not intend to ratify Kyoto. The two articles present different views as to who is to blame for the U.S. withdrawing its support.

Clearly for Chakravarthi Raghavan it is the United States that is at fault. The protocol needs 55 ratifications if it is to come into force, including those of the industrialized countries accounting for at least 55 percent of the total 1990 carbon dioxide emissions. The United States, the largest producer of carbon dioxide, has refused to ratify. Although Kyoto could still go ahead if Russia joins the ratifying nations, the author believes that without U.S. support "attempts to forge ahead would not be very effective."

By contrast, Patrick J. Michaels believes that the European Union (EU) is out of step with the rest of the world. He rejects European criticism of the United States and blames the Europeans for blocking the treaty's "last best chance" for implementation. Europeans blocked U.S. proposals to compensate for carbon dioxide production, including through technology transfer and planting trees. Kyoto is set to fail, therefore, because of EU intransigence and inflexibility. It is also set to be ineffectual, because it does not include developing nations such as China and India. In Michaels's view the United States is merely "siding with the majority" in its view that Kyoto would damage domestic economies were it to come into force.

FURTHER INFORMATION:

Books:

Donnelly, Jack, *Universal Human Rights in Theory and Practice*. Ithaca, NY: Cornell University Press, 2002.

Useful websites:

http://www.brainyencyclopedia.com/encyclopedia/i/in/international_law.html
E-encyclopedia entry on international law. Looks at background, issues, and other aspects.
http://www.deathpenaltyinfo.org/article.php?scid=17&did=806
Article on the death penalty and international influence on the United States.
http://www.globalissues.org/EnvIssues/GlobalWarming/Kyoto.asp
Article on Kyoto conference. Discusses America's role on the conference.

The following debates in the Pro/Con series may also be of interest:

In this volume:

Part 4: The United States and international law, pages 174–175

The Kyoto Protocol, pages 188–189

Topic 15 Is the United States the ultimate defender of international human rights?

DOES THE UNITED STATES HAVE TOO MUCH INFLUENCE ON INTERNATIONAL LAW?

YES: America is "unsigning" or stalling on ratification of a number of treaties; for example, it is the only UN member (apart from Somalia) not to have ratified the Rights of the Child Convention

YES: U.S. citizens are entitled to be subject to the jurisdiction of their own courts in all cases

INTERNATIONAL COMMUNITY
Is the United States out of step with the international community in international law?

SOVEREIGNTY
Is international law a threat to national sovereignty?

DOES THE UNITED STATES HAVE TOO MUCH INFLUENCE ON INTERNATIONAL LAW?
KEY POINTS

NO: In refusing to ratify certain treaties, the United States often stands up for smaller, less powerful nations

NO: International courts only take cases that national courts are demonstrably unable or unwilling to prosecute

YES: The United States has a moral obligation to use its power to look after the planet and everyone on it

YES: Since the United States is the world's dominant power, its support is vital if international laws are going to work

RESPONSIBILITY
As the only superpower, should the United States act in international rather than U.S. interests?

UNDERMINING
Does lack of U.S. support undermine international laws and treaties?

NO: If the United States does not put itself first, other nations will exploit its selflessness for their own gain

NO: Other nations are capable of acting without the United States, as they did to create the International Criminal Court, for example

THE KYOTO PROTOCOL

"I oppose the Kyoto Protocol because it exempts 80 percent of the world, including major population centers such as China and India, from compliance, and would cause serious harm to the U.S. economy."
—PRESIDENT GEORGE W. BUSH (2001–)

The Kyoto Protocol is a proposed amendment to an international treaty on global warming—the United Nations Framework Convention on Climate Change, which was adopted in 1992. The protocol was adopted at the third session of the Conference of the Parties (COP-3) in Kyoto, Japan, in December 1997. It contains emissions targets for industrialized countries to achieve by the period 2008–2012. These targets will be legally binding on all countries that have ratified the protocol by the time it comes into force—should it ever do so.

The ultimate aim of the convention is to prevent "dangerous anthropogenic [human-made] interference with the climate system." In Kyoto the developed nations committed themselves to reducing collective emissions of six important greenhouse gases by an average of 5.2 percent below 1990 levels, but the protocol left a number of issues open. In late 2000 COP-6 in The Hague, Netherlands, was suspended after it failed to resolve these issues because of disputes between the European Union (EU), which favored a tougher agreement, and the United States, Canada, Japan, and Australia, which all wanted the protocol to be more flexible.

The United States and the protocol

In March 2001 President George W. Bush declared that the United States would not ratify the protocol as it stood. Changes to the treaty, accepted by participants during the resumption of COP-6 in Bonn, Germany, in July 2001, permit industrialized nations to include nature reserves and parks as "sinks"—which act by removing and storing carbon dioxide from the atmosphere—as part of a country's strategy to meet its obligations. These modifications were successful in enlisting the support of Japan. The United States, however, maintained its opposition, demanding that restrictions on the emission of carbon dioxide apply equally to developed and developing countries. It also argued that because emissions levels of many industrialized nations have risen, the reductions required would be much higher than the agreed targets. For example, in 1997 the United States committed itself to a reduction of greenhouse gases by 7 percent compared to 1990 levels. This target represents a cut of more than 30 percent compared to the emissions levels expected by 2010 had there been no protocol. The United States is concerned that meeting such a target would damage its economy.

As things stand, the United States has neither ratified nor withdrawn from the protocol altogether. As the world's largest producer of carbon dioxide emissions, at 31 percent, America's withdrawal of its intention to ratify has put significant pressure on the EU to secure the support of other nations yet to ratify, particularly Russia. If Russia also fails to ratify, it is unlikely that the accord could ever be brought into force.

Developing countries

The protocol targets the developed countries because their factories were the originators of gas emissions during the Industrial Revolution, and because they are in a financial and technological position to make reductions. The protocol also reaffirms the principle of the convention that developed countries must pay for and supply technology to help other nations with climate-related projects. The U.S. intransigence has provoked much anger in developing countries such as India because these nations stand to lose billions of dollars worth of investment if Kyoto fails to go ahead. President Bush's position on the protocol struck many in the international community as galling since the U.S. population—barely 5 percent of humanity—is responsible for nearly one-third of all carbon dioxide emissions.

In addition, many people believe that the effects of climate change will be felt most in the developing world. Marginal populations will be made more vulnerable in the face of extreme events such as floods, droughts, and cyclones. Some low-lying island nations, such as the Maldives, may disappear completely if the sea level rises appreciably because of global warming.

TARGETS AND TIMETABLES

Under the protocol there are national targets for reducing greenhouse gas emissions. The United States originally committed itself to reductions of 7 percent, while Canada and Japan must achieve reductions of 6 percent. The EU states aim to reduce emissions by an average of 8 percent. Some countries, such as Russia and New Zealand, need only stabilize emissions, while others—Australia and Norway, for example—may increase emissions up to a certain level.

The most important greenhouse gases—carbon dioxide (CO_2), methane (CH_4), and nitrous oxide (N_2O)—are to be measured against a base year of 1990. The other gases—hydrofluorocarbons (HFCs), perfluorocarbons (PFCs), and sulfur hexafluoride (SF_6)—can be measured against either a 1990 or a 1995 base. Each nation's target must be achieved by 2008–2012, calculated as an average over those five years.

The protocol cannot enter into force until it has been ratified by at least 55 parties to the convention, including industrialized nations representing at least 55 percent of the total 1990 carbon dioxide emissions from this group. By April 2004, 122 countries, including Canada, China, India, Japan, and the EU member states, had ratified the protocol, representing just 44.2 percent of emissions.

Topic 15

IS THE UNITED STATES THE ULTIMATE DEFENDER OF INTERNATIONAL HUMAN RIGHTS?

YES
"SPEECH AT HEARINGS, UN HUMAN RIGHTS COMMISSION"
BEFORE THE SENATE FOREIGN RELATIONS COMMITTEE INTERNATIONAL OPERATIONS
AND TERRORISM SUBCOMMITTEE, WASHINGTON, D.C., MAY 24, 2001
PAULA DOBRIANSKY

NO
"LETTER TO PRESIDENT GEORGE W. BUSH"
WWW.HRW.ORG, DECEMBER 26, 2002
HUMAN RIGHTS WATCH

INTRODUCTION

The United States has a long tradition of protecting the rights of its own people. The Constitution, and the Bill of Rights in particular, guarantees rights such as freedom of speech and the right to a fair trial. The nation has also long promoted democracy and human rights in its foreign policies. It fought in World War II (1939–1945) against the forces of fascism, for example. After the war it played a leading role in drafting the UN's Universal Declaration of Human Rights (UDHR). Today the Universal Declaration is accepted almost worldwide and is the foundation of international human rights law.

With such a background it is not surprising that some people today see the United States as the world's leading defender of human rights. They argue, for example, that U.S. military power can be used to protect the vulnerable against abuse by oppressive dictatorships. This interpretation has been used to justify U.S. policy in places such as Latin America and the Middle East. In Afghanistan in 2002, for example, the United States and its allies overthrew the nondemocratic Taliban regime and replaced it with an elected government. After overthrowing the dictatorship of Saddam Hussein in 2003, the United States planned to do the same in Iraq by creating a representative Iraqi governing body.

To many Americans, among others, such actions are proof of a U.S. commitment to the establishment of its democratic, libertarian values around the world. A strand in U.S. political thought, labeled the neoconservative, or "neocon," tendency, sees it as the role of U.S. foreign policy to use economic and military dominance to establish democracy and free markets around the world. Such thinking emerged in the idealistic peace settlements proposed by President Woodrow Wilson after World War I (1914–1918) and remained a strong influence throughout the 20th century.

> *"America did not invent human rights.... Human rights invented America."*
>
> —JIMMY CARTER (1924–),
>
> HUMAN RIGHTS AMBASSADOR

U.S. attempts to promote its values around the world have as many critics as supporters, however. There are those who argue, for example, that any attempt to promote human rights in other countries is not inspired by any regard for those rights in themselves but by practical considerations of strengthening U.S. alliances around the world with states with similar value systems or for economic gain. For such critics, for example, the 2003 invasion of Iraq was more about access to oil reserves than about establishing democracy. Indeed, they argue, the torture of Iraqi prisoners by U.S. military personnel proves that human rights are not high on the U.S. agenda. Supporters of the invasion argue that local breakdowns of discipline do not lessen the justness of the cause.

Further criticism of U.S. intervention overseas comes from those who denounce certain elements of the U.S. legal system, such as its application of the death penalty or the apparent bias of the judicial system against minorities.

Critics assert that elements of the War on Terrorism launched by President George W. Bush in 2001 also undermine human rights. The detention of more than 600 prisoners from the war in Afghanistan, for example, without trial at a base at Guantanamo Bay in Cuba has caused much controversy. Critics also believe that U.S. attempts to enforce human rights through military force actually undermine citizens' rights. They further claim that the United States is not consistent in its foreign policy: It tolerates human rights abuses in certain countries in order to preserve beneficial alliances. One such example is its relationship with the People's Republic of China, with which, critics argue, it enjoys a most-favored-nation trading status. Similarly, some observers say that U.S. support for Israel has actually hindered peace initiatives between the Israelis, the Palestinians, and other Arab nations. In the past the United States has also been willing to support revolts against democratically elected governments it considered too left-wing or potentially harmful to U.S. interests, as seen in its role in the 1973 overthrow of the democratically elected socialist government in Chile of Salvador Allende.

In May 2001 the United States was voted off the United Nations Commission for Human Rights for the first time since the commission's creation in 1947. Many observers saw the move as an expression of other nations' disapproval of the U.S. human rights record. Others, however, argue that the United States was being punished precisely because it had strongly defended human rights.

The following articles address some of the issues in the debate, focusing on the United Nations and Iraq.

SPEECH AT HEARINGS, UN HUMAN RIGHTS COMMISSION...
Paula Dobriansky

Paula Dobriansky became under secretary of state for global affairs in May 2001 and addressed the Senate Foreign Relations Committee in the same month.

Critics of the United States often allege that it places national interest before human rights. Are they the same thing, or are they mutually incompatible?

The Helsinki Final Act of 1975 laid out the basis for the dealings of the Organization for Security and Cooperation in Europe (OSCE), which includes all European states, the United States, and Canada. The Community of Democracies is a group of 106 governments committed to the spread of democracy around the world.

YES

☑ **Mr. Chairman, Members of the Foreign Relations Committee,**

It is an honor to be here to discuss the Bush Administration's democracy promotion and human rights policy and the importance of maintaining our leadership in this field. This is my first chance to address this committee since I became the Under Secretary of State for Global Affairs. I look forward to future discussions with you on these important issues. My purpose today is to highlight the Bush Administration's commitment to democracy and human rights promotion and the policies we intend to pursue in support of them.

U.S. commitment to human rights dates from the Declaration of Independence and our nation's founding. This reflects our nation's values and our deeply rooted belief in the importance of developing and maintaining democratic governments, subject to the rule of law, that respect and protect individual liberty. At the same time, the defense of human rights clearly serves our national interest.

A century of commitment

As the history of the past century has shown, the strongest, most stable, tolerant, and prosperous countries are precisely those which respect universal human rights. For that reason, we have long made the promotion of human rights a focus of our foreign policy and our foreign assistance programs.

Since the end of the Second World War, the United States has been without equal in articulating a vision of international human rights and having the grit to carry it out. Whether crafting the United Nations Charter and the Universal Declaration of Human Rights, championing freedom and democracy throughout the Cold War, insisting on human rights in the Helsinki Final Act, compiling the Country Reports on Human Rights Practices for the past 25 years, or helping establish the Community of Democracies in Warsaw last year, the United States has been the country that has set the agenda and has done the heavy lifting. Throughout these years, our message has not wavered. Promoting democracy

Eleanor Roosevelt was the chair of the United Nations Commission on Human Rights. In 1958 she presented members with a guidebook on the 10th anniversary of the U.S. observance of the UDHR.

and protecting the individual against the excesses of the state is the policy of the United States.

Fortunately, that effort has been successful. The U.S. vision has come to be shared by many other states, and is now a fundamental component of NATO, the Organization for Security and Cooperation in Europe, and the Organization of American States and the Summit of the Americas, and in the basic laws of many states that have emerged since the end of World War II. It is increasingly an important factor in decisions of countries in other regions, for example in Africa.

Let me turn now to a subject that has been much in the news recently: the United Nations Commission on Human Rights. I am sure you are all aware of the UN Economic and Social Council vote in New York on May 3, which resulted in the United States losing its seat for the first time since the Commission was created in 1947 under the chairmanship of Eleanor Roosevelt.

The UN Commission on Human Rights has 53 elected seats, of which four are reserved for advanced western nations. Some people saw the U.S. exclusion as a punishment for its poor human rights record; others argued that in fact it reflected the U.S. readiness to criticize the records of other countries on the commission.

Paying a price

As President Bush said on Cuban Independence Day last week at the White House:

> *Last month, the UN Human Rights Commission called on Castro's regime to respect the basic human rights of all its people. The United States' leadership was responsible for passage of that resolution. Some say we paid a heavy price for it, but let me be clear: I'm very proud of what we did. And repressed people around the world must know this about the United States: We might not sit on some commission, but we will always be the world's leader in support of human rights.*

The President was right: we did pay a price for taking forthright, principled positions at the Commission this year. Secretary of State Colin Powell spoke about this when he addressed the Senate Appropriations Subcommittee on Foreign Operations May 15, and he stressed that the future policy of the United States toward the Commission would be the result of a review and ultimately a decision by the President. This review is now under way....

As the President said, the United States will remain committed to human rights. It will be a crucial part of our approach to China, Cuba, Indonesia, the Balkans, Iran, Sudan and all the other places where fundamental freedoms are at stake. We are working ever closer with our friends and allies at the UN, the OSCE, OAS, NATO, and other multilateral organizations, and the State Department remains strongly committed to its round-the-clock, round the year, round-the-world human rights monitoring portfolio.

We shall continue to be the world's leading advocate for democracy and human rights. We shall continue to meet foreign government officials, and insist that our views on human rights be known. We shall speak up for the dissidents, the victims of persecution, the tortured and the dispossessed. We shall continue to tell the truth when we submit our Country Reports on Human Rights Practices to Congress and to the millions who now access them via the Internet. We shall continue our reports on International Religious Freedom, now in its third cycle, and a new report on Trafficking in Persons to be released on June 1.

Is this easy? No. Is it always appreciated by our friends and allies? Unfortunately, not. But it is necessary. It is worthwhile. To quote the President again:

The United States was reelected to its seat on the commission in 2002.

If U.S. attempts to support human rights only lead to criticism from other nations, would it be better off looking after its own interests? Or do you think the United States has a duty to take a lead?

The Country Reports on Human Rights Practices are published each year by the State Department. Go to http://www.state.gov/g/drl/hr/c1470.htm to access them.

History tells us that forcing change upon oppressive regimes requires patience. But history also proves, from Poland to South Africa, that patience and courage and resolve can eventually cause oppressive regimes to fear and then to fall."

The United States was criticized for not imposing sanctions on South Africa to force it to end apartheid. Apartheid was finally ended in 1994.

The vote by the member states of ECOSOC has limited our role in one highly visible forum, but it has hardly crippled us: Those states which voted against us in the hope that they would prevent us from being forceful advocates for human rights were sadly mistaken. Indeed, in the policy review, to which I earlier referred, we are taking a close look at new approaches and new opportunities to pursue our human rights objectives worldwide. We may be forced, for a time, to shift our tactics, but we will never abandon our goal.

"A deal's a deal"

I would like to say a brief word about the proposal by some to link the payment of our arrears to the outcome of the Commission election. The Administration believes strongly that any attempt to link U.S. payments to the UN—now or in the future—to U.S. membership in or support for the Commission is counterproductive. Not only will withholding money or adding additional conditions on arrears payments provide ammunition to our adversaries, but it will also frustrate our efforts to further U.S. political interests and push for reform of the institution and its agencies. In the words of the President, "a deal's a deal."

Congress withheld $244 million of U.S. contributions to the UN after the United States lost its seat on the Human Rights Commission until it regained its seat.

Do you think that Dobriansky is right to agree with the president that "a deal's a deal"? The United States is the biggest funder of the UN. Is it therefore understandable that it should use its economic wealth to try to influence the decisions of organizations such as the UN?

While the Commission on Human Rights (CHR) is far from a perfect institution, it has done much good over the years. It established Special Rapporteurs on country situations like the former Yugoslavia or Iraq, and on crucial thematic issues such as torture or the independence of judges and lawyers. These special mechanisms of the CHR are among the activities of the Office of the UN High Commissioner for Human Rights, former Irish President Mary Robinson, which also maintains field offices in trouble spots like Congo and Colombia.

We would caution against penalizing the UN, the UN human rights program, or the Office of the High Commissioner, for the vote by a small number of UN Member States in the Economic and Social Council over membership in the CHR. I strongly urge the Committee to proceed very cautiously in this regard.

Thank you.

LETTER TO PRESIDENT GEORGE W. BUSH
Human Rights Watch

Human Rights Watch was set up in 1978 to monitor human rights around the world. This letter, sent on December 26, 2002, refers to reports of prisoner mistreatment during the war in Afghanistan in 2002.

Go to http://www. washingtonpost. com/ac2/ wp-dyn?pagename =article&contentId= A37943-2002Dec25 &notFound=true to read the article in The Washington Post.

In 2004 there was widespread criticism of U.S. abuse and torture of prisoners in Iraq. Do you think that such episodes have ruined America's image overseas?

NO

Dear President Bush:

Human Rights Watch is deeply concerned by allegations of torture and other mistreatment of suspected Al Qaeda detainees described in *The Washington Post* ("U.S. Decries Abuse but Defends Interrogations") on December 26. The allegations, if true, would place the United States in violation of some of the most fundamental prohibitions of international human rights law. Any U.S. government official who is directly involved or complicit in the torture or mistreatment of detainees, including any official who knowingly acquiesces in the commission of such acts, would be subject to prosecution worldwide.

Human Rights Watch urges you to take immediate steps to clarify that the use of torture is not U.S policy, investigate *The Washington Post*'s allegations, adopt all necessary measures to end any ongoing violations of international law, stop the rendition of detainees to countries where they are likely to be tortured, and prosecute those implicated in such abuse.

I. Prohibitions against torture

The Washington Post reports that persons held in the CIA interrogation centers at Bagram air base in Afghanistan are subject to "stress and duress" techniques, including "standing or kneeling for hours" and being "held in awkward, painful positions." The *Post* notes that the detention facilities at Bagram and elsewhere, such as at Diego Garcia, are not monitored by the International Committee of the Red Cross, which has monitored the U.S. treatment of detainees at Guantánamo Bay, Cuba.

The absolute prohibition against torture is a fundamental and well-established precept of customary and conventional international law. Torture is never permissible against anyone, whether in times of peace or of war.

The prohibition against torture is firmly established under international human rights law. It is prohibited by various treaties to which the United States is a party, including the International Covenant on Civil and Political Rights (ICCPR), which the United States ratified in 1992, and the Convention against Torture and Other Cruel,

Inhuman or Degrading Treatment or Punishment, which the United States ratified in 1994. Article 7 of the ICCPR states that "No one shall be subjected to torture or to cruel, inhuman or degrading treatment or punishment." The right to be protected from torture is non-derogable, meaning that it applies at all times, including during public emergencies or wartime.

> Why should the United States sign such conventions? Do they limit its ability to look after its national interests?

Prisoners of war or just prisoners?

International humanitarian law (the laws of war), which applies during armed conflict, prohibits the torture or other mistreatment of captured combatants and others in captivity, regardless of their legal status. Regarding prisoners-of-war, article 17 of the Third Geneva Convention of 1949 states: "No physical or mental torture, nor any other form of coercion, may be inflicted on prisoners of war to secure from them information of any kind whatever. Prisoners of war who refuse to answer may not be threatened, insulted, or exposed to any unpleasant or disadvantageous treatment of any kind." Detained civilians are similarly protected by article 32 of the Fourth Geneva Convention. The United States has been a party to the 1949 Geneva Conventions since 1955.

> The Geneva Conventions set international rules of wartime. The first rules (1864) were for the treatment of injured on the battlefield; the second (1906) applied to warfare at sea. The third convention (1949) established rules for dealing with prisoners of war. A fourth convention in 1949 set rules for the treatment of civilians in wartime.

The United States does not recognize captured Al Qaeda members as being protected by the 1949 Geneva Conventions, although Bush administration officials have insisted that detainees will be treated humanely and in a manner consistent with Geneva principles. However, at minimum, all detainees in wartime, regardless of their legal status, are protected by customary international humanitarian law. Article 75 ("Fundamental Guarantees") of the First Additional Protocol to the Geneva Conventions, which is recognized as restating customary international law, provides that "torture of all kinds, whether physical or mental" against "persons who are in the power of a Party to the conflict and who do not benefit from more favorable treatment under the [Geneva] Conventions," shall "remain prohibited at any time and in any place whatsoever, whether committed by civilian or military agents." "[C]ruel treatment and torture" of detainees is also prohibited under common article 3 to the 1949 Geneva Conventions, which is considered indicative of customary international law.

> The United States argues that Al Qaeda fighters do not count as prisoners of war. But if they were captured during fighting in Afghanistan, how else should they be treated?

II. Possible U.S. complicity in torture

It is a violation of international law not only to use torture directly, but also to be complicit in torture committed by other governments. The *Post* reports being told by U.S.

Can the United States really be held accountable for the actions of its allies? Does the importance of the War on Terrorism justify America's alliances with politically or morally suspect nations? Does it really matter as long as terror is defeated?

officials that "[t]housands have been arrested and held with U.S. assistance in countries known for brutal treatment of prisoners." The Convention against Torture provides in article 4 that all acts of torture, including "an act by any person which constitutes complicity or participation in torture," is an offense "punishable by appropriate penalties which take into account their grave nature."

The *Post* article describes the rendition of captured Al Qaeda suspects from U.S. custody to other countries where they are tortured or otherwise mistreated. This might also be a violation of the Convention against Torture, which in article 3 states: "No State Party shall expel, return ('refouler') or extradite a person to another State where there are substantial grounds for believing that he would be in danger of being subjected to torture…. For the purpose of determining whether there are such grounds, the competent authorities shall take into account all relevant considerations including, where applicable, the existence in the State concerned of a consistent pattern of gross, flagrant or mass violations of human rights."

Uzbekistan and Pakistan both border Afghanistan and offered important support during the 2002 war. Does that mean that the United States should turn a blind eye to their rights records?

The U.S. Department of State annual report on human rights practices has frequently criticized torture in countries where detainees may have been sent. These include Uzbekistan, Pakistan, Egypt, Jordan and Morocco. The United States thus could not plausibly claim that it was unaware of the problem of torture in these countries.

III. International prosecutions for torture and command responsibility

Direct involvement or complicity in torture, as well as the failure to prevent torture, may subject U.S. officials to prosecution under international law.

The willful torture or inhuman treatment of prisoners-of-war or other detainees, including "willfully causing great suffering or serious injury to body or health," are "grave breaches" of the 1949 Geneva Conventions, commonly known as war crimes. Grave breaches are subject to universal jurisdiction, meaning that they can be prosecuted in any national criminal court and as well as any international tribunal with appropriate jurisdiction.

The United States has refused to back the creation of an international court. But would such a court help prevent torture and abuse of prisoners?

The Convention against Torture obligates States Parties to prosecute persons within their jurisdiction who are implicated or complicit in acts of torture. This obligation includes the prosecution of persons within their territory who committed acts of torture elsewhere and have not be extradited under procedures provided in the convention.

Should senior U.S. officials become aware of acts of torture by their subordinates and fail to take immediate and effective steps to end such practices, they too could be found criminally liable under international law. The responsibility of superior officers for atrocities by their subordinates is commonly known as command responsibility. Although the concept originated in military law, it now is increasingly accepted to include the responsibility of civil authorities for abuses committed by persons under their direct authority. The doctrine of command responsibility has been upheld in recent decisions by the international criminal tribunals for the former Yugoslavia and for Rwanda.

Do you think that it is right for senior officials to take responsibility for their subordinates? Where should the buck stop?

There are two forms of command responsibility: direct responsibility for orders that are unlawful and imputed responsibility, when a superior knows or should have known of crimes committed by a subordinate acting on his own initiative and fails to prevent or punish them. All states are obliged to bring such people to justice.

Clarification required

The allegations made by *The Washington Post* are extraordinarily serious. They have put the United States on notice that acts of torture may be taking place with U.S. participation or complicity. That creates a heightened duty to respond preventively. As an immediate step, we urge that you issue a presidential statement clarifying that it is contrary to U.S. policy to use or facilitate torture. The *Post*'s allegations should be investigated and the findings made public.

Would a presidential statement clarify the position? Or would America's enemies use it to suggest that torture has taken place in the past?

Should there be evidence of U.S. civilian or military officials being directly involved or complicit in torture, or in the rendition of persons to places where they are likely to be tortured, you should take immediate steps to prevent the commission of such acts and to prosecute the individuals who have ordered, organized, condoned, or carried them out. The United States also has a duty to refrain from sending persons to other countries with a history of torture without explicit and verifiable guarantees that no torture or mistreatment will occur.

Thank you for your attention to these concerns.

Sincerely,
Kenneth Roth, Executive Director

Summary

The first article is a speech given on behalf of the Bush administration by Paula Dobriansky, in which she reasserts U.S. human rights policy following the loss of its seat on the UN Human Rights Commission in May 2001. In her view the United States has for a long time been "without equal in articulating a vision of international human rights and having the grit to carry it out." President George W. Bush and his colleagues believe that the United States maintains its position regardless of whether or not it has a seat on the commission and despite the actions of some UN member states that hope to curtail future American involvement on human rights issues. Although its stance might make it unpopular, the United States is and will continue to be the world's leading advocate for dissidents, victims of persecution, the tortured, and the dispossessed.

The second article contains the text of a letter to President George W. Bush from Kenneth Roth of Human Rights Watch. Roth highlights reports of abuse of prisoners in *The Washington Post* on December 26, 2002. He argues that torture and abuse are forbidden under international law and lists various pieces of legislation to clarify the position. Roth argues that the United States is breaking international law by sending prisoners to countries with known records of prisoner abuse. He urges Bush to issue a statement condemning the use of torture, to stop the torture and prosecute the perpetrators should the allegations be true, and to reaffirm the United States' commitment not to send people to countries that have a history of torture.

FURTHER INFORMATION:

Books:

Forsythe, David P. (ed.), *The United States and Human Rights: Looking Inward and Outward (Human Rights in International Perspective)*. Lincoln, NE: University of Nebraska Press, 2000.

Steiner, Henry, and Philip Alston, *International Human Rights in Context*. New York: Oxford University Press, 2000.

Useful websites:

www.amnesty.org

Amnesty International monitors human rights abuses around the world. It has produced several report on America and international human rights.

http://hrw.org/doc/?t=usa

Human Rights Watch site on the United States. Features recent articles, reports, and links to other relevant material.

The following debates in the Pro/Con series may also be of interest:

In this volume:
  Part 4: The United States and International Law,
pages 174–175

Topic 14 Does the United States have too much influence on international law?

In *Human Rights*:
  Part 4: Human rights and the United States

IS THE UNITED STATES THE ULTIMATE DEFENDER OF INTERNATIONAL HUMAN RIGHTS?

YES: U.S. citizens' rights are guaranteed under the Constitution. The whole history of the republic has been based on the idea of essential personal liberties.

YES: The United States has taken the minimum steps necessary to fight terrorism without affecting rights—but the right of citizens to security outweighs the rights of terrorists

HEAL THYSELF
Do human rights in the United States justify a leading role abroad?

A JUST WAR
Has the United States upheld human rights in its pursuit of the War on Terrorism?

NO: The death penalty and the detention of prisoners at Guantanamo Bay without trial are both rights abuses. People in glass houses should not throw stones.

NO: It has eroded both the rights of U.S. citizens under legislation such as the USA PATRIOT Act and the rights of noncitizens who have been detained without trial

IS THE UNITED STATES THE ULTIMATE DEFENDER OF INTERNATIONAL HUMAN RIGHTS?

KEY POINTS

YES: The establishment of governments that respect human rights is not only morally right; it is often in the United States' best interests

YES: Military victory in World War II and in Afghanistan in 2002 and Iraq in 2003 paved the way for the introduction of government based on civil rights

MOTIVATION
Does the United States really care about human rights?

BARREL OF A GUN
Can warfare ever improve human rights?

NO: The United States is only concerned with its own interests, as demonstrated by its role in overthrowing democratic governments it does not like

NO: The suffering inflicted by warfare always results in the reduction of human rights, not their improvement. Alleged abuses by U.S. personnel also did not help matters.

Topic 16
IS THE U.S. WAR ON TERRORISM A VIOLATION OF INTERNATIONAL LAW?

YES
"LAWLESS WAR"
LE MONDE DIPLOMATIQUE, APRIL 2003
IGNACIO RAMONET, TRANSLATED BY ED EMORY

NO
"LEGAL BASIS FOR USE OF FORCE AGAINST IRAQ"
HOUSE OF LORDS OFFICIAL REPORT (HANSARD)
MARCH 17, 2003
LORD GOLDSMITH

INTRODUCTION

The U.S.-led War on Terrorism was launched by President George W. Bush at a joint session of Congress nine days after the terrorist attacks of September 11, 2001. Bush declared: "Our war on terror begins with Al Qaeda, but it does not end there. It will not end until every terrorist group of global reach has been found, stopped, and defeated." In January 2002 Bush identified an "axis of evil"—Iran, Iraq, and North Korea— as rogue states that sponsored terrorists. The list was later expanded to include Cuba, Libya, and Syria.

The War on Terrorism, Bush warned, would take many years and have many aspects. They include tracing terrorist funding in the international banking system, using diplomatic pressure to prevent states from harboring terrorist organizations, and possibly covert operations that Bush said would remain "secret even in success." The USA

PATRIOT Act was introduced to allow closer monitoring of the activities of residents of the United States.

The most visible part of the War on Terrorism was military action. In October 2001 the United States led an international coalition in an attack on Afghanistan, where the Taliban regime was harboring Al Qaeda terrorists. The Taliban was overthrown, but the Al Qaeda leaders escaped. In March 2003 the United States invaded Iraq, justifying the attack by claiming that Saddam Hussein abused human rights, may have been implicated in the 9/11 attacks, possessed weapons of mass destruction that represented a threat to the United States, and had failed to comply with numerous United Nations resolutions. The war resulted in a rapid victory and the overthrow of Hussein. In June 2004 the United States handed control of Iraq back to an Iraqi government.

The War on Terrorism has received broad international backing: The campaign in Afghanistan involved 36 nations, for example. However, observers have queried the legitimacy of various aspects of the U.S. campaign.

At home, civil liberties organizations have vigorously protested some of the provisions of the USA PATRIOT Act, for example, arguing that it compromises free speech, the right to privacy, and the right to due process. There has also been criticism of the detention of prisoners from the Afghanistan conflict at Guantanamo Bay in Cuba. Many have been held for years without trial. Critics argue that such abuses sacrifice the very freedoms for which America is fighting and provide ammunition for its enemies around the world.

> *"We will take defensive measures against terrorism to protect Americans."*
> —GEORGE W. BUSH,
> 43RD PRESIDENT (2001–)

The most controversial part of the War on Terrorism is the 2003 invasion of Iraq and its aftermath. The United States and its allies invaded Iraq without the explicit backing of the United Nations, although the UN had itself threatened Iraq with "serious consequences" for failure to comply with UN resolutions. The U.S. action had allies, most notably Britain and Spain, but it was also widely condemned. Critics argued that it was illegal: Customary international law condemns attacks that are launched

to prevent a possible future threat, as opposed to preemptive attacks launched in the face of an imminent threat. They also claimed that the United States was less interested in fighting terror in Iraq than in gaining access to its rich oil supplies. Advocates of the invasion countered both that Iraq's weapons of mass destruction (WMD) offered an immediate threat to the United States and that in any case the 9/11 attacks necessitated a new definition of legal preemptive action.

Critics believe that their opposition was justified by the failure to discover WMDs in Iraq—the government blamed "faulty" intelligence—and by the failure to make any positive links between Iraq and Al Qaeda. Supporters of military action, however, maintain that the overthrow of a brutal dictator and moves toward the establishment of a democratic system in Iraq justify the invasion, as did Iraq's noncompliance with UN demands to prove that it had abandoned its WMDs.

Controversy continued when it was revealed that U.S. personnel had allegedly abused and tortured Iraqi prisoners. To critics this was further proof that the United States was acting illegally, as was its refusal to submit its military personnel to the jurisdiction of the International Criminal Court (ICC) set up to punish such abuses. Supporters of the invasion counter that the actions of rogue individuals should be punished but do not undermine the legitimacy of the War on Terrorism as a whole. They also assert that were U.S. personnel subject to the ICC, they would likely become victims of malicious prosecutions brought by America's political enemies.

The following two articles consider the legality of the War on Terrorism.

LAWLESS WAR
Ignacio Ramonet

YES

The preamble to the United Nations Charter—the shared law of our planet—states: "We the peoples of the United Nations, determined to save succeeding generations from the scourge of war, and to ensure, by the acceptance of principles and the institution of methods, that armed force shall not be used, save in the common interest, have resolved to combine our efforts to accomplish these aims." The first article of the Charter says that the purpose of the UN is to "maintain international peace and security" and to suppress "acts of aggression or other breaches of the peace".

A preventive war is considered legally as being different from a preemptive war. See Topic 4 Is it legal for one nation to attack another preemptively?

So, when the United States and its British allies launched their "preventive war" on Iraq at dawn on Thursday 20 March, in invading that country without a UN mandate and without the authorisation of any other international body they were violating international legality, wiping their feet on the most basic principles of the UN, and behaving as aggressors.

Faced with this crime against peace the world community finds itself in an unprecedented position. Never since the creation of the UN in 1945 have we seen two countries that are founder members of that organisation, permanent members of the Security Council, among the world's oldest democracies, so brutally flouting international law and thereby making themselves, under the terms of that law, into delinquent states.

World order

The prospect of war in Iraq occasioned huge popular protests in February 2003. Around 6 to 10 million people protested in up to 60 countries, including 100,000 in New York City and 200,000 in San Francisco. They were the largest antiwar demonstrations since the Vietnam era in the 1960s.

World order has been inverted. Not the hierarchy of power, because US power remains incontestable. But in political values. The protests of millions of people around the world, even within the US and Britain, against this war were motivated by the feeling that it is immoral. People may not have many illusions, but they do expect the most powerful country in the world to be guided by ethics, to champion respect for the process of law and to be a model of obedience to the law. At the very least they don't expect it to turn its back on the basic principles of political morality.

Protestors against the war on Iraq show their opposition in one of the many antiwar demonstrations held around the world.

Italian Renaissance thinker Niccolò Machiavelli (1469– 1527) argued in The Prince (1513) that rulers sometimes have to take action that is not otherwise morally justified.

What motives might such countries have for not supporting the United States?

Does it matter who U.S. allies are as long as the cause of the war is just?

In June 2004 the official commission investigating the 9/11 attacks said that there was no link between the attacks and the Iraqis. Many Americans continued to believe that such a link existed. Why might that have been?

However, it seems that since the attacks of 11 September 2001 the US, under the administration of President George Bush, has arrived at a cynical definition of proper behaviour by governments. Perhaps with an eye on Machiavelli—"to maintain his state a prince is often forced to act in defiance of good faith, of charity, of kindness, of religion" [*The Prince*]—Bush and the hawks surrounding him decided to take action which is against morality, human rights and international law.

After an unprecedented diplomatic disaster in which the US hyperpower was incapable of rallying support within the Security Council from countries that have long been within its sphere of influence (Mexico, Chile and Pakistan), the US had another big setback when Turkey, an ally of long standing, refused to allow US troops to cross through its territory. Regardless, Bush maintained his project of aggression against Iraq and claimed the support of a "coalition" of 40 in which former communist countries figure largely, including Uzbekistan and Turkmenistan, two of the most sinister neo-totalitarian states. Saddam Hussein may be odious and tyrannical, but Bush and his entourage have hardly distinguished themselves for their morality. Their contempt for international law and the arrogance engendered by the force of their military power have caused the biggest wave of anti-Americanism since the Vietnam war (1961–75).

The Geneva-based International Commission of Jurists, a consultative body within the UN, warned on 18 March 2003 against attacking Iraq without a UN mandate, referring to an "outright illegal invasion of Iraq, which amounts to a war of aggression". (These words had been preceded by similar warnings from lawyers' associations in Britain, France, Belgium and Spain.) It said there was no possible juridical basis for such an intervention. In the absence of authorisation from the Security Council, no state may have recourse to force against another state except in legitimate defence, in response to an armed attack.

Legal argument

The US has invoked legitimate defence to justify its attack on Iraq, but for domestic public consumption—trying to link the 11 September attacks to the Baghdad regime (an unproven case)—and not for the Security Council. The view of the Council, up to 20 March, was that Iraq was not an immediate threat of the kind that would justify an immediate war. Moreover the legitimate defence argument presupposes the existence of a prior armed aggression, which Iraq has not committed. And legitimate preventive defence is not admitted under international law.

Bush has also justified his invasion of Iraq by the need for regime change, getting rid of Saddam Hussein. Admirable as such an intention may be, it is not enough under the UN Charter to justify a unilateral recourse to force. As to the US claim that it is installing democracy in Iraq, this has no status as a legal justification for aggression. In the 17th century the jurist Grotius, founding father of human rights, wrote that "wanting to govern others against their will, under the pretext that it is good for them" was the most frequent justification for unjust wars.

Dutchman Hugo Grotius (1583–1645) wrote De jure belli ac pacis *(On the Laws of War and Peace) in 1625. Do you think that his argument is still relevant?*

LEGAL BASIS FOR USE OF FORCE AGAINST IRAQ
Lord Goldsmith

NO

In a written Parliamentary Answer, the Attorney General, Lord Goldsmith, has set out his view of the legal basis for the use of force against Iraq:

"Authority to use force against Iraq exists from the combined effect of resolutions 678, 687 and 1441. All of these resolutions were adopted under Chapter VII of the UN Charter which allows the use of force for the express purpose of restoring international peace and security:

1. In resolution 678 the Security Council authorised force against Iraq, to eject it from Kuwait and to restore peace and security in the area.

2. In resolution 687, which set out the ceasefire conditions after Operation Desert Storm, the Security Council imposed continuing obligations on Iraq to eliminate its weapons of mass destruction in order to restore international peace and security in the area. Resolution 687 suspended but did not terminate the authority to use force under resolution 678.

3. A material breach of resolution 687 revives the authority to use force under resolution 678.

4. In resolution 1441 the Security Council determined that Iraq has been and remains in material breach of resolution 687, because it has not fully complied with its obligations to disarm under that resolution.

5. The Security Council in resolution 1441 gave Iraq "a final opportunity to comply with its disarmament obligations" and warned Iraq of the "serious consequences" if it did not.

6. The Security Council also decided in resolution 1441 that, if Iraq failed at any time to comply with and cooperate fully in the implementation of resolution 1441, that would constitute a further material breach.

COMMENTARY: The Second Persian Gulf War

One of the most controversial aspects of the War on Terrorism was the U.S.-led invasion of Iraq in March 2003, in the Second Persian Gulf War. The United States declared victory in the war on May 1, 2003. The Iraqi leader Saddam Hussein was overthrown and later captured. The war's origins and its aftermath were both controversial, however.

Case for war

After the terrorist attacks of September 11, 2001, in the United States President George W. Bush argued that Iraq's known hostility to the United States and its determination to develop weapons of mass destruction (WMDs) meant that it should be disarmed as soon as possible. The United Nations passed a resolution demanding that Iraq admit international arms inspectors. Iraq allowed inspectors, but Bush and his leading ally, British Prime Minister Tony Blair, insisted that it hindered their operations and still maintained WMDs. Millions of people around the world marched to protest a war that increasingly seemed inevitable. On March 17, 2003, Bush controversially abandoned possible diplomatic solutions and gave Saddam Hussein only 48 hours to leave Iraq. When Saddam failed to do so, U.S. aircraft began bombing the Iraqi capital, Baghdad.

The U.S. action was widely condemned by citizens in many countries, including the United States—protest marches around the world involved millions of people—for not having the explicit backing of the United Nations. It caused a diplomatic rift with important former allies, such as France, Germany, and Russia, and was condemned virtually throughout the Arab and Islamic world as an example of U.S. imperialism. However, the United States claimed the support of more than 30 countries, which provided various levels of backing. The most important military allies were Great Britain, Australia, and Spain, although countries such as Poland and the Czech Republic also sent troops. Other countries such as Japan promised financial support for Iraq's recovery from war.

Rapid victory

Coalition troops advanced through Iraq from the south. While the British focused on the southern city of Basra, U.S. fighters reached the outskirts of Baghdad by April 4, when they captured the airport. Five days later resistance in the city collapsed. By April 13 Saddam's last stronghold of support—his home city of Tikrit—had fallen to U.S. forces.

In the aftermath of victory order broke down throughout much of Iraq, which the U.S. occupiers seemed to be unable to prevent. There was also a guerrilla campaign by Saddam loyalists and others against U.S. forces, of whom more than a hundred were killed in the 12 months after the proclaimed "end" of the war.

7. It is plain that Iraq has failed so to comply and therefore Iraq was at the time of resolution 1441 and continues to be in material breach.

8. Thus, the authority to use force under resolution 678 has revived and so continues today.

9. Resolution 1441 would in terms have provided that a further decision of the Security Council to sanction force was

U.S. marines lead a group of Iraqi prisoners of war in March 2003. American and British troops launched an assault on Iraq in a bid to topple Saddam Hussein. Many observers questioned the legality of the attack.

required if that had been intended. Thus, all that resolution 1441 requires is reporting to and discussion by the Security Council of Iraq's failures, but not an express further decision to authorise force.

I have lodged a copy of this answer, together with resolutions 678, 687 and 1441 in the Library of both Houses.

Lord Goldsmith

The United States disagreed with many members of the UN about the interpretation of resolution 1441. Should it have discussed the resolution again at the UN?

211

Summary

Both the foregoing articles consider the legality of the War on Terrorism in particular regard to one of its most controversial elements, the 2003 U.S.-led invasion of Iraq.

In the first article Ignacio Ramonet states that invasion was not a justified attempt to forestall potential aggression by Baghdad, as the coalition claimed. It was a war of aggression and as such was a breach of international law. He says that the United States launched the war even after it had failed to persuade the United Nations (UN) to take military action against Iraq, as it had successfully done before the 1991 Gulf War. In doing so it ignored warnings from, among others, the International Commission of Jurists that such action was illegal. The U.S. justification that Iraq was linked to Al Qaeda was unproven. A further claim by President George W. Bush that the invasion aimed to bring about regime change in Iraq by ousting Saddam Hussein may be "laudable" but in itself is not sufficient grounds to justify military action.

In the second article, written by Britain's chief law officer, the attorney general outlines a legal basis for the invasion of Iraq. He cites three resolutions passed by the UN Security Council. The first two, dating from the 1991 Persian Gulf War, obliged Iraq to "eliminate its weapons of mass destruction." In 2003 a new resolution again called on Iraq to do so without further delay. When Iraq failed to respond satisfactorily, the original resolutions came back into force. Lord Goldsmith argues that the 2003 invasion was therefore a continuation of the Gulf War, which the UN had authorized, rather than a new campaign that required separate justification.

FURTHER INFORMATION:

 Books:

Hamilton, John, *Behind the Terror (War on Terrorism)*. Edina, MN: Abdo and Daughters, 2002.

Useful websites:

http://www.amconmag.com/10_21/iraq.html
Article on preemptive war by Paul W. Schroeder, published on *The American Conservative* site.
http://www.cdi.org/news/law/preemptive-war.cfm
Article by Stephen C. Welsh looking at international law and preemptive strikes.
http://hrw.org/doc/?t=usa
Human Rights Watch site on the United States. Features recent articles and reports.
http://www.prospect.org/print/V13/17/galston-w.html
2002 *American Prospect* article by William Galston. Looks at the U.S. position regarding attacking Iraq.

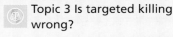

The following debates in the Pro/Con series may also be of interest:

In this volume:
Topic 3 Is targeted killing wrong?

Topic 4 Is it legal for one nation to attack another preemptively?

Topic 15 Is the United States the ultimate defender of international human rights?

IS THE U.S. WAR ON TERRORISM A VIOLATION OF INTERNATIONAL LAW?

YES: Members of the UN are committed to avoiding warfare wherever possible; actions such as the 2003 invasion of Iraq should be resolved by diplomacy

YES: There are no links between, say, Al Qaeda and Iraq. The United States is simply targeting countries with whose policies it disagrees, or whose resources it requires.

THE UNITED NATIONS

Is the United States obliged to act through the United Nations?

TERROR

Has the War on Terrorism failed to target terrorists and their supporters?

NO: The UN Charter does not forbid nations from making preemptive strikes if they believe that they are in immediate danger

NO: The possible targets outlined by the United States are rogue states in which terrorists and their supporters can prosper

IS THE U.S. WAR ON TERRORISM A VIOLATION OF INTERNATIONAL LAW?

KEY POINTS

YES: Both prisoner abuse in Iraq and the detention of prisoners without trial at Guantanamo Bay in Cuba seem to be official U.S. policy. They both violate international law and the conventions that govern military conflict.

YES: No WMDs have been found in Iraq, which shows that it presented no immediate threat to the United States; a preemptive strike was therefore illegal

ABUSE

Does prisoner abuse or detention without trial undermine the legality of the whole war?

PREEMPTIVE STRIKE

Was the invasion of Iraq an illegitimate preemptive strike?

NO: Such incidents are isolated and do not reflect the U.S. intention that its actions in all cases be humane, fair, and legal

NO: Iraq's hostility toward the United States and its possession of WMDs made it an immediate threat and, as such, a legitimate target

GLOSSARY

Amnesty International (AI) an international organization working for the release of "prisoners of conscience," people who have been arrested for their convictions, race, ethnicity, or religious beliefs.

Andean Free Trade Agreement (AFTA) this 1991 agreement abolished or reduced duty on imports to the United States from Bolivia, Colombia, Ecuador, and Peru. It expired in 2001. *See also* GATT, WTO.

Caravan of death following the overthrow of Salvador Allende's government in Chile, in October 1973 the Caravan of Death occurred when an army unit toured the country by helicopter torturing and killing around 3,000 Allende supporters.

Commission on the Status of Women (CSW) founded in 1946 by the UN, it monitors the situation of women around the world.

Convention on the Elimination of All Forms of Discrimination against Women (CEDAW) endorsed by the United Nations (UN) in 1992, it defines violence against women as discrimination and requires governments to prevent and punish these acts.

crimes against humanity defined by Article 1 of the Rome Statute, they include murder, enslavement, torture, and rape when committed as part of a systematic attack against a civilian population. *See also* ethnic cleansing, genocide.

customary law rules of conduct widely agreed to be universally applicable.

cyberspace the virtual environment created by the Internet.

Declaration on the Elimination of Violence against Women adopted by the UN in 1993, it states that violence against women is a violation of human rights and a form of discrimination against women.

diplomacy the art and practice of carrying out negotiations between nations.

diplomatic immunity the legal principle that ambassadors and other officials of a foreign state are not subject to the jurisdiction of the country in which they are present.

ethnic cleansing action intended to remove or extinguish an ethnic group from a country or region. *See also* genocide.

free trade international trade that is not subject to restrictions or barriers.

General Agreement on Tariffs (GATT) an organization formed in 1948 to agree the easing of trade restrictions on countries.

Geneva Conventions international rules of wartime. The first (1864) set rules for the treatment of injured on the battlefield; the second (1906) applied to warfare at sea. The third convention (1949) established rules for dealing with prisoners of war, and a fourth (1949) for the treatment of civilians in wartime.

genocide action intended to destroy or kill an entire national or ethnic group.

greenhouse gases gases produced by burning fossil fuels that can trap the sun's heat in earth's atmosphere; many scientists believe that they contribute to global warming.

Hague Convention on the Civil Aspects of International Child Abduction passed in 1980, this acts to discourage parental child abduction and to ensure that children who are abducted are returned to their country of residence. *See also* human rights.

human rights the rights people have irrespective of citizenship, nationality, race, ethnicity, language, sex, sexuality, or abilities, enforceable when they are codified as covenants or treaties. *See also* Amnesty International.

International Criminal Court (ICC) founded in 1998 with jurisdiction over persons committing serious crimes in the international community. By 2003, 139 nations had signed up to its establishment, and 92 states had ratified it.

International Monetary Fund (IMF) formed in 1945 to promote monetary cooperation and economic growth.

Kyoto Protocol a proposed amendment to an international treaty on global warming first adopted in 1992. It contains emissions targets for industrialized countries to achieve by the period 2008–2012. *See also* greenhouse gases.

Libyan embassy siege On April 18, 1984, a group of protestors were fired on from the Libyan embassy in London, England. Police Constable Yvonne Fletcher was killed. The British government insisted that Libya waive its diplomatic immunity, but it refused. *See also* diplomatic immunity.

money laundering the processing of income earned from crime to disguise its origins.

Movement for Democratic Change main opposition to Robert Mugabe's ruling ZANU-PF party in Zimbabwe.

national sovereignty the freedom of a country to conduct its internal affairs without external interference.

North American Free Trade Agreement (NAFTA) an agreement between Canada, Mexico, and the United States establishing a free trade zone in North America from 1994.

North Atlantic Treaty Organization (NATO) a military alliance of 26 European and North American nations, including the United States, Germany, Spain, and the UK.

political asylum the right of an individual who has been forced to flee his or her country to receive sanctuary, or "asylum," in a foreign state.

preemptive attack a military attack launched in order to prevent an enemy launching an attack of its own.

Protocol to Prevent, Suppress, and Punish Trafficking in Persons, Especially Women and Children this 2000 protocol requires states to protect victims of human trafficking, particularly women and children.

"shell" banks banks that exist only on paper. They have no staff, branches, or other physical holdings. They are common in offshore financial centers (OFCs).

Taliban an Islamic fundamentalist political and religious group that emerged in Afghanistan in the mid-1990s following the withdrawal of occupying Soviet troops.

tax haven a country with low taxation where overseas investors can keep their money to avoid paying higher taxes.

transition economies developing free-market economies, such as China and the former states of the Soviet Union.

transnational corporation (TNC) an enterprise that operates in a number of different countries, and that has production facilities outside its home country.

Treaty of Westphalia (1648) a peace treaty among European nations that established the principle that rulers were free to impose their own rule in their countries without interference from other countries.

tyrannicide the killing of a tyrant by his or her subjects.

Universal Declaration of Human Rights (UDHR) UN declaration in 1948 establishing that human rights apply to all people. The UDHR asserts that no one will be subjected to torture or "cruel, inhuman, or degrading treatment of any kind." *See also* Geneva Conventions, human rights.

USA PATRIOT Act (2001) introduced after the terrorist action of September 11, 2001, this law allowed for the arrest and detainment of immigrants, and extended the powers of the Military Order to allow tribunals to try noncitizens who have been charged with terrorism. *See also* human rights, terrorism.

War on Terrorism (the War on Terror) the effort of the United States and its allies to neutralize international terrorist groups and axis-of-evil nations.

World Trade Organization (WTO) founded in 1995, the WTO monitors trading policies, handles trade disputes, and enforces the GATT agreements. *See also* GATT.

Acknowledgments

1. Does the International Criminal Court Undermine National Sovereignty?

Yes: "ICC—New Threat to U.S. Sovereignty" by David Davenport, Newsmax.com, August 27, 2003. Copyright © UPI, used under license. iCopyright Clearance License 3.5981.2327442-46434.
No: "The International Criminal Court Will Strengthen Australia's Global Standing" by Andrew MacLeod and Greg Barns, Onlineopinion.com June 15, 2002. Used by permission.

2. Should Heads of State Be Prosecuted for Crimes against Humanity?

Yes: "New Bid to Arrest Mugabe" by Peter Tatchell, www.petertatchell.net. Used by permission.
No: "War Crimes Trials and Errors" by Butler Shaffer, www.lewrockwell.com, December 19, 2003. Used by permission.

3. Is Targeted Killing Wrong?

Yes: "Assassination and Display in Iraq: The Killings of Uday and Qusai Hussein in International Law" by Marjorie Cohn, *Jurist*, July 29, 2003. Used by permission.
No: "Reviving the Assassination Option" by David Silverstein, originally published in *The American Enterprise*, December 2001. Used by permission.

4. Is It Legal for One Nation to Attack Another Preemptively?

Yes: "International Law and the Preemptive Use of Force against Iraq" by David M. Ackerman. Report of the Congressional Research Service available at the website of Rep. Boozman (www.boozman.house.gov). Public domain.
No: "Make Love, Not War: The Upside-Down World" by Edourdo Galeano, *The Progressive*, September 2003. Used by permission.

5. Are Women's Adequately Protected by International Law?

Yes: "International Justice for Women: the ICC Marks a New Era" by Human Rights Watch, Backgrounder, July 1, 2002.
No: "15 Steps to Protect Women's Human Rights" by Amnesty International (www. amnesty.org). Used by permission.

6. Has the Hague Convention Been Effective in Settling International Parent–Child Abduction Cases?

Yes: "Statement of Maura Harty, Assistant Secretary, Bureau of Consular Affairs, United States Department of State on International Child Abduction Before the Subcommittee on Human Rights and Wellness Committee on House Government Reform" by Maura Harty, July 9, 2003. Public Domain.
No: "Germans Don't Budge Even after Plea by Clinton" by Ray Moseley, *The Chicago Tribune*, September 7, 2000. Copyright © 2000, Chicago Tribune Company. All rights reserved. Used with permission.

7. Do International Trade Laws Favor the Rich?

Yes: "Divide and Conquer: Bilateral Trade Agreements" by Yuill Herbert, *The Dominion*, April 6, 2004. Used by permission.
No: "Bilateral Deals Are No Threat to Global Trade" by Daniel Griswold, The Cato Institute. Published in *The Financial Times*, July 27, 2003. Used by permission.

8. Should Cyberspace Be Treated as International Space?

Yes: "The Cyberspace Revolution" by David G. Post, Keynote address, Computer Policy and Law Conference, Cornell University, July 9, 1997. Used by permission.
No: "Boomtown: The Hot New Field of Cyberlaw Is Just Hokum, Skeptics Argue" by Lee Gomes, *The Wall Street Journal*, July 1, 2002. Reprinted by permission of *The Wall Street Journal*, Copyright © 2002 Dow Jones & Company, Inc. All Rights Reserved Worldwide. License number 1018251337949.

9. Does the Program for Eradicating Illicit Crops Violate Human Rights?

Yes: "WOLA Delegation in Putumayo Told: 'Stop the Fumigation!'" by Joe Eldridge, *Colombia Update* (newsletter of Colombia Human Rights Network), Winter 2000/Spring 2001. Used by permission.
No: "Aerial Eradication of Illicit Crops: Frequently Asked Questions" by Bureau for International Narcotics and Law Enforcement Affairs, Fact Sheet, March 24, 2003. Public domain.

10. Do Extradition Treaties Violate Human Rights?

Yes: "Letter to the Senate Foreign Relations Committee Urging Opposition to Ratification of the Revised United States–United Kingdom Extradition Treaty Signed by Attorney General John Ashcroft and Home Secretary David Blunkett" by American Civil Liberties Union (www.aclu,org), December 18, 2003. Used by permission.

No: "Killing of Innocent Civilian Not 'Political' Crime" by Kenneth Ofgang, *Metropolitan News-Enterprise*, March 11, 2004. Copyright © 2004 Metropolitan News Company. All rights reserved. Used by permission.

11. Should Tax Havens Be Made Illegal?

Yes: "Tax Havens: Releasing the Hidden Billions for Poverty Eradication" by Oxfam United Kingdom. Adapted from Executive summary, June 2000, with the permission of Oxfam GB, 274 Banbury Road, Oxford, OX2 7DZ, www.oxfam.org.uk.

No: "The Moral Case for Tax Havens" by Robert Stewart, www.LewRockwell.com, October 30, 2002. Used by permission.

12. Is Money Laundering Too Easy?

Yes: "U.S. Senators Seek Crackdown on Money Laundering" by Andrew Clark/Reuters, (russianlaw.org). Used under iCopyright Clearance License 3.5398.2339986-47714.

No: "U.S., Colombia, Canada and United Kingdom Jointly Announce Dismantling of Massive International Money-Laundering Ring" by U.S. Drug Enforcement Administration (www.dea.gov). Used by permission.

13. Should Diplomatic Immunity Be Retained?

Yes: "Privilege of Diplomatic Immunity Facing Challenges from All Sides" by John Shaw, *The Washington Diplomat,* March 2002. Used by permission.

No: "Diplomatic Immunity Should End" by Geoffrey Robertson, *The Guardian*, July 9, 1999. Geoffrey Robertson QC is the author of *Crimes against Humanity* (Penguin 2002) and is now a United Nations Appeals Judge for the Special War Crimes Court in Sierra Leone. Used by permission.

14. Does the United States Have Too Much Influence on International Law?

Yes: "Saving Kyoto, in Name or Substance?" by Chakravarthi Raghavan, *South-North Development Monitor*, 2001. Used by permission.

No: "The Kyoto Killers" by Patrick J. Michaels, The Cato Institute, August 2001. Used by permission.

15. Is the United States the Ultimate Defender of International Human Rights?

Yes: "Speech at Hearings, UN Human Rights Commission" by Paula Dobriansky, before the Senate Foreign Relations Committee International Operations and Terrorism Subcommittee, Washington, D.C., May 24, 2001. Public domain.

No: From "United States: Reports of Torture of Al Qaeda Suspects" by Human Rights Watch, December 27, 2002. Copyright © 2002 Human Rights Watch. Used by permission.

16. Has the U.S. War on Terrorism Violated International Law?

Yes: "Lawless War" by Ignacio Ramonet, translated by Ed Emory, *Le Monde diplomatique* (English edition), April 2003. Used by permission. To subscribe to Le Monde diplomatique's English edition e-mail: lmdsubs@granta.com or visit www.mondediplo.com.

No: "Legal Basis for Use of Force against Iraq" by Lord Goldsmith. House of Lords Official Report (Hansard), March 17, 2003: Column WA 2 (Volume No:646 Part no 65). Public domain.

The Brown Reference Group plc has made every effort to contact and acknowledge the creators and copyright holders of all extracts reproduced in this volume. We apologize for any omissions. Any person who wishes to be credited in further volumes should contact The Brown Reference Group plc in writing: The Brown Reference Group plc, 8 Chapel Place, Rivington Street, London EC2A 3DQ, U.K.

Picture credits

Cover: Robert Hunt Library
Corbis: David Bebber/Reuters 170, Bettmann 193, Manuela Hartling/Reuters 184, Ted Horowitz 122/123, Brooks Kraft 93, Reuters 34/35, 113, 210/211; **Digital Vision:** 179,188/181; **Rex Features:** 13, Andrew Aiken 18/19, Everett Collection 55, Nils Jorgensen 153, LKA 56, Jussi Nukari 129, Ron Sachs 157, 205, Sipa Press 105, 133, Richard Young 25; **Robert Hunt Library:** 6/7

SET INDEX